West German Steam

An atmospheric evening scene in August 1971.
John Dove/Online Transport Archive

West German Steam
in colour 1955–1975

Andrew Fox

UNIQUE
BOOKS

First published by Unique Books 2018

A CIP record for this book is available from the British Library

Unique Books is an imprint of Unique Publishing Services Ltd, 3 Merton Court, The Strand, Brighton Marina Village, Brighton BN2 5XY.

www.uniquepublishingservices.com

Printed in Poland

ISBN: 978 0 9957493 3 7

Contents

Glossary of German Terms & Abbreviations

Hbf = Hauptbahnhof	Main station
Gbf = Güterbahnhof	Freight yard/freight depot
Rbf = Rangierbahnhof	Marshalling yard
Umbauwagen	Carriages produced in large quantities from 1953 onwards by placing new all-steel bodies on pre-war coach chassis. They were of either six-wheel (Type 3yg) – sometimes adding a third axle to a four-wheel chassis – or bogie configuration (Type 4yg).
Silberling	Stainless steel bodied coach built in large numbers from 1959.
Donnerbüchse	'Thunder box' – pre-war metal-bodied four-wheel carriages
Verbrennungskammer	The literal translation is 'combustion chamber'. However, its common use with reference to a feature of the post-war boilers retro-fitted to certain pre-war 'Einheitslokomotiven' does not relate to a true combustion chamber, but rather to an extension of the rear lower firebox into the lower part of the boiler, giving a significant additional direct heating area, which materially increased the boiler's steam generating capacity.
Mischvorwärmer	Mixing feed water heater. The more modern, post-war design, in which exhaust steam and the feed water are mixed in a mixing tank.
Oberflächenvorwärmer	Surface feed water heater. The traditional version, in which exhaust steam passes through pipes which transfer heat to the surrounding feed water.
Grube/Zeche	Mine
Heeresfeldbahn	Military light railways
Kleinbahn	Minor/light railway
Länderbahn	Pre-DRG railway belonging to one of the German 'Länder' (states)
Privatbahn	Private/independent railway
Einheitslokomotive	Standard locomotive (DR) – plural Einheitslokomotiven
Neubaulokomotive	New type locomotive (DB) – plural Neubaulokomotiven
Königlich Bayerische Staatseisenbahnen	Royal Bavarian State Railways
Königlich Preußische Eisenbahn-Verwaltung (KPEV)	Royal Prussian Railways
Königlich Württembergische Staats-Eisenbahnen	Royal Württemberg State Railways

Deutsche Reichsbahn Gesellschaft (DRG)	German Imperial Railways (1920–49)
Deutsche Bundesbahn (DB)	German Federal Railways (1949–94)
Deutsche Dampflokomotiv-Museum	German Steam Locomotive Museum
Verkehrsmuseum Nürnberg	Nürnberg Transport Museum
Bayern	Bavaria
Braunschweig	Brunswick
Franken	Franconia
Köln	Cologne
Mosel	Moselle river
Niedersachsen	Lower Saxony
Nordrhein-Westfalen	North Rhine-Westfalia
Nürnberg	Nuremberg
Ostfriesland	East Fresia

Note on Deutsche Bundesbahn steam locomotive numbering:
On its formation in 1949 the steam locomotives of the Deutsche Bundesbahn continued with the previous Deutsche Reichsbahn numbering system. With effect from 1 January 1968, as mentioned in some captions, DB locomotives and rolling stock were renumbered in line with the standard UIC numbering system. In most cases the alteration consisted simply of adding 0 to the class number (thus Class 44 became Class 044), and a computer check digit suffix to the running number. Thus, No 44 380 became 044 380-4. Some exceptions are described in the following pages. Some class numbers changed under the new numbering system to distinguish between coal-and oil-fired members of the same basic class. Again, examples of this are described in the body of the book. Some locomotives continued to run for many months with the old pattern numbers.

A note on the photographs
All of the illustrations in this book have been drawn from the collection of the Online Transport Archive, a UK-registered charity that was set up to accommodate collections put together by transport enthusiasts who wished to see their precious images secured for the long-term. Further information about the archive can be found at: www.onlinetransportarchive.org or email secretary@onlinetransportarchive.org

Introduction

In the 1950s and 1960s West Germany offered a railway scene of fascinating variety, especially with the range of different steam locomotives in use. Whilst ever more diesel and electric locomotives were being introduced, the last of the Länderbahn classes survived in use even into the 1970s, side by side with 'Einheit' locomotives from the 1930s and 40s and modern 'Neubau' locomotives featuring a range of technical developments that were intended to improve further the performance and efficiency of steam traction, and to improve the crews' working conditions.

Many independent 'Privatbahn' lines survived into the 1960s with true minor railway atmosphere, offering scenes that had often hardly changed in 50 years. It was still possible to experience steam operating on various narrow gauge lines into the 1960s, with traditional narrow gauge character.

But this would not last for long. In the 1960s, with the relentless onset of modernisation and the steady drift – especially of passengers but also of freight – from rail to road, many minor and narrow gauge lines were either modernised with new motive power and rolling stock, rationalised or often simply closed. Even the main line 'Neubau' classes introduced by the Deutsche Bundesbahn in the 1950s and the pre-war classes modernised with new high-performance boilers, oil firing and other developments, would all be swept away within 25 years, some having remarkably brief lives.

With such a wealth of subject matter it is not possible to give thorough coverage of every class and location, but this volume sets out to illustrate this variety and the changing steam scene over a fascinating period, and to present a now vanished world from the late 1950s to the end of steam.

Everyone with an interest in steam and the railways of Germany should find something of interest in the following pages – whether it be large express or freight locomotives on the main line, possibly less prestigious but nonetheless interesting branch lines, private, narrow gauge or industrial lines.

Andrew Fox, September 2018

No 023 100-1 is seen running light near Ellwangen on 15 September 1970.
John Worley/Online Transport Archive

No 023 085-4 brings a long passenger train consisting of bogie 'Umbauwagen' through the small station at Itzelberg, a few miles south of Aalen, on 4 August 1970. She was built by Jung in 1957, and had been allocated to Crailsheim since 23 November 1966. *Alan Murray Rust/Online Transport Archive*

On 4 August 1970 No 050 112-2 brings a short passenger train through Unterkochen south of Aalen. Built by Henschel in 1940 as No 50 112, she was allocated to Ulm from 1 February 1970 to 28 September 1971. Subsequently she was at Heilbronn shed for two years, and then at Crailsheim from October 1973, where she was placed in store on 24 April 1974, and withdrawn on 18 September 1974. *Alan Murray Rust/Online Transport Archive*

No 023 085-4 leaves Heidenheim an der Brenz on 4 August 1970 with a train towards Itzelberg and Aalen. Although the locomotive was not even 13 years old (built by Jung in 1957, and first taken into stock by DB in November 1957) she only had another eight months left in service, being placed in store at Crailsheim on 6 April 1971, and withdrawn on 2 June 1971.
Alan Murray Rust/Online Transport Archive

No 078 256-5 leaves Aalen light engine heading south, also on 4 August 1970. The locomotive is on a section of mixed gauge track where the metre gauge Härtsfeldbahn left Aalen station and shared the trackbed with the standard gauge for a short distance.
Alan Murray Rust/Online Transport Archive

Opposite above: Nos 051 620-3 and 052 759-8 leave Crailsheim with a double-headed engineering train on 15 September 1970. No 051 620-3 (originally No 50 1620) was placed in store at Rottweil on 7 March 1974, and withdrawn on 9 June 1974. No 052 759-8 (originally No 50 2759) survived more than a year longer, and was not placed in store until 22 August 1975, being withdrawn on 22 October 1975.
John Worley/Online Transport Archive

Opposite below: Nos 023 012-8 and 044 565-0 wait for their next duties at Crailsheim shed on 15 September 1970. At the end of 1969 there were no fewer than 39 members of Class 23 at Crailsheim. Three years later in 1972 the planned withdrawal of the '23s' began, and in December 1975 the last three examples – Nos 023 023, 023 029 and 023 058 – were taken out of service at Crailsheim.
John Worley/Online Transport Archive

Above: Nos 051 722-7 and 044 477-8 (both allocated to Nürnberg Rbf at the time) leave Crailsheim with a freight for Nürnberg on 11 March 1970.
Les Folkard/Online Transport Archive

With an impressive exhaust No 044 558-5 leaves Crailsheim on 11 March 1970 with a freight towards Schwäbisch Hall. When it was placed in store in December 1972 the locomotive had been at Crailsheim for more than 25 years since November 1947, being finally withdrawn on 12 April 1973.
Les Folkard/Online Transport Archive

2-10-0s Nos 050 830-9 and 051 540-3 leave Crailsheim light engine on 11 March 1970. Within a year No 050 830-9 (originally 50 830) was placed in store at Crailsheim on 14 January 1971, and was withdrawn on 2 June 1971. No 051 540-3 (originally 50 1540) remained in use for a full five years more, being placed in store on 23 April 1976, also at Crailsheim, and withdrawn on 11 June 1976.
Les Folkard/Online Transport Archive

No 052 613-7 leaves Eutingen on 8 June 1972 with a train for Horb consisting of three 'Silberling' coaches. She was allocated to Tübingen from 3 January 1971 to 12 October 1972. *Both: Les Folkard/Online Transport Archive*

Left: The clock on the tower of the Protestant church in the Bahnhofstraße at Hausach (built in 1904 in the Gothic Revival style) shows 15.11 as No 038 382-8 moves off towards the turntable.
John Dove/Online Transport Archive

Below: When Deutsche Bundesbahn locomotives and rolling stock were given computerised numbers on 1 January 1968, the individual running number could have only three characters, and no numbers could appear twice. In most cases the original three digits were simply re-used in the new number. The 'thousand' digit was simply dropped or was included in the class number. However, sometimes two locomotives, had the same three-digit running number, which had to be changed to accommodate this. This applied in the case of No 38 2383, as No 38 3383 was also still in service, and had been allocated the new number 038 383-6. As no members of the class remained on the DB with the last three digits 382, No 38 2383 became 038 382-8. In October 1968 No 038 382-8 was allocated to Tübingen shed, then in June 1973 to Rottweil, where she was withdrawn one year later. She is seen waiting to depart from Hausach.
John Dove/Online Transport Archive

No 038 382-8 catches the rays of the evening sun as she leaves Horb with a train consisting of four six-wheel 'Umbauwagen'. Built by Henschel in 1919 as Works No 16539, she entered service as Königlich Preußische Eisenbahn-Verwaltung 'Elberfeld 2535'.
John Dove/Online Transport Archive

No 38 3559 waits at Freudenstadt with a passenger train in June 1968. The Locomotive is still carrying its old number without the 0 prefix and computer check digit.
Harry Luff/Online Transport Archive

'P8' No 038 313-3 (formerly 38 2313) stands at Rottweil depot in June 1971. At the time she was allocated to Tübingen shed. Just a few months later, on 26 November 1971, she was placed in store at Tübingen. After spending some time as a stationary heating boiler at Friedrichshafen and allocated to Lindau, she returned to Tübingen in February 1972, where soon afterwards she was withdrawn on 21 April 1972.
Harry Luff/Online Transport Archive

No 38 3845 arrives at Calw in June 1962 with a passenger service. Calw lies on the Nagold valley line in the northern Black Forest, which links Pforzheim with Hochdorf (near Horb) and largely follows the valley of the River Nagold. Due to the geological features in the Nagold valley the 56.6 km long line features many significant pieces of civil engineering. There are no fewer than 21 bridges and viaducts that are more than 20 metres in length. In addition, there are nine tunnels, including the Hochdorfer tunnel, by far the longest tunnel on the network of the Royal Württemberg State Railways. No 38 3845, which had been built by Borsig in 1911, was withdrawn, five years after this photograph was taken, at Tübingen shed in July 1967.
W. J. Wyse/LRTA (London Area) Collection/Online Transport Archive

No 064 491-4 is engaged in
shunting at Lauda station on
5 August 1970. She had been
built by O&K 30 years earlier in
1940 and entered service with
the Reichsbahn as No 64 491.
Apart from a short period at
Ulm in November 1972, she
was based at Heilbronn
between 1 January 1968 and
2 June 1973. From 3 June 1973
her home depot was
Crailsheim, where she was
placed in store on 3 May 1974,
and eventually withdrawn on
18 September of that year. She
survives in preservation, once
again carrying her original
number, and in 1993 received a
new boiler at Meiningen works.
*Both: Alan Murray Rust/Online
Transport Archive*

No 064 136-5 stands with a passenger train at Lauda on 5 August 1970. Built by O&K in 1928, she was placed in store on 10 May 1973 after 14 years based at Heilbronn depot, and withdrawn on 24 July 1973.
Alan Murray Rust/Online Transport Archive

Nos 050 965-3, built by Krupp in 1941, and 052 759-8, built by Henschel in 1942, are prepared for their next duties at Lauda shed on 5 August 1970.
Alan Murray Rust/Online Transport Archive

No 050 492-8 (built by Borsig in 1940, Works No 14940) has charge of a long freight near Geroldshausen on 8 June 1972. The following year the locomotive was placed in store at Heilbronn on 14 August 1973, but was not officially withdrawn until 6 March 1974.
Les Folkard/Online Transport Archive

No 023 012-8 leaves Heilbronn Hauptbahnhof on 17 September 1970. She had been supplied to the Bundesbahn by Henschel in February 1951. As with the other members of the first series of Class 23, as well as members of Class 65, after only a short period in service she suffered from boiler damage and distortion around the base of the dome, and as a result spent several months out of service in 1952 until a dome strengthening ring could be fitted. From June 1969 she was allocated to Crailsheim, where she was placed in store on 22 May 1975 with a damaged steam chest, and was withdrawn on 26 June 1975.
John Worley/Online Transport Archive

No 064 018-5 leaves an impressive exhaust over Bad Friedrichshall station in September 1970 with a local train to Rappenau and Sinsheim. The time is 17.40. At this time the locomotive was allocated to Heilbronn depot.
John Worley/Online Transport Archive

It is June 1968, and No 038 273-9 will soon depart from platform 6 at Bad Friedrichshall with a short passenger train. Previously numbered 38 3273, the locomotive had received its new number with 0 prefix and computer check digit only a few months earlier, with the implementation of the International Union of Railways (UIC) system on 1 January 1968.
Harry Luff/Online Transport Archive

No 044 386-1 has charge of a heavy freight train on the sunny 8 June 1972. Built by Krupp in 1942 she was put in service by the Reichsbahn as No 44 1384, and was renumbered as 044 386-1 on 1 January 1968. Between 1951 and 1973 she was allocated to Crailsheim. On 1 August 1973 she moved to her last depot at Gelsenkirchen-Bismarck, where she was placed in store on 24 September 1973 and withdrawn on 6 March 1974.
Les Folkard/Online Transport Archive

No 050 646-9 brings a passenger train through the long curve before Schwäbisch Hall-Hessental station on the evening of 8 June 1972.
Les Folkard/Online Transport Archive

No 050 646-9 is seen again with the same train at Grossaltdorf, en route from Schwäbisch Hall to Crailsheim. The lightweight train, consisting of just four six-wheel Umbauwagen, does not challenge the powerful locomotive unduly.
Les Folkard/Online Transport Archive

Above: There is hardly a trace of smoke or steam from Nos 050 450-6 and 051 430-7, which are making leisurely progress with a freight near Gailenkirchen on 8 June 1972.
Les Folkard/Online Transport Archive

Left: No 023 027-6 has an easy task near Gailenkirchen on 8 June 1972, hauling a train of just three Umbauwagen. The locomotive was built by Jung in 1954. She was allocated to Crailsheim from 9 March 1971, until she was placed in store with a damaged frame on 13 February 1974 following an accident, and finally withdrawn on 9 June 1974.
Les Folkard/Online Transport Archive

No 038 631-8 stands at Tübingen with a passenger train in June 1971. She was built by Humboldt in 1919 for the Königlich Preußische Eisenbahn-Verwaltung (KPEV) as 'Essen 2509'. During World War 2 she travelled as far as Vienna and even Kiev, but returned to Germany after the war, where she spent the 10 years from 1946 to 1956 at Freiburg im Breisgau, and then the nine years from 1956 to 1965 at Ulm, before moving on several occasions between Crailsheim, Ulm, Tübingen and Heilbronn. From 10 June 1970 her last shed was at Tübingen, where she was placed in store in April 1972 and withdrawn in July 1972.
Harry Luff/Online Transport Archive

No 038 772-0 and a member of Class 078 are at rest on shed in August 1971. No 038 772-0, the former No 38 1772, was built for the Königlich Preußische Eisenbahn-Verwaltung in 1915 as 'Königsberg 2459'. She was based at Tübingen between 30 May 1967 and 2 June 1973, before being placed in store on 3 June 1973 and withdrawn at Rottweil on 31 December 1974.
John Dove/Online Transport Archive

No 078 246-6 is hauling a passenger train of six-wheel Umbauwagen in August 1971. She was built by the Stettiner Maschinenbau-AG Vulcan in 1922 for the Königlich Preußische Eisenbahn-Verwaltung.

Rottweil was her last shed, where she was allocated from 7 February 1970 until her withdrawal in December 1974.
John Dove/Online Transport Archive

No 050 560-2 leaves Altoberndorf with a long freight towards Rottweil on 9 June 1972. Not long after this she was taken out of traffic on 3 August 1972, and

withdrawn three months later on 8 November 1972 at Rottweil.
Les Folkard/Online Transport Archive

Until the 1970s a modern Esslingen 0-6-0T (built 1952, Works No 5054) survived at the Albbruck paper mill in the district of Waldshut, operating the connection between the paper mill and Albbruck station. In October 1976 she stands with a tank wagon and two wagons with DB containers on the steep gradient at the mill entrance. Although very short, the connection between the station and the mill was extremely demanding. Over a distance of

30 metres the gradient was reportedly no less than 1 in 13.5, followed by 100 metres at 1 in 16, with the result that that the steam locomotive was limited to three wagons. Taken out of use in the 1970s, she moved to the Eisenbahnfreunde Zollernbahn preservation group, and operated at several preserved lines in the 1980s and 90s.
Harry Luff/Online Transport Archive

Zabergäubahn

The Zabergäubahn was a 20.2km long 750mm gauge line from Lauffen am Neckar to Leonbronn, which was built by the Königlich Württembergische Staats-Eisenbahnen. It left the standard gauge Frankenbahn from Stuttgart to Würzburg via Heilbronn at Lauffen. The line was opened from Lauffen am Neckar to Güglingen on 28 August 1896, and was extended to Leonbronn in October 1901.

From 1954 the Deutsche Bundesbahn started a railway bus service in parallel with the narrow gauge line, and reduced the railway passenger service with the objective of closing the line, although in some cases the railway buses were slower than the trains. On 20 June 1959 a serious accident occurred, when a fully occupied railway bus was hit by a train on a level crossing with the Frankenbahn at Lauffen. This led to the founding of the 'Zabergäu Action Group', which successfully campaigned for passenger traffic to be returned to the railway, for modernisation of the route, and its conversion to standard gauge. The rebuilding took place in phases between May 1964 and July 1965.

Between 1923 and 1927 the Deutsche Reichsbahn ordered a total of 47 locomotives based on the original Saxon VI K Class 99[64–65], which were built in several batches as Class 99[67–71], numbered 99 671-717. The new build locomotives differed only slightly from their predecessors. Externally the most obvious difference was the much less rounded dome casing. Some of these locomotives operated in Württemberg on the Bottwartalbahn and the Zabergäubahn. Nos 99 679-683 were delivered direct to Württemberg, and later Nos 99 671, 672, 698, 701, 704 and 716 were transferred from Saxony to Württemberg. Most of these locomotives were in use with the Deutsche Bundesbahn into the 1960s. After being withdrawn in May 1965, No 99 716 was preserved at Güglingen, and since 1993 has been part of the Öchsle preserved railway collection.

On a fine day in August 1961 Nos 99 672 (Henschel, built 1923) and 99 704 (Karlsruhe, built 1926) stand outside the locomotive shed at Güglingen.
Phil Tatt/Online Transport Archive

In August 1961 a well-kept No 99 704 stands at the inspection pit in Güglingen. The buffer beam shows the date of her last 'L3' repair on 4 May 1960. She was withdrawn on 22 May 1967 as the last example of the new build series.
Phil Tatt/Online Transport Archive

Öchslebahn

The 'Öchsle', a 750mm gauge railway between the Oberschwaben (Upper Swabia) cities of Biberach (Riß) and Ochsenhausen was opened on 29 November 1899 between Warthausen and Ochsenhausen (19km). The remaining 3.2km to Biberach followed on 1 March 1900.

In 1954 the Deutsche Bundesbahn began rationalising services through timetable reductions and the use of buses, and on 31 May 1964 passenger services were withdrawn on the whole line, after its purpose had been undermined by the growth of private transport as well as by the Memmingen via Ochsenhausen to Biberach post bus service. Shortly afterwards the Biberach to Warthausen section was

dismantled. Nonetheless, there was a growth in freight traffic in the 1960s. At the end of 1964 the Class VI K steam locomotives were replaced by two Class V 51 diesels (reclassified as Class 251 from 1968). The remaining occasional use of steam ended completely in 1969.

Although DB considered converting the line to standard gauge, instead of pursuing this, closure procedures commenced in 1981, and all services were withdrawn with effect from 31 March 1983. However, the route was acquired by the towns along the line together with the Rural District of Biberach, and since 1985 the remaining section from Warthausen to Ochsenhausen has operated as the 'Öchsle' preserved railway.

No 99 651, seen shunting van No 157 at Biberach in August 1961, was one of the original Saxon VI K locomotives, which were easily distinguished from the later builds by the round-topped dome casing. Class VI K was originally designed for the military authorities, with 15 of the class being built by Henschel for use on Polish narrow gauge lines, but in the event this intended use never took place. In 1919 the Sächsische Staatseisenbahnen purchased all 15 locomotives for use on its narrow gauge lines. Under the Deutsche Reichsbahn they became Class 99$^{64-65}$, being numbered 99 641-655.

In 1928 Nos 99 650 and 99 651 were transferred to the DB's Stuttgart division, which allocated them

to Ochsenhausen. Until the end of passenger services on 31 May 1964 these two locomotives were the regular motive power on the 'Öchsle'. Subsequently they moved to the Bottwartalbahn as the last examples of their type on the Deutsche Bundesbahn, where they were withdrawn in May 1967 (99 650) and September 1969 (99 651). No 99 651 – the last of the class in service – was subsequently preserved at Steinheim an der Murr as the last example of the original series. In 2016 she moved to the 'Öchsle' preserved railway at Ochsenhausen.
Phil Tatt/Online Transport Archive

No 99 651 (built by Henschel in 1918, Works No 16132) awaits departure from the narrow gauge platform at Biberach with a short train.
Phil Tatt/Online Transport Archive

In August 1961 No 99 651 has arrived at the terminus at Ochsenhausen with a mixed train. At the end of 1964 No 99 651 was transferred from the 'Öchsle' to the Bottwartalbahn, later going on loan to the Federseebahn at Buchau from January to June 1969. She was taken out of use in August 1969 as the DB's last narrow gauge steam locomotive, and officially withdrawn the following month.
Phil Tatt/Online Transport Archive

Federseebahn

The Federseebahn was a 29.3km long line in Oberschwaben, which connected Schussenried with Riedlingen. The section from Schussenried to Buchau (9.4km) opened on 13 October 1896. The further section to Riedlingen (29.3km) opened in November 1915. Buchau to Riedlingen was the last section of narrow gauge line to be opened by the Königlich Württembergische Staats-Eisenbahnen. Traffic levels on this section, however, were very disappointing.

Apart from the immediate post-war years, traffic levels were modest during the DB era. As a result, the Buchau to Riedlingen section was closed on 2 October 1960, and shortly afterwards the track was removed between Kappel and Riedlingen. On 31 May 1964 passenger traffic ended between Schussenried and Bad Buchau, but freight services continued for the time being. This section eventually closed to all traffic on 1 January 1969, although a narrow gauge locomotive continued to be allocated until early 1970 to shunt connecting lines at Bad Schussenried. Subsequently all narrow gauge rails were removed, except from Bad Schussenried to the turf works, which was converted into a standard gauge connection.

In August 1961 No 99 633 stands with its train at Buchau, terminus of the line since October 1960. She was built by Maschinenfabrik Esslingen for the Königlich Württembergische Staats-Eisenbahnen in 1899, was placed in store on 31 October 1968 and withdrawn on 3 March 1969.
Phil Tatt/Online Transport Archive

Members of Württemberg Class Tssd, 0-4-4-0T compound Mallets, constituted the principal motive power on the Federseebahn. No 99 633 awaits its next duty in August 1961. No 99 637 is preserved at the site of the former station at Bad Buchau as a memorial to the narrow gauge line.
Phil Tatt/Online Transport Archive

No 99 633 has its coal supply replenished at the basic coaling stage at Schussenried.
Phil Tatt/Online Transport Archive

Mosbach to Mudau

The metre gauge 27.5km long Mosbach to Mudau line was opened on 31 May 1905. The line started on the forecourt of Mosbach station. It ran parallel to the Neckarelz to Osterburken line for approximately two kilometres, before it crossed this on a bridge and continued through a sometimes heavily wooded region before arriving at Mudau. From 1 May 1931 operations were taken over by the Karlsruhe division of the Deutsche Reichsbahn. Freight traffic was significant, with standard gauge wagons being carried on narrow gauge transporter wagons.

After World War 2 the line became part of the Deutsche Bundesbahn. In the 1950s and 60s it increasingly lost traffic to the growing number of private cars, as well as to bus routes which ran parallel to the railway. The Bundesbahn itself transferred most passenger traffic to railway buses, and from 1964 there was only one return rail service.

However, the state of Baden-Württemberg attempted to ensure the future of the line, by financing the acquisition of two Class V 52 diesel locomotives and new bogie coaches in 1964, which replaced the line's four steam locomotives and four-wheel coaches. Although the new diesel locomotives were a success, it did not prove possible to achieve an adequate level of revenue either from passenger or freight traffic, and various rationalisation measures were also unsuccessful. In the end the electrification of the main line sealed the fate of the narrow gauge line, which crossed the standard gauge on a bridge which was too low to allow for the installation of overhead wires. As a result, all traffic was withdrawn with effect from 3 June 1973.

Four non-superheated 0-6-0Ts were built for the line by Borsig in 1904 as Works Nos 5324-5327. These were responsible for most of the traffic on the line until dieselisation in 1964. The Deutsche Reichsbahn numbered them as 99 7201-7204. No 99 7203 is at the head of a short train to Mudau in August 1961.
Phil Tatt/Online Transport Archive

No 99 7203 stands outside the locomotive shed at Mudau in August 1961.

After the steam locomotives were taken out of service in 1964, No 99 7203 was acquired by the Albtal-Verkehrs-Gesellschaft (AVG) to meet the requirement for a suitable locomotive to operate works trains for the demolition of the Albtalbahn between Ittersbach and Langensteinbach, and the conversion of the section between Langensteinbach to Busenbach from metre to standard gauge. Its use on the Albtalbahn lasted only from November 1964 to August 1965, after which it was laid aside at Busenbach.
Phil Tatt/Online Transport Archive

The locomotives were transported to and from overhaul on standard gauge transporter wagons, as illustrated by No 99 7202 on its return to Mosbach in August 1961. Happily, all four locomotives have survived; this includes No 99 7203 in operating condition on the Amstetten to Oppingen line, known as the 'Albbähnle', and No 99 7202 preserved at the former terminus of Mudau. Several items of rolling stock have also survived on various preserved railways.
Phil Tatt/Online Transport Archive

No 052 475-1, built by Krupp in 1942 as No 50 2475, pauses with a passenger train at Miltenberg, Unterfranken (Lower Franconia) in June 1971. She was allocated to Nürnberg Rbf from May 1966 to January 1973, subsequently from February 1973 to January 1974 to Hof, and from January 1974 to Lehrte. She was placed in store on 1 June 1976, and withdrawn 10 days later.
Harry Luff/Online Transport Archive

The well-kept No 001 202-1, built by Henschel of Kassel in 1937 as No 01 202, leaves Hof with an express in August 1971. From October 1959 she was allocated to Hof, where she was placed in store on 17 February 1973, and subsequently withdrawn on 12 April 1973. After her withdrawal she saw temporary use as a stationary boiler, was then purchased by a private individual and restored to working order over many years. *John Dove/Online Transport Archive*

The driver watches attentively from the footplate of No 052 890-1, as it passes a modern road overbridge in August 1971 with a long freight. *John Dove/Online Transport Archive*

No 052 417-3 arrives at Aschaffenburg Hauptbahnhof in
May 1973. She was built by Krauss-Maffei in 1942
(Works No 16292) and entered service as Deutsche
Reichsbahn No 50 2417. From December 1972 she was
allocated to Schweinfurt, until being placed in store on
3 February 1975, and then withdrawn on 16 May 1975.
Harry Luff/Online Transport Archive

Three members of Class 50 stand ready for service at Nürnberg Rbf on 7 June 1965, with No 50 1954 in the foreground. No 50 1954 was allocated to Nürnberg Rbf between April 1950 and June 1973.
Les Folkard/Online Transport Archive

No 44 1178, built by Krupp in 1942, stands on the turntable at Nürnberg Rbf on 12 June 1964. At this time she was allocated to Würzburg depot. Subsequently she moved on to Schweinfurt, Nürnberg Rbf, Betzdorf, and finally to Gelsenkirchen-Bismarck in October 1975, where she was withdrawn on 21 February 1977 after more than 34 years in service.
Les Folkard/Online Transport Archive

No 78 526 stands on the turntable at Nürnberg Hbf depot on 13 September 1964, with sister locomotive No 78 164 in the background. No 78 526 was built by Stettiner Maschinenbau-AG Vulcan in 1924, and from September 1958 to June 1965 was allocated to Nürnberg Hbf. Older sister No 78 164 was built in 1919 by the same maker. She was allocated to Nürnberg Hbf for almost 14 years from September 1951 until June 1965. No 78 526 was withdrawn as early as March 1966 from Schweinfurt, shed but No 78 164 survived until being withdrawn as No 078 164-1 at Rottweil in December 1971.
Les Folkard/Online Transport Archive

Class 01 Pacific No 01 213 was built by Henschel in 1937. She was placed in store as early as December 1968, and withdrawn at Hof on 3 March 1969. On 13 September 1964 she is waiting for her next duty at Nürnberg Hbf depot.
John Dove/Online Transport Archive

On 15 September 1970 fireless loco No 1 (built by Krauss in 1923, Works No 8072) is shunting at the Glanzstoff AG factory at Obernburg on the line from Aschaffenburg to Miltenberg.
John Worley/Online Transport Archive

The 'Schiefe Ebene'

The 'Schiefe Ebene' is a famous section of line on the Ludwig-Süd-Nord-Bahn from Bamberg to Hof (Saale) in the Oberfranken region. It begins to the east of Neuenmarkt-Wirsberg station, and ends at Marktschorgast, featuring inclines of up to 1 in 40. It was built between 1844 and 1848, and opened in November 1848.

In steam days the 'Schiefe Ebene' was a challenge for both man and machine. Most trains received assistance from banking locomotives, which were stationed at Neuenmarkt-Wirsberg depot. At the start of the 1970s it was one of the last stamping grounds of the celebrated '01' Pacifics.

Leaving Neuenmarkt Wirsberg at the start of the 'Schiefe Ebene', No 001 008-2 passes the Steinerne Brücke ('stone bridge') of 1892 at km 75.3 in May 1972. Built by Borsig in 1926 (Works No 12000) as No 01 008, one of the first members of Class 01, she was allocated to Hof from May 1968, was placed in store on 1 November 1973, and withdrawn on 15 December 1973. The attractive semaphores were replaced by colour light signals the following year. *John Dove/Online Transport Archive*

Running light engine, No 001 008-2 storms up the incline at the 80.4km post in May 1973. She had been allocated to Hof shed since May 1968, was placed in store on 1 November 1973 and was withdrawn on 12 December 1973. Soon afterwards she was purchased by the Deutsche Gesellschaft für Eisenbahn Geschichte (DGEG). *Harry Luff/Online Transport Archive*

Above: No 051 057-8 approaches Marktschorgast with a train of three Umbauwagen and parcels vans in May 1973. She is about to crest the summit of the 'Schiefe Ebene' at km 81.7. No 051 057 had only another six months of active life left, as she would be taken out of service on 26 November 1973, and withdrawn on 6 March 1974.
Harry Luff/Online Transport Archive

Left: With a well-stocked tender, No 001 131-2 passes Marktschorgast at the summit of the 'Schiefe Ebene' in May 1973. No 001 131-2 was built by Henschel in 1935 and entered service as No 01 131. She was allocated to Hof from 24 May 1967 until she was placed in store on 3 June 1973, and then withdrawn on 24 August 1973.
Harry Luff/Online Transport Archive

No 001 150-2, built by Henschel in 1935, sets off downgrade after leaving Marktschorgast in May 1973. Next to the locomotive is a stainless steel 'Silberling' coach, of which approximately 5,000 were built from 1959 onwards. No 001 150-2 was allocated to Hof from 16 June 1972, but was placed in store on 5 November 1973 and withdrawn eight days later. Since then she has led a varied life in preservation, restored to operating condition and returned to her original identity as No 01 150.
Harry Luff/Online Transport Archive

Nos 001 180-9 and 001 008-2 stand at Neuenmarkt-Wirsberg in May 1973. No 001 180-9 had been rebuilt at Frankfurt Nied works in 1960 with a 'Verbrennungskammer' fitted boiler, fitted with a 'Mischvorwärmer' and a single valve superheater regulator. Shortly after this photograph she was taken out of service at Hof on 31 May 1973, and withdrawn on 24 August 1973. Her older sister, No 001 008-2 remained in traffic a little longer, being taken out of service on 1 November 1973, and withdrawn six weeks later on 15 December 1973. Both locomotives have survived in preservation; No 001 008-2 with the Eisenbahnmuseum Bochum collection at Bochum-Dahlhausen, and No 001 180-9, restored to running order since November 2014, at the Bayerisches Eisenbahnmuseum.
Harry Luff/Online Transport Archive

Neustadt-Eslarn

The line from Neustadt (Waldnaab) to Eslarn was a 49.8km long branch line, connected the eastern part of the present day district of Neustadt an der Waldnaab in the northern Oberpfalz. The first part of the line from Neustadt an der Waldnaab via Floß to Vohenstrauß was opened by the Königlich Bayerische Staats-Eisenbahnen in October 1886. In August 1900 the line reached Waidhaus on the Czech border, from where it turned southwards to terminate at Eslarn in October 1908. With a total length of almost 50km it was the longest branch line in the Oberpfalz region. Its remote location in the hills of the Oberpfalz forest often led to disruption to services in the winter months. During and immediately after World War 2 there was heavy passenger traffic on the line, which continued to operate until 1 June 1975. From that date it was limited to the section from Weiden to Floß, closing completely on 29 May 1992.

No 064 337-9 stands at the terminus of Eslarn on 13 March 1970. The locomotive had been built by Krauss-Maffei in 1934 as No 64 337. From 1 August 1966 war she was allocated to her last depot at Weiden in der Oberpfalz. After almost 38 years in service she was stored on 7 June 1972 and withdrawn on 8 November 1972. *Les Folkard/Online Transport Archive*

No 064 337-9 waits to depart from Eslarn with the 15.55 to Weiden, consisting of four six-wheel Umbauwagen on 13 March 1970. *Les Folkard/Online Transport Archive*

Sekundärbahn Erlangen-Gräfenberg

The Erlangen to Gräfenberg local railway from Erlangen via Neunkirchen am Brand (12.3km) and Eschenau (19.0km) to Gräfenberg (28.0km) opened in November 1886. For financial reasons the line was built largely on or alongside the roads, and ran through the centre of Erlangen as well as other narrow towns and villages. Only in Neunkirchen am Brand was this not the case because of the very densely built town centre.

The local population's nick-name for the line, the 'Seku' or 'Seekuh' (sea cow), supposedly results from an occasion when a painter was painting the words 'Restauration zur Sekundärbahn' ('The Local Railway Café' on the wall of the station restaurant, but had not finished

when he stopped work for the evening, with the result that over the weekend the text read 'Restauration zur Seku' 'Seku Café').

With the growth of the motor car the 'Seku' declined progressively in the years following World War 2, not least because the railway had to give way at junctions where the road had priority, and also because the maximum speed was reduced to 15km/h due to the frequent accidents with road traffic. The section from Neunkirchen am Brand to Eschenau was closed to all traffic on 1 May 1961, and less than two years later the remaining section lost its passenger traffic in February 1963. The last freight train ran on 31 December 1963, and shortly after this the track was removed as far as Eschenau. The section from Eschenau to Gräfenberg survived as part of the Nürnberg to Gräfenberg line.

No 98 839 stands with a freight train at Neunkirchen am Brand in August 1961. On the left stands a three-car Uerdinger railbus set. The line had terminated here since May 1961. *Phil Tatt/Online Transport Archive*

At Neunkirchen am Brand station nothing moves. No 98 839 sizzles quietly, while the railcar waits hopefully for passengers to Erlangen. Since the closure of the 'Seku', the former station building has been authentically restored by its new owners. *Phil Tatt/Online Transport Archive*

On a rainy day in August 1961 No 98 839 has arrived at Uttenreuth, 6.7km from Erlangen, with its passenger train. The line would remain open until February 1963 for passenger traffic, and until December 1963 for freight.
Phil Tatt/Online Transport Archive

A close-up view of No 98 839 at Uttenreuth. Built by Krauss, München in 1922, she was delivered to the Bayerische Staatseisenbahnen as their No 2589, Class GtL 4/4 (later Deutsche Reichsbahn Class 98$^{8-9}$). From November 1954 she was allocated to Nürnberg Hbf shed until being taken out of service on 11 April 1962, and withdrawn on 1 August 1962.
Phil Tatt/Online Transport Archive

Right: Class 01[10] Pacific No 01 1068 stands at Hamburg Hauptbahnhof in September 1968 with an afternoon train to Osnabrück.
John Worley/Online Transport Archive

Below: Class 03 Pacific No 03 114, built by Henschel in 1933, receives attention from its crew at Hamburg Altona shed on 2 September 1968. From 30 May 1961 until 28 September 1968 she was allocated to Bremen Hbf shed. She then spent just a week at Lehrte before moving to Braunschweig from October 1968 to the start of June 1970. Finally she was transferred to Ulm, where she was immediately placed in store, and then withdrawn on 30 September 1970.
John Worley/Online Transport Archive

Above: A fine parade of Pacifics at Hamburg Altona on 2 September 1968 consisting, from left to right, of Nos 03 259, 03 262, 03 184, and 01 1088. None of the four locomotives is carrying a smokebox numberplate; instead they all have their running numbers painted – in the case of the '03s', not very elegantly – on their smokebox doors. At the time all three '03s' were allocated to Hamburg Altona. Since July 1955 the home shed of No 01 1088 had been Osnabrück Hbf, but on 29 September 1968, four weeks after this scene, she also moved to Altona, where she was placed in store on 9 November 1969, and officially withdrawn one year later, on 27 November 1970.
John Worley/Online Transport Archive

Right: No 03 296, built by Borsig in 1937, stands outside the shed at Hamburg Altona on 2 September 1968. Since 28 June 1966 she had been allocated to Altona shed, where she was placed in store on 1 October 1969, and eventually withdrawn on 4 March the following year.
John Worley/Online Transport Archive

Opposite above: No 01 1104, which had been fitted with a 'Verbrennungskammer' boiler at Braunschweig works in March 1954, and converted to oil firing in May 1957, stands on the turntable at Hamburg Altona, where the locomotive was allocated from April 1967 until September 1972. From September 1972 her last shed was Rheine, where she was placed in store on 22 May 1974, and withdrawn on 18 September 1974.
John Worley/Online Transport Archive

Opposite below: On 2 September 1968 No 78 246 stands outside the shed at Hamburg Altona depot, where she was allocated from 1 June 1968 to 14 April 1969. Subsequently she moved to Aalen depot until February 1970, and then to Rottweil from 7 February 1970. On 30 December 1974 she was placed in store at Rottweil, and withdrawn the following day.
John Worley/Online Transport Archive

Above: No 50 020, built by Henschel in 1939, takes a break at Hamburg Rothenburgsort shed in September 1968. She had been allocated to Rothenburgsort since 24 September 1967, being placed in store there in October 1970, and subsequently withdrawn on 27 November 1970.
John Worley/Online Transport Archive

On 2 September 1968 No 94 1378 stands at Hamburg Rothenburgsort depot, temporarily stored in serviceable condition together with other members of Class 94$^{5-17}$ (the former Prussian Class T 16.1). She was allocated to Rothenburgsort until 31 May 1969, then moving to Flensburg, where she was placed in store on 11 January 1971, and eventually withdrawn on 9 September 1971. *John Worley/Online Transport Archive*

When No 094 937-0 and a sister locomotive stood cold and with covered chimneys at Rothenburgsort shed in October 1971 the end was almost in sight. In the 1960s steam allocations at Hamburg had diminished progressively, and had been concentrated on Rothenburgsort. In the winter of 1964/65 Hamburg Eidelstedt closed to steam, in the winter of 1967/68 Hamburg Wilhelmsburg followed, and in the winter of 1968/69 it was the turn of Hamburg Harburg, whose steam locomotives were all transferred to Rothenburgsort. On 31 October 1972 the end came for steam allocations in the Hamburg Bundesbahndirektion when Hamburg Rothenburgsort itself finally closed. No 094 937-0 was still at Rothenburgsort on the last day, although already in store. Built by Schwartzkopff in 1920, she was placed in store in August 1972, and withdrawn on 8 November 1972 after a working life of 52 years. *Harry Luff/Online Transport Archive*

No 82 017 stands at Bergedorf with an engineering train on 2 September 1968. Built by Krupp in 1951, she was allocated to Hamburg-Wilhelmsburg between May 1951 and September 1967, when she moved to Rothenburgsort. The records show that she was placed in store on 21 September 1968, but not officially withdrawn until 27 November 1970. *John Worley/Online Transport Archive*

No 78 521 departs Aumühle with a push-pull train in September 1968. She had been allocated to Hamburg Altona since 1 June 1966, but was placed in store on 23 September 1968, just three weeks after this photograph was taken. Withdrawal followed on 11 December 1968. *John Worley/Online Transport Archive*

No 78 521 waits to depart Aumühle with a train for Bergedorf. The electric S-Bahn service from Altona to Bergedorf had already commenced in 1959, and from 1969 it would be extended from Bergedorf to Aumühle. Preparatory work for this has already begun.
John Worley/Online Transport Archive

No 50 1023 has charge of an engineering train at Aumühle in September 1968. As can be seen, she was one of the 735 members of Class 50 that were fitted with a cabin tender for use by the guard.
John Worley/Online Transport Archive

No 78 248 waits at Aumühle for her next turn of duty in September 1968. She had been allocated to Hamburg Altona depot since 10 March 1967, where she would remain until being placed in store on 23 July 1969, and subsequently withdrawn on 19 September 1969.
John Worley/Online Transport Archive

Two-cylinder 2-8-2 No 41 206, built by Henschel in 1940, stands at Bremen Hauptbahnhof in September 1968. She had been rebuilt at Braunschweig works in 1960 with a 'Verbrennungskammer'-fitted boiler, 'Mischvorwärmer', single valve superheat regulator and oil firing. Between 23 November 1960 and 28 September 1968 she was allocated to Kirchweyhe, then moved to Rheine, where she was withdrawn in May 1977 as 042 206-3.
John Worley/Online Transport Archive

No 39 162, built by Henschel in 1924 as Works No 20213, stands at Frankfurt am Main Hauptbahnhof on the sunny 6 September 1958. At the time of this photograph she was allocated to Frankfurt am Main 1 depot, which was her home shed between 2 June 1958 and 20 January 1959.
John McCann/Online Transport Archive

The Moselstrecke from Koblenz via Cochem (47.7km), Bullay (59.2km) and Wittlich (76.5km) to Trier (111.6km) was built between 1874 and 1879. Although originally promoted partly for strategic political purposes, the line rapidly developed into an important traffic artery with prestigious main line passenger trains, significant local passenger services and heavy freight traffic. Confined between the Mosel and steep valley sides, it also traverses an important wine producing area.

The line features several notable pieces of civil engineering, in particular the Güls viaduct over the Mosel at Koblenz, the Kaiser-Wilhelm tunnel, the Mosel viaduct at Bullay, and the Pünderich viaduct. The line was electrified between 1972 and 1973, and the start of electric services on 7 December 1973 spelt the end of steam along the Mosel valley.

No 044 270-7 charges southwards past the vineyards with its freight in September 1970. Since June 1965 she had been allocated to Koblenz-Mosel shed, where she was taken out of service on 10 December 1971 and formally withdrawn in April 1972.
John Worley/Online Transport Archive

A Class 044 three-cylinder 2-10-0 thunders across the Mosel viaduct with its freight in September 1970. The 314m viaduct, built between 1875 and 1878, was Germany's first double-deck bridge. The steel girder construction, with a total weight of 1,400 tonnes, crosses the Mosel with six spans and five supporting columns.

After passing Bullay and crossing the river by the Mosel viaduct, the railway plunges into the 459m long Prinzenkopf tunnel. At the west end of the tunnel follows the 786m long Pünderich hanging viaduct, the longest such structure in Germany.
John Worley/Online Transport Archive

During World War 2 the viaduct was an important route for transporting supplies to Germany's western front, and therefore from 1944 was often the target of raids by allied bombers. On 10 February 1945 it was severely damaged during an attack by the

USAAF, with three of the six spans being torn from the supporting pillar at one of their ends. The viaduct was rebuilt after the war, and reopened to traffic on 24 April 1947.
Harry Luff/Online Transport Archive

No 044 670-8 (built by Krupp in 1943, and originally No 44 1668) is seen on a freight near Neef in September 1971. This had been one of her regular routes since 1951, being allocated between 1951 and 1955 to Koblenz-Mosel shed, between 1955 and 1959 to Koblenz-Lützel, and then Koblenz-Mosel again, where she was placed in store on 3 May 1973 and officially withdrawn on 24 August 1973.
John Worley/Online Transport Archive

No 044 595-7 brings a long northbound freight off the viaduct and into the station at Bullay on a September evening in 1971. From October 1963 to June 1972 she was allocated to Ehrang shed at Trier, at the southern end of the Mosel line.
John Worley/Online Transport Archive

No 044 888-6 makes a fine sight with a long coal train from the Ruhr in September 1970. From February 1966 to November 1973 she was allocated to Koblenz-Mosel shed at the northern end of the Mosel line.
John Worley/Online Transport Archive

'P8' No 38 3541, built by Humboldt in 1921, stands on the turntable at Trier depot in the evening sun on 11 September 1959. Just two days earlier, on 9 September, she had received an 'L2' repair.
John McCann/Online Transport Archive

Opposite above: No 86 844 glows in the sun at Trier depot in March 1959. She was placed in store at Trier as early as December 1964, and withdrawn on 1 September 1965.
Les Folkard/Online Transport Archive

Opposite below: Nos 86 316 and 38 1596 slumber inside the shed at their home depot of Trier in March 1959. Both of these locomotives, like No 86 844, were withdrawn on 1 September 1965.
Les Folkard/Online Transport Archive

On a rainy Monday
23 February 1970
No 001 128-8 waits at
Cochem at 13.50 with a
passenger train towards
Trier. After leaving the
station the 1935 built
Pacific and its train will
plunge into the 4,205m
Kaiser-Wilhelm tunnel
(also known as the
Cochem tunnel), built
between 1874 and
1877.
*Les Folkard/Online
Transport Archive*

No 044 380-4 brings a
heavy mixed freight
through Cochem on
23 February 1970. She
had been allocated to
Ehrang shed since
1 January 1969, being
placed in store on
7 June 1973 and
withdrawn on
24 August 1973.
*Les Folkard/Online
Transport Archive*

Nos 050 647-7 and 050 023-1 (both allocated to Mayen) await their next duties at Mayen shed on 12 September 1971. *John Worley/Online Transport Archive*

Five Class 50s in a line at Mayen shed on the sunny Sunday 12 September 1971. From left to right they are Nos 050 592-5, 052 272-2, 050 214-6, 050 047-0 and 050 545-3. *John Worley/Online Transport Archive*

On 18 July 1967 an '044' brings its long train of high capacity bogie coal hoppers past Ehrang signalbox.
John Worley/Online Transport Archive

No 50 136 leaves Ehrang on 18 July 1967. She was allocated to Ehrang shed until 31 March 1969.
John Worley/Online Transport Archive

Leaving an impressive exhaust in its wake, No 50 1738 departs Ehrang with an engineering train in July 1967.
John Worley/Online Transport Archive

Two 'Jumbos' – Nos 44 482 and 44 1277 – are serviced at Ehrang in July 1967. Both were allocated to Ehrang at the time, but whilst No 44 482 spent almost 26 years there from April 1948 to January 1974, No 44 1277 moved between sheds several times over the same period. It was only in October 1965 that she had come to Ehrang from Dillenburg, and stayed there until September 1972, before moving to Crailsheim.
John Worley/Online Transport Archive

The Rheine to Norddeich Mole line runs from Rheine through Lingen, Meppen, Papenburg and Leer to Emden and then on to Norddeich Mole in Ostfriesland (East Fresia). The section from Rheine to Emden is often referred to as the Emsland line, as it follows the River Ems for almost its entire length.

This line was the last DB route with scheduled steam services. From the summer 1973 timetable until 31 May 1975 it had the last DB express passenger services diagrammed for steam traction, hauled by Class 012 Pacifics, whilst freight was operated by two-cylinder 2-8-2s of Class 042 and three-cylinder Class 043/044 2-10-0s until the autumn of 1977. The 2,000 and 4,000 tonne ore trains between Emden and the Ruhr, which finally went over to diesel traction in September 1977, were particularly well known to railway enthusiasts. The last steam locomotives were finally taken out of service on 26 October 1977.

No 01 1054 awaits the departure time at Leer on 7 March 1971. From 15 October 1968, now renumbered 012 054-3, she was allocated to Rheine, where she was placed in store on 15 March 1972, and finally withdrawn on 15 August 1972.
Les Folkard/Online Transport Archive

No 012 100-4 (built by BMAG in 1940 as No 01 1100) passes Papenburg with a Norddeich to Essen express on 16 September 1971. She had been transferred from Hamburg Altona to Rheine just a few days earlier on 10 September. In 1956 she had received a new 'Verbrennungskammer' boiler, and had been the first '01^{10}' to be equipped for oil firing. She was withdrawn at Rheine on 26 June 1975.
John Worley/Online Transport Archive

No 043 326-8 has charge of a long train of bogie hoppers near Papenburg in September 1971. The former No 44 326 had been converted to oil firing in March 1960. From September 1969 to Mai 1974 she was allocated to Rheine depot before being transferred to Emden on 1 June 1974, where she remained in service until the very end of steam in October 1977.
John Worley/Online Transport Archive

Two 'Jumbos' – Nos
044 618-7 and
044 591-6, both from
Emden depot – thunder
through Lingen with a
block train of bogie
hoppers on
15 September 1971.
*John Worley/Online
Transport Archive*

Fresh out of the works
at Lingen No 050 541-2
undertakes a test run on
15 September 1971.
She had just received
an 'L2' repair.
*John Worley/Online
Transport Archive*

No 094 640-0
(Schwartzkopff 1923)
stands outside Lingen
works on 15 September
1971. At the time she
was allocated to
Hamburg Rothenburgs-
ort, but after spells at
Lehrte and Ottbergen
moved to Emden in
February 1974, where
she was withdrawn in
December 1974.
*John Worley/Online
Transport Archive*

No 012 068-3 (formerly
No 01 1068) heads
south with the 10.55
Emden to Münster on
15 September 1971.
Allocated to Rheine
since 29 September
1968, she was placed in
store on 23 January
1974, and withdrawn on
9 June of the same year.
*John Worley/Online
Transport Archive*

Nos 043 381-3 and
050 599-0 bring their
freight through Meppen
on 15 September 1971.
Originally numbered
44 381, No 043 381-3
had been converted to
oil firing at Braunschweig
works in 1960.
*John Worley/Online
Transport Archive*

No 050 173-4 of Emden
shed brings its freight
into Meppen on
15 September 1971.
*John Worley/Online
Transport Archive*

On 16 September 1971 No 050 173-4 of Emden
shed storms through Oldersum, east of Emden with
its train for Rheine.
John Worley/Online Transport Archive

Oil-fired No 043 665-9
of Rheine shed is seen
working hard with a long
train of high capacity
ore hoppers from the
cab of a train bound in
the opposite direction.
*John Dove/Online
Transport Archive*

No 050 132-0 receives
works attention in
January 1972.
*John Dove/Online
Transport Archive*

No 41 206 is seen with a freight near Vehrte in May 1968. Between November 1960 and September 1968 she was allocated to Kirchweyhe shed near Bremen. From 29 September 1968, by now running as No 042 206-3, she moved to Rheine, where she was withdrawn on 10 Mai 1977.
Harry Luff/Online Transport Archive

No 41 113 is seen with a freight near Vehrte on the same day. From September 1960 to September 1968 No 41 113 was also allocated to Kirchweyhe shed. On 29 September 1968 she also moved to Rheine, now numbered 042 113-1, where she remained in traffic until the last day of steam operations on 26 October 1977.
Harry Luff/Online Transport Archive

On 3 June 1968 No 01 1064 speeds through Vehrte, roughly 12km north-east of Osnabrück, at the head of an express. She had been allocated to Osnabrück shed since May 1957. From 29 September 1968 she moved to Rheine, where she was placed in store in October 1972, and withdrawn on 29 December 1972. *Les Folkard/Online Transport Archive*

No 23 073 waits at Osnabrück Hauptbahnhof, platform 12, with the 15.10 departure to Bad Bentheim. A product of Jung in 1956, she was placed in store at Saarbrücken on 6 February 1975, and withdrawn on 16 May 1975. *Harry Luff/Online Transport Archive*

No 50 2224, built by Borsig in 1942, awaits the right-away at Helmstedt on Monday 3 March 1969. Two years later she was placed in store at Braunschweig on 2 April 1971, and withdrawn two months later on 2 June 1971.
Les Folkard/Online Transport Archive

Also on the cold, sunny 3 March 1969 No 50 937 is seen at Helmstedt with a train of 'Silberling' coaches. Until 27 May 1972 she also was allocated to Braunschweig. On 12 April 1973 she was taken out of service at Lehrte shed, and subsequently withdrawn on 24 August 1973.
Les Folkard/Online Transport Archive

Pacific No 03 111 of 1933 leaves Köln Hauptbahnhof in September 1959. At the time she was allocated to Köln Deutzerfeld shed, and still had many years of service left before she was eventually placed in store on 3 December 1970 as 003 111-2, and finally withdrawn on 9 June 1971.
W. J. Wyse/LRTA (London Area) Collection/Online Transport Archive

A Class 38 (Prussian 'P 8') and a Class 03 Pacific bring a train into Köln Hauptbahnhof early in the morning of a September day in 1959.
W. J. Wyse/LRTA (London Area) Collection/Online Transport Archive

A short time later No 78 112, a Prussian 'T 18', built in 1918 by Stettiner Maschinenbau-AG Vulcan, rolls light engine into Köln Hauptbahnhof. At the time she was allocated to Köln Nippes shed.
W. J. Wyse/LRTA (London Area) Collection/Online Transport Archive

No 041 253-6 stands at her home shed of Köln Eifeltor on a fine autumn day in October 1969. Although she appears well looked after, the 2-8-2 was placed in store less than a year later on 9 September 1970, and subsequently withdrawn on 27 November.
Les Folkard/Online Transport Archive

No 051 360-6 stands at Köln Eifeltor shed on the same day in October 1969. The front bufferbeam shows the date of its last 'L3' repair in November 1967. In the background can be seen classmate No 051 778-9.
Les Folkard/Online Transport Archive

No 051 039-6 waits with its lengthy mixed freight at Köln Eifeltor yard on 6 October 1959.
Les Folkard/Online Transport Archive

A grimy No 044 668-2 rests at Köln Gremberg shed in October 1971. Gremberg was the last of various sheds around Köln with steam locomotive allocations. The end of steam came eventually with the start of the 1975/76 winter timetable, when the last locomotives (Class 050/051/052) were either transferred away or withdrawn at the start of October 1975.
Harry Luff/Online Transport Archive

On Saturday 30 June 1962 a group of British and German railway enthusiasts is visiting Köln Deutzerfeld shed, where a variety of steam locomotives is on view. From left to right can be seen Nos 23 092, 39 064, 78 227, 03 077 and 38 2263.
Les Folkard/Online Transport Archive

Smartly turned out locomotive No 4 of the Theodor Wuppermann GmbH steelworks at Leverkusen-Schlebusch, seen in September 1973, was built in 1949 by Krupp (Works No 2825). She remained in use until 1981, and has survived at the Dieringhausen railway museum. A total of 12 locomotives of this type were built between 1949 and 1961; for delivery to eight different customers in Germany.
Author's Collection

No 78 443 seen departing from platform 8 at Essen Hauptbahnhof on 3 June 1963 had been allocated to Essen Hauptbahnhof shed since 3 October 1960. The front buffer beam shows that she had received an 'L2' repair at Nied works, Frankfurt am Main, 10 months previously in August 1962. She was placed in store on 27 July 1964, and finally withdrawn on 10 March 1965.
Les Folkard/Online Transport Archive

Above: No 050 606-3, fitted with a tender cabin, runs into the shed at Wuppertal Vohwinkel on 13 September 1970. She was allocated to Vohwinkel from 1 June 1970 to 30 September 1972.
John Worley/Online Transport Archive

Below: On Sunday 13 September 1970 Nos 052 781-2, 052 857-0, 052 188-0 and 050 439-9 stand ready for Monday's freight trains at Wuppertal Vohwinkel shed.
John Worley/Online Transport Archive

Standing at Mönchengladbach Hauptbahnhof with a train to Aachen on 15 April 1968, No 03 169 of Mönchengladbach shed is admired by a man and two young boys.
Les Folkard/Online Transport Archive

Coal production began at Alsdorf in 1854, and in 1863 'Grube Anna' mine was acquired by the Eschweiler Bergwerksverein (EBV). In 1871 Grube Anna was connected to the Rheinische Eisenbahn line to Stolberg, and was progressively expanded over the following years. For more than 100 years EBV's coal production at Alsdorf was an important and highly visible operation, and featured a significant steam locomotive fleet into the 1980s. Coal production at Grube Anna ended in December 1983. Until 1992 coke was produced from coal at Alsdorf, but the closure of the coke ovens spelt the end of the story of the coal industry at Alsdorf.

Three members of Class 050 stand at Alsdorf on 24 April 1973, with No 051 421 front right. All three are fitted with tender cabins.
Alan Murray Rust/Online Transport Archive

EBV *Grube Anna No 1* of Class D 600 was built
by Henschel in 1949 and delivered to the
Steinkohlenbergwerk Westfalen AG, Westfalen mine
at Ahlen. She came to Grube Anna at Alsdorf in
1972, where she is seen on 24 April 1973.
Alan Murray Rust/Online Transport Archive

Grube Anna No 2 III, a member of the 0-8-0T Class D 500, was built by Henschel in 1947 as Works No 29884. Originally delivered to the Hersfelder Kreisbahn, from 1954 she changed locations several times until moving to the EBV, Grube Anna at Alsdorf in 1970, where she is seen in 1971.
Harry Luff/Online Transport Archive

Opposite above: Grube Anna No 9 II, a 0-6-0T of the 'Hannibal' class, was built by Krupp in 1939 as Works No 1845, and delivered to IG Farben in Ludwigshafen. In 1959 she moved to Grube Anna, Alsdorf, where she was photographed in 1971. She was taken out of service on 28 October 1972.
Harry Luff/Online Transport Archive

Opposite below: Grube Anna No 3 III, another member of Class D 600, was built by Henschel in 1949 as Works No 25169 for the Rheinische AG für Braunkohlenbergbau and Brikettfabrikation, Köln, where she operated as No 321 of the Rheinische Braunkohlenwerke. In 1965 she moved to Grube Anna, where she is seen in 1971.
Harry Luff/Online Transport Archive

The Ruhrkohle AG (RAG) was established in 1968 as a single company for the coal mining industry in the Ruhr region, to respond to a continuing decline in the coal market. It was divided into seven separate mining companies – 'Bergbauaktiengesellschaften' (BAG).

1 Niederrhein

2 Oberhausen

3 Gelsenkirchen

4 Herne/Recklinghausen

5 Essen (closed 11 January 72)

6 Dortmund

7 Westfalen

Each BAG numbered the locomotives in its region in its own numerical sequence, starting with the respective BAG number. There were different prefix letters for the different types of motive power, with the letter D being used for steam locomotives. Thus, steam locomotives belonging to BAG 7 (Westfalen) were numbered in the D 7xx sequence. BAG 3 (Gelsenkirchen), BAG 6 (Dortmund), and above all BAG 7 (Westfalen) had the most significant steam fleets. Regular steam operations ended in 1977.

The Ruhrkohle AG workshops at Kamen-Heeren, located within BAG 7 (Westfalen) were responsible for the locomotives used at various RAG sites. These included five former members of DB Class 945-17, (Prussian 'T 18') numbered D 791-D 795, and seven examples of Class 80, numbered as D 721-D 727.

Zeche Heinrich Robert D 718 in the Ruhrkohle AG numbering scheme, seen in September 1973, was built by Krupp in 1944 and delivered to Steinkohlenbergwerk (coal mine) Heinrich Robert AG. On the smokebox door she still displays her previous identity as No 7.
Author's Collection

Ruhrkohle AG No D 781, built by Henschel in 1940 as Works No 25279 (previously Klöckner-Werke AG, Zeche Königsborn No 4) standing in front of the Kamen-Heeren workshops in September 1973. She was taken out of use almost two years later, on 18 August 1975. Behind No D 781 and on the right are two former DB Class 94[5-17] (Prussian T 16.1) 0-10-0Ts. On the right of the picture is No D 794, formerly No 94 1219).
Author's Collection

Ruhrkohle AG No D 723 (formerly No 8) seen at the Kamen-Heeren workshops in September 1973 was formerly Deutsche Bundesbahn No 80 038, which had been withdrawn by the DB in March 1960. She was subsequently acquired by Klöckner-Bergbau Königsborn-Werne AG in December 1960 and entered service as their No 3. Subsequently she was moved to Zeche Königsborn 3/4 at Altenbögge-Bönen, and remained in service with Ruhrkohle AG until 1976.
Author's Collection

No 50 464 of Saarbrücken shed replenishes its water supply beside the turntable on 19 July 1967. She was placed in store at Saarrbrücken on 29 December 1972, and withdrawn on 12 April 1973. *John Worley/Online Transport Archive*

No 78 047 stands at Saarbrücken turntable on the same day. The last examples of the Prussian 'T 18' with the DB were withdrawn in the mid-1970s at Rottweil. No 78 047 by contrast would be placed in store just two weeks later on 1 August 1967, and withdrawn on 12 March 1968. *John Worley/Online Transport Archive*

No 23 001 stands at Saarbrücken depot in July 1967. In all 105 members of Class 23 were built between 1950 and 1959. Towards the end members of Class 23 were allocated to Saarbrücken, Crailsheim and Kaiserslautern sheds. No 23 058 was withdrawn from Crailsheim in December 1975 as the last representative of the class.
John Worley/Online Transport Archive

No 023 100-1 stands at Saarbrücken station on the evening of 23 February 1970. She was supplied to the Bundesbahn on 1 September 1959, and would be one of the last members of the class in service. She was allocated to Saarbrücken from 4 December 1968, where she was taken out of service on 5 September 1973 after just 14 years of use following an accident at Ehrang.
Les Folkard/Online Transport Archive

Königlich Bayerischen Staatsbahn Class S 3/6 were four-cylinder compound 4-6-2 express passenger locomotives, of which a total of 159 were built in various batches over almost 25 years; 89 being built by the Bavarian State Railways and 70 by the Deutsche Reichsbahn. The final batches were:

- 30 members of Series k, built by Maffei in 1923 and 1924, renumbered as Nos 18 479-508 in 1926.
- 12 members of Series l, built in 1927 as Nos 18 509-520, and eight members of Series m, built in 1927 - 28 as Nos 18 521-528.
- Two members of Series n, built by Maffei as Nos 18 529 and 530 before its insolvency, and 18 examples built 1930/31 by Henschel as Series o numbered 18 531 - 548.

30 members of Series l to o were rebuilt between 1953 and 1957 with 'Verbrennungskammer'-fitted boilers, multi-valve superheated steam regulators and new cabs, being numbered 18 601-630, and used on express passenger duties. During the rebuild brackets were welded directly to the boiler, which gave rise to cracks in the boiler barrel, because of which the boiler pressure was reduced by 12.5%, significantly compromising the locomotives' performance. As a result, although they proved to be both powerful and economical in service, all 30 locomotives were withdrawn between 1961 and 1965. The last members of the class were withdrawn in 1965 at Lindau.

All non-rebuilt members of Class S 3/6 were withdrawn by 1962, with the exception of No 18 505, which remained in use at the Lokomotiv-Versuchsamt (LVA) at Minden until 1967, and was not withdrawn until 1969.

No 18 605, one of the 30 locomotives that were rebuilt between 1953 and 1957, leaves Ulm on 14 September 1958. She had been built in 1930 as No 18 530, being the last of the class to be constructed by Maffei. She was rebuilt with a new boiler at Ingolstadt works in 1954 and renumbered as No 18 605. She was placed in store at Lindau on 22 November 1962, and withdrawn on 28 May 1963. *John McCann/Online Transport Archive*

The first members of Preußische Staatseisenbahnen Class P 8 were built in 1906. Construction of these very successful locomotives continued until 1930. From 1906 to 1918 a total of 1,887 were built for the various German state railways and the military railway directorate. A further 1,669 examples followed between 1919 and 1923, making a total of 3,556 members of the class built for the different German companies and administrations. The Karlsruhe division ordered a further 40 examples to address the locomotive shortage that followed World War 1.

After World War 1 a total of 627 members of the class had to be handed over to the victorious powers, which made their way to Poland, Belgium, France, Lithuania, Italy, Rumania and Greece, but by 1923 the newly formed Deutsche Reichsbahn replenished the ranks of 'P 8s' through construction of further locomotives. Under the Deutsche Reichsbahn they became Class 38¹⁰⁻⁴⁰.

From 1954 the DB modified 41 examples for push-pull operation. In addition to Class 52 tub-style tenders, they also received the Class 52 loco-tender coupling and enclosed cabs. These push-pull operations ended in April 1965.

The last DB examples were not withdrawn until 1974.

No 38 2272, built by Henschel in 1918, stands at Limburg on 9 September 1959. Allocated to Limburg shed between May 1955 and November 1960, she was placed in store on 28 December 1966 at Nürnberg Hbf shed, and eventually withdrawn on 22 May 1967.
John McCann/Online Transport Archive

No 038 772-0 is seen at rest in August 1971. Built in 1915 as KPEV No 2459, she became Deutsche Reichsbahn No 38 1772. From 30 May 1967 to 2 June 1973 she was allocated to Tübingen shed, and subsequently to Rottweil from 3 June 1973 until her withdrawal on 1 January 1975.
Both: John Dove/Online Transport Archive

No 38 3412, built by Henschel in 1921, running with an ex-Class 52 'Kreigslok' tub tender at Mannheim in June 1962. At the time she was allocated to Darmstadt. Placed in store at Rottweil on 6 June 1967, No 38 3412 was withdrawn on 14 November 1967.
W. J. Wyse/LRTA (London Area) Collection/Online Transport Archive

The later Class 39 was the last passenger locomotive developed by the Preußische Staatseisenbahnen as Class P 10. They were intended for use on heavy express services, as well as on stopping passenger services in semi-mountainous areas to avoid the need for uneconomic double-heading. The formation of the Deutsche Reichsbahn led to delivery of the first examples being delayed until 1922.

The three-cylinder 2-8-2 class were the most powerful passenger locomotives of any of the German 'Länderbahn' companies, and further examples were ordered by the Deutsche Reichsbahn. However, they exceeded the specified maximum axle loading of 17 tonnes, with the result that they could only be fully deployed after certain routes had been upgraded. By 1927 a total of 260 had been built.

Of the 152 examples inherited by the Deutsche Bundesbahn, the last three locomotives, allocated to Stuttgart, were withdrawn in 1967.

Many examples were fitted with Witte smoke deflectors, including No 39 238, built by Krupp in 1926, which is seen awaiting her next duty in June 1962. She was placed in store in May 1965, and was withdrawn on 1 September 1965.
W. J. Wyse/LRTA (London Area) Collection/Online Transport Archive

The members of Bayerische Staatsbahn Class G 3/4 H were built between 1919 and 1923. Notable changes compared to the earlier Class G 3/4 N were that they were fitted with superheating and a feed water heater, had a larger and higher situated boiler and an Adams axle instead of the Krauss-Helmholtz version. The early locomotives had the steam dome and sand-box within a combined, angular casing. From No 7166 onwards (DR No 54 1656) the dome and sand-box were separated and

had rounded casings. At the same time the boiler size was increased. The locomotives were renumbered as Nos 54 1501-1725 in the final Reichsbahn numbering scheme.

Most of the class survived World War 2, and all but a few made their way to the Deutsche Bundesbahn. The last example (No 54 1632) was only withdrawn in 1966 at Nürnberg.

No 54 1632 (built in 1920 by Krauss, München) is seen running light engine near Nürnberg Rangierbahnhof on 12 September 1964. *Les Folkard/Online Transport Archive*

Nine months later No 54 1632 is seen at Nürnberg Hauptbahnhof shed on 7 June 1965. She had been allocated to Nürnberg Rangierbahnhof shed since 30 November 1956, was placed in store on 13 October 1965, and finally withdrawn on 4 March 1966. *Les Folkard/Online Transport Archive*

The Prussian Class G 8¹ was a development of the Class G 8, with a larger boiler and increased tractive effort. Because of its high axle loading, however, the class was restricted to main line routes. The 'G 8.1' was the most numerous 'Länderbahn' class, and the second most numerous class in Germany. No fewer than 4,958 examples were built for the Preußische Staatseisenbahnen and later the Deutsche Reichsbahn. In 1925 the Reichsbahn inherited some 3,121 Prussian locomotives as Class 55²⁵⁻⁵⁶, numbered 55 2501-5622. In World War 2 their ranks were increased by many further examples from Poland and Lithuania, as well as others from Belgium.

Between 1934 and 1941 a total of 691 examples were fitted with a leading pony truck in order both to increase the maximum speed and to reduce the average axle loading, becoming Class 56²⁻⁸.

After World War 2 there were still more than 1,000 examples in existence. In 1968 the Deutsche Bundesbahn still had 50 examples, known as Class 055 from 1968, with the last example being withdrawn on 21 December 1972.

The smartly presented No 55 3599 is seen at Neuss on 1 June 1963. Built by Borsig in 1917, she spent the years between the two world wars from 1918 to 1939 in Poland. In her last years she was allocated to Nürnberg Rbf shed from May 1961 until October 1967, then Gießen until 27 September 1968, finally moving to Dillenburg, where she was placed in store on 4 January 1969 and withdrawn on 10 July 1969. *Les Folkard/Online Transport Archive*

Between 1934 and 1941 the Deutsche Reichsbahn rebuilt 691 members of Class 55²⁵⁻⁵⁶ (Prussian Class G 8.1), with a leading pony truck as Class 56²⁻⁸, being now 2-8-0s. The pony truck allowed the locomotives' maximum speed to be increased from 55 km/h to 70 km/h loco-first, enabling their use on stopping passenger services. In addition, it reduced the average axle loading, allowing the class to be used on secondary lines. In the course of the rebuild the boiler was moved forward in the frames by 720mm and raised by 80mm, and a ballast weight was added above the front driving wheels. The rebuilt locomotives were renumbered as 56 201-891.

After World War 2 the Deutsche Bundesbahn inherited 368 examples, of which the last (No 56 241) was withdrawn in 1968.

No 56 742 stands at Gießen shed on 22 May 1965. She had been built by Jung in 1916 as Works No 2486, and was originally KPEV 'Köln 5191'. Before being rebuilt from Class 55²⁵⁻⁵⁶ in 1938 she was DR No 55 4364. *Les Folkard/Online Transport Archive*

Seen on 6 September 1958, No 56 815 was built by Arthur Koppel AG in 1916 as Works No 8125, and put in service by the KPEV as 'Essen 5732'. Prior to being rebuilt from Class 55²⁵⁻⁵⁶ to Class 56²⁻⁸ in 1939 she was DR No 55 4196. *John McCann/Online Transport Archive*

The Class G 10 freight locomotives were based on the chassis of the Prussian 'T 16' tank locomotive and the boiler of the 'P 8' passenger locomotive. In addition to the boiler, the cab was also largely based on the 'P 8' design. The 'G 10s' were intended for main line heavy freight duties, but because of their low axle weight they had a better route availability than the Prussian 'G 8.1' class of similar power. They were occasionally also used on passenger duties.

Between 1910 and 1924 a total of 2,615 examples were supplied to the Preußische Staatseisenbahnen and the Deutsche Reichsbahn. 35 went to the state railways in Alsace-Lorraine and 27 to the railways of the Saar region. The Deutsche Reichsbahn inherited most of the locomotives from Prussia and continued building 'G 10s' until 1924. The Reichsbahn numbered the members of Class G 10, which were to be found almost everywhere in Germany, as 57 1001-2725 and 57 2892-3524.

Further examples from Poland and Luxembourg were absorbed into DR stock during World War 2.

In 1950 the Deutsche Bundesbahn had more than 600 examples in its fleet, which were renumbered as Class 057 from January 1968, which were all withdrawn by 1970.

No 57 2566, built by Borsig in 1922, is serviced at Trier on 11 September 1959. She was withdrawn on 1 August 1962 at Koblenz-Mosel after a working life of 40 years.
John McCann/Online Transport Archive

Class T 12 was a Preußische Staatseisenbahnen passenger tank design, which was a superheated version of the 'T 11'. Although four prototypes were built in 1902, series production did not begin until 1905. Example were also acquired by the state railways in Alsace-Lorraine, as well as the Lübeck-Büchener Eisenbahn and the Halberstadt-Blankenburger Eisenbahn. Their principal area of use was on the Berlin Stadtbahn, Ringbahn and Vorortbahn, the predecessor of the electrified S-Bahn. 1921 A further 40 examples were built by Borsig in 1921. Following the electrification of most S-Bahn lines

between 1924 and 1929 they were used for shunting duties, or on short-distance passenger and freight services. The tendency for the powerful engines to over-tax the boilers at higher outputs, and their limited water supply, meant that they were unsuited for use over longer distances.

In 1925 the Reichsbahn inherited 899 examples as Class 74⁴⁻¹³, numbered 74 401- 300, except for No 74 544. A further 11, numbered 74 1311-1321, came from the Lübeck-Büchener Eisenbahn in 1938.

The Bundesbahn withdrew all members of the class by 1968.

Nos 74 1114 and 74 838 are at rest at Trier shed on 11 September 1959. No 74 1114 had only been transferred to Trier on 17 July 1959, whereas No 74 838 had been allocated there since 10 June 1952. Both locomotives were withdrawn at Trier on 1 August 1962. *Les Folkard/Online Transport Archive*

No 74 508 is engaged in shunting at Koblenz on 15 May 1959. She was allocated to Koblenz Mosel from 22 June 1956 to 31 May 1959. From 1 June 1959 she was based at Bingerbrück, where she was placed in store on 30 May 1960 and withdrawn four months later, on 30 September. *Paul de Beer/Online Transport Archive*

In 1908 the Königlich Württembergische Staats-Eisenbahnen placed an order for a powerful passenger tank locomotive. This superheated 'T 5' class, intended for use on both main line and secondary routes in Württemberg had a very long fixed wheelbase of 4,000mm to ensure a smooth ride. By 1920 a total of 96 examples had been built. The Württemberg 'T 5s' proved successful and were occasionally even used on express trains on the Gäubahn between Immendingen and Stuttgart.

The Deutsche Reichsbahn inherited 93 examples, numbered 75 001-093, of which 89 passed later to the Deutsche Bundesbahn. Withdrawals began in 1959. The last example was taken out of service in 1963 and retained for preservation at Aulendorf until 1968, but was then also scrapped.

On 14 September 1958 the photographer has captured this view of No 75 035 at Ulm. She was built by Maschinenbaugesellschaft Heilbronn in 1915 for the Königlich Württembergische Staats-Eisenbahnen, as No 1237. She was withdrawn on 29 July 1961.
John McCann/Online Transport Archive

Class T 18 was the last passenger tank locomotive design for the Preußische Staatseisenbahnen, and was developed as the existing 'T10' and 'T12' classes were not capable of dealing with increasing loads. The new class was required to be comparable in performance, axle loading and maximum speed with the 'P 8'. The choice of a 4-6-4T design was driven by the desire to avoid the need for the use of turntables at the end of journeys, and for equally good running properties in both directions.

A total of 534 examples were delivered to German railways between 1912 and 1927, of which the Deutsche Bundesbahn inherited 424. Various locomotives were modified for push-pull operations on shorter commuter routes – for example between Frankfurt and Wiesbaden, and around Hamburg.

The last members of the class were withdrawn from Rottweil shed in the mid-1970s.

No 078 297-9 of Aalen shed is seen shunting at Crailsheim on 15 September 1970. She was placed in store on 21 December 1971 and withdrawn on 18 April 1972. *John Worley/Online Transport Archive*

In the 1960s nearly all members of Class 78 allocated to Hamburg Altona were fitted with push-pull equipment, including No 78 248 seen at Schwarzenbek, east of Hamburg, on 2 June 1968. Until electrification, the push-pull fitted Altona '78s' were used especially on the Aumühle to Bergedorf line. They could be identified by the push-pull control connections with the plug and socket, as well as the additional air reservoir connection, with four air pipes instead of two. No 78 248 was allocated to Altona from 10 March 1967 until being placed in store on 23 July 1969, and subsequently withdrawn on 19 September 1969. *Les Folkard/Online Transport Archive*

On 23 April 1972 a special train, organised by the Kölner Eisenbahn Club, ran from Köln-Deutz to Neuerburg (Eifel) and return with No 78 192 from Rottweil shed. The last 25.4 km were on the Pronsfeld to Neuerburg line, also known as the Enztalbahn. The train is seen leaving the Neuerburger tunnel on arrival at Neuerburg. *John Dove/Online Transport Archive*

No 78 192 is seen again on 23 April 1972 on the return journey. From 1966 to 1970 No 78 192 was based at Aalen, and then moved to Rottweil, where withdrawal came in August 1973. *John Dove/Online Transport Archive*

The Preußische Staatseisenbahnen und Württembergische Staats-Eisenbahnen 'T 14.1' class were 2-8-2T freight locomotives, which later became Deutsche Reichsbahn Class 93⁵⁻¹². The objective with the new class was to address the major design flaw of the Prussian 'T 14' class – the excessive axle loading of 17.3 tonnes on the front carrying axle against 14.2 tonnes for the driving axle, which was only partially achieved. Both the coal and water storage capacity were increased compared with the 'T 14'.

After World War 1 the Württembergische Staats-Eisenbahn ordered new locomotives, which it classified as 'T 14', based on the Prussian 'T 14.1' design, from which it differed only in details.

Between 1918 and 1924 the Preußische Staatseisenbahnen and the Prussian divisions of the Deutsche Reichsbahn received a total of 729 examples; during 1921 and 1922 the Württembergischen Staats-Eisenbahnen and the Stuttgart division together received 39 examples. Under the Deutsche Reichsbahn the 'T 14.1s' became Nos 93 501-1261 (Class 93⁵⁻¹²).

In 1952 the Deutsche Bundesbahn had a total of 423 members of Class 93⁵⁻¹². In 1968 it became Class 093 under the new numbering scheme, but the last examples were withdrawn during the same year.

No 93 640, built in 1920 by Hohenzollern, stands at Osnabrück Hauptbahnhof in 1960. From 1 April 1951 to 17 June 1960 she was allocated to Osnabrück Hbf shed, before she moved to Rheine, where she was placed in store on 7 November 1961, and withdrawn on 18 June 1962. *Phil Tatt/Online Transport Archive*

No 93 849, built in 1923 by Maschinenfabrik Esslingen, waits for her next duty in June 1962. On 1 October 1962 she was transferred from Kornwestheim to Altenkirchen, where she spent her last days in service. Placed in store on 4 November 1963, she was formally withdrawn on 10 March 1963. *W. J. Wyse/LRTA (London Area) Collection/Online Transport Archive*

Class T 16.1 was a Preußische Staatseisenbahn tank locomotive for use on freight services, which was an improved version of the 'T 16'. Amongst other changes, the frames were strengthened and lengthened, and coal and water storage capacity were increased.

In addition to shunting duties Class T 16.1 was also used on lines with steep gradients. Locomotives used on such lines were equipped with a Riggenbach counter-pressure brake. Through the use of members of Class T 16.1 on steeply graded lines it was possible to dispense with the expense and inconvenience of rack operation on lightly constructed routes. Between 1913 and 1924 a total of 1,236 examples were built. Of these, some 1,119 entered DR stock as Class 94⁵⁻¹⁷, numbered as 94 502-1380 and 94 1501-1740. In addition to these came Saarländische Eisenbahnen Nos 94 1381-1384 in 1935, as well as some of the Polish PKP locomotives in World War 2, which were taken into DR stock as Nos 94 1385-1416.

With the introduction of the new numbering scheme from 1 January 1968 the remaining Deutsche Bundesbahn locomotives became Class 094. The last examples were withdrawn in 1974.

No 94 1379 was built by SACM in 1915 as Works No 6816. On 15 May 1959 the 0-10-0T is seen shunting at Wiesbaden. Her last depot was Koblenz-Mosel, where she was placed in store just over a year later, on 29 June 1960, but not officially withdrawn until 12 November 1962.
Paul de Beer/Online Transport Archive

On 13 September 1970 No 094 651-7 slumbers in the shed at Wuppertal Vohwinkel, her last home depot. She was built by Schwartzkopff in 1923 as Works No 8217. On 28 May 1967 she moved from Hagen Gbf shed to Wuppertal Vohwinkel, where she was placed in store on 20 October 1971, and withdrawn less than two months later, on 15 December 1971.
John Worley/Online Transport Archive

Class 97.5 were 0-10-0RT locomotives, built for the Königlich Württembergische Staats-Eisenbahnen as its Class Hz by Maschinenfabrik Esslingen, in 1922 (Nos 97 501 and 502) and 1925 (Nos 97 503 and 504). They operated on the rack line from Honau to Lichtenstein, where they spent their working lives until withdrawal in 1956 (97 503) and 1962 (97 501, 502 and 504). The locomotives had a Winterthur system rack drive with one upper and one lower pair of cylinders. In adhesion mode they operated like conventional steam locomotives, driven by the lower pair of cylinders. Before entering the

rack section live steam was admitted to the upper pair of cylinders. Once the pinion wheel was engaged with the rack, the exhaust steam from the lower cylinders was diverted to the upper cylinders so that the locomotive was now operating as a compound.

Nos 97 502 and 504 were modernised from 1952, with steel fireboxes and strengthening of the frames, especially around the rack engine.

Three of the four locomotives have survived, including No 97 501 with the Verein der Freunde der Zahnradbahn Honau-Lichtenstein at Reutlingen, restored to working order since 2012.

No 97 502 stands at Lichtenstein in March 1961. In less than 18 months she would be withdrawn, on 10 August 1962, together with sister locomotives Nos 97 501 and 97 504.
Both: Phil Tatt/Online Transport Archive

After withdrawal in August 1962, No 97 504 was kept at Reutlingen until February 1965. Afterwards she was stored at Horb until 1972 together with No 97 504, and then until 1981 in the shed at Freudenstadt (Schwarzwald) depot. In May 1981 she was moved to Kornwestheim, and finally in June 1988 to Berlin, where she was destined for the Museum für Technik and Verkehr (later the Deutsche Technikmuseum). On 9 June 1972 No 97 504 stands at Horb whilst No 044 402-6 passes through the station on a freight.
Les Folkard/Online Transport Archive

Class 98[10] were superheated locomotives built by the Deutsche Reichsbahn. As the Bavarian Class GtL 4/4 had proved itself reliable, it was decided to build further examples. However, as the class was required to be capable of a speed of 40 km/h, the new build, often known as Class GtL 4/5, was turned out as a 0-8-2T with a trailing carrying axle, which was joined with the rear coupled axle in a Krauss-

Helmholtz truck. Between 1929 and 1931 Krauss built a total of 21 members of the class. The remainder were supplied between 1932 and 1933 by the newly established company Krauss-Maffei. After World War 2 all 45 members of Class 98[10] were inherited by the Deutsche Bundesbahn. The class was withdrawn between 1957 and 1966.

No 98 1026, built by Krauss-Maffei in 1935, is seen at rest in Lindau shed. She was transferred to Lindau on 1 October 1952, where she would see out the remainder of her days. She was taken out of traffic on 7 August 1966, and withdrawn a few weeks later on 27 September 1966
Harry Luff/Online Transport Archive

Class PtL 2/2 of the Bayerische Staatsbahn were lightweight and compact superheated locomotives for use on branch lines. Two variants were inherited by the Deutsche Reichsbahn as Class 98³. Both had a semi-automatic firing system, which permitted one-man operation, and balconies fitted with handrails, which enabled safe access for members of the crew from the locomotive to the train. The locomotives had a large cab with three windows on each side, which surrounded the boiler up to the smokebox. They were nicknamed 'Glaskasten' ('glass case').

In 1908/09 Krauss delivered 29 locomotives with outside motion, that drove onto a jackshaft between the axles. Two further batches of nine and four locomotives followed in 1911 and 1914 respectively, where the jackshaft was dispensed with, and the wheelbase was reduced. The Deutsche Reichsbahn inherited 22 locomotives numbered 98 301-322, of which nine were from the first series with the jackshaft drive. After World War 2 most members of the class became part of the Deutsche Bundesbahn fleet; the majority being withdrawn during the 1950s.

No 98 307, for many years allocated to Nürnberg Hauptbahnhof shed, remained in use between Spalt and Georgensgmünd until 1963, where she was known as the 'Spalter Bockerl' or 'Spalt Goat'. She was taken out of service on 8 October 1962, and officially withdrawn on 1 July 1963. Subsequently she was placed on loan by the Verkehrsmuseum Nürnberg to the Deutsche Dampflokomotiv-Museum at Neuenmarkt-Wirsberg. No 98 307 is seen at Nürnberg on 13 September 1964 following withdrawal.
Les Folkard/Online Transport Archive

The term 'Einheitsdampflokomotive' denotes the new steam locomotive classes that were ordered by the Deutsche Reichsbahn-Gesellschaft between 1925 and the end of World War 2. They were developed on the basis of largely standardised design features.

Class 01 was a two cylinder 4-6-2 design intended for heavy express passenger services. Between 1926 and 1938 a total of 231 members of the class were supplied to the Deutsche Reichsbahn. For comparison purposes 10 members of the two-cylinder Class 01 were ordered, as well as 10 members of the four-cylinder compound version Class 02. The eventual decision went in favour of the two-cylinder design. A further 10 members of Class 01 were created between 1937 and 1942 through conversion of the Class 02 locomotives to the two-cylinder version.

On its formation the Deutsche Bundesbahn inherited 165 members of Class 01. In 1950-51 five were rebuilt with 'Mischvorwärmer' and turbine-driven feed water pumps. In addition, the boiler was equipped with a 'Verbrennungskammer' and the smoke deflectors were replaced by Witte pattern deflectors. From 1957 onwards 50 locomotives were fitted with high performance welded boilers. In addition, a 'Mischvorwärmer' was installed in the smokebox, and many plain bearings were replaced by roller bearings. Changes to the running plate, the lower chimney, removal of the feed water dome and front apron, together with changes to the frames, gave the rebuilt locomotives a distinctly different appearance, but they retained their existing numbers, and were not separately classified.

From the end of the 1960s the last examples in service were based at Hof depot, where they operated over the famous 'Schiefe Ebene' (see pages 40-42). The last members of Class 01 were withdrawn in June 1973.

The first Class 01 to enter traffic was not 01 001, but instead No 01 008, which was built by Borsig in 1926 as Works No 12000. She was withdrawn from Hof shed on 15 December 1973, and sold to the Deutsche Gesellschaft für Eisenbahngeschichte. No 01 008 is seen at Trier in July 1967.
John Worley/Online Transport Archive

No 01 150 was built by Henschel in 1935. On the frosty 14 March 1970 as No 001 150-2 she has charge of the 07.10 Hof to Nürnberg. She was taken out of traffic at Hof in November 1973, and withdrawn a few days later. Shortly afterwards she began her new life in preservation.
Les Folkard/Online Transport Archive

No 001 169-2 was built by Henschel in 1935, and entered traffic with the Deutsche Reichsbahn as No 01 169. In August 1961 she was rebuilt at Frankfurt Nied works, being fitted with a 'Verbrennungskammer' boiler, 'Mischvorwärmer' and single valve superheated steam regulator. She is seen in rebuilt condition on 27 May 1970. She was placed in store just 10 months later in March 1971, and officially withdrawn at Hof on 15 December 1971.
W. J. Wyse/LRTA (London Area) Collection/Online Transport Archive

In the 1930s the Deutsche Reichsbahn had a requirement for a powerful express passenger locomotive with a top speed of 150 km/h. To achieve improved starting performance a design with a smooth-running three cylinder chassis was selected, with streamlined casing being fitted to reduce air resistance. A total of 204 examples were ordered in 1939, but due to the war only 55 were built. Because of developments in the war all class members were moved to Western Germany in 1944.

After World War 2 the '01[10]s' were in a very run down condition, and all members of the class were withdrawn from service with effect from 20 June 1945. Because of the acute motive power shortage, however, some members of the class without major faults were temporarily reinstated. In 1949 a decision was made to refurbish the locomotives, with the streamlined casing being removed, and Witte style smoke deflectors being fitted.

To address problems with the boilers, which suffered from damage as a result of metal fatigue and at welding points, 56 new high performance 'Verbrennungskammer' welded boilers were supplied between 1953 and 1956. In 1956 No 01 1100 received a new boiler and was equipped for oil firing, which significantly improved its performance, and gave improved efficiency. As a result, from 1957 a further 33 examples were converted to oil firing. In 1968 the coal-fired locomotives became Class 011, whilst the oil-fired version became Class 012.

Until electrification, the class was used on all major routes. The last examples were withdrawn from Rheine depot on 31 May 1975.

On 4 April 1970 No 011 091-6 is seen at Papenburg with an enthusiasts' special. She was fitted with a 'Verbrennungskammer' boiler at Braunschweig works in August 1955, but as soon as June 1958 received a replacement 'Verbrennungskammer' boiler. From 1 April 1967 the locomotive was allocated to Rheine, where she was placed in store on 15 September 1971, and withdrawn three months later on 15 December.
John Worley/Online Transport Archive

No 01 1058 has a clear road in 1967. After a long period out of service she was refurbished for further use by Henschel between January and April 1949. Five years later she received a 'Verbrennungs-kammer' boiler and Heinl feed water heater at Braunschweig works from January to February 1954. In September 1957 she was one of the '01[10]s' to be equipped for oil firing. She was placed in store at Rheine on 20 December 1972, and withdrawn on 12 April 1974.
John Dove/Online Transport Archive

A total of 298 members of Class 03 were built between 1930 and 1938 as a standard express class for routes with a maximum axle loading of 18 tonnes. The lower weight of the locomotives in comparison with Class 01 was achieved through the use of lightweight bar frames, a smaller boiler and smaller cylinders. No 03 193 was given full streamlined casing in order to provide a reasonably comparable reserve locomotive for Nos 05 001 and 05 002. In addition, Nos 03 204 and 03 205 were given experimental motion casing.

In 1959 the Deutsche Bundesbahn had 145 members of Class 03 in service. In 1968 there were still 45 members of what was now Class 003 in service with the DB. From 1971 the last 10 members of the class operated out of Ulm, and the last three were withdrawn in 1972.

No 03 251 stands at Aachen Hauptbahnhof on 12 April 1968 with a train for Mönchengladbach. Built by Krupp in 1936 (Works No 1570), she was placed in store in March 1971, and withdrawn at Ulm on 2 June 1971.
Les Folkard/Online Transport Archive

No 03 281, built by Borsig in 1937 (Works No 14673), awaits departure time in 1958. She was placed in store in July 1971, and withdrawn at Ulm on 15 December 1971. *Phil Tatt/Online Transport Archive*

No 03 111, built by Henschel in 1933, Works No 22162, leaves Köln Hauptbahnhof in September 1959. She was placed in store in December 1970, and was withdrawn at Hohenbudberg on 2 June 1971. *W. J. Wyse/LRTA (London Area) Collection/Online Transport Archive*

Two prototypes of a 2-8-2 design were delivered as Nos 41 001 and 41 002 in January 1937 in response to the requirement for a new class of fast freight locomotive. They immediately impressed through their power, smooth ride and acceleration. In October 1938 the Reichsbahn placed an order for the first production series Class 41 locomotives. However, very soon the 20 bar (290lb/sq in) boiler exhibited serious problems with cracks and fractures so that in August 1941 the DR ordered the boiler pressure of the affected locomotives to be reduced to 16 bar (232lb/sq in), which enabled the damage to be contained. At the same time orders were placed for replacement boilers.

Because of the war existing orders for further Class 41 locomotives were cancelled in January 1941, and the last example was delivered on 2 June 1941. In just under four years no fewer than 366 examples had been built, of which 216 passed to the Bundesbahn after the war.

Between 1957 and 1961 a total of 107 members of the class were given fully welded 'Verbrennungskammer' boilers, which produced considerably more steam than the original boilers. In addition, 40 locomotives were converted to oil firing. In 1968 these oil-fired locomotives were all transferred to Rheine and reclassified as Class 042. The remaining coal-fired locomotives became Class 041 in 1968, but were all withdrawn by 1971.

No 042 113-1 was withdrawn at Rheine in October 1977 as the last member of the class.

No 41 166 is seen at the head of a freight train at Twistringen between Bremen and Osnabrück on 1 June 1968. No 41 166 was allocated to Kirchweyhe between March 1967 and September 1968. She had received a replacement boiler in November 1957, and from August 1958 was equipped as an oil burner. She was allocated to Rheine from 29 September 1968 as No 042 166-9, was placed in store in July 1975, and withdrawn on 21 August 1975.
Les Folkard/Online Transport Archive

Palindrome locomotive No 042 024-0 is seen with cylinder drain cocks open running light engine at Emden on 4 April 1970. Built by Henschel in 1939 as No 41 024, she was fitted with a 'Verbrennungs-kammer' boiler, feed water heater, single valve superheated steam regulator and oil firing at Braunschweig works between December 1960 and January 1961. She was placed in store at Rheine on 21 February 1977, and withdrawn three days later.
John Worley/Online Transport Archive

Class 44 was a 2-10-0 heavy freight locomotive design. For comparison purposes both two-cylinder (Class 43) and three-cylinder (Class 44) versions were built simultaneously, with 10 examples of each being ordered in 1926. Further members of Class 44 were not ordered until 1937, with Class 44 being selected as the increased traffic requirements could be better met by the three-cylinder version. A total of 1,989 examples were built between 1926 and 1949.

After the war 1,242 members of Class 44 passed to the Deutsche Bundesbahn. 36 of these were converted to oil firing from 1958, becoming Class 043 in 1968, whilst the coal-fired examples became Class 044.

The most obvious change that the class underwent was the replacement of the original Wagner smoke deflectors with the Witte style. The nickname 'Jumbo' was applied to Class 44 by railway staff on account of the locomotives' considerable power.

The last coal-fired Class 044 was withdrawn from Gelsenkirchen-Bismarck in May 1977. On 26 October 1977 No 043 903-4 operated a working consisting of a breakdown train equipment van from Oldersum to Emden as the very last diagrammed steam-hauled Deutsche Bundesbahn train.

No 44 578, built by Krupp in 1941, stands at Trier shed on 11 September 1959. She was placed in store in August 1968, and withdrawn on 11 December 1968 at Ehrang.
John McCann/Online Transport Archive

No 044 573-4 runs light engine through Cochem on 23 February 1970. Between December 1967 and November 1973 she was allocated to Koblenz Mosel shed. After this she moved for a short time to Rheine, and from December 1973 to Emden, where she was placed in store in February 1975, and withdrawn on 16 May 1975.
Les Folkard/Online Transport Archive

The two-cylinder 2-10-0 Class 50, of which the first 12 examples were built between April and July 1939, was intended to replace elderly Länderbahn freight locomotives on secondary lines. World War 2 gave rise to an increased requirement for freight locomotives, resulting in Class 50 being built in large quantities. No fewer than 3,164 examples were built between 1939 and 1948. After the war a total of 2,159 serviceable examples were inherited by the Bundesbahn, which were used not only for freight traffic but also on passenger services. Thanks to their low axle loading they could also be used on lightly-built branch lines.

After the war many examples were fitted with Witte style smoke deflectors, and 735 members of Class 50 received tenders with guards' cabins. One example was rebuilt as a Franco-Crosti locomotive in 1954, and a further 30 followed from 1958.

At the start of 1968 a total of 1,452 examples survived in traffic to be included in the new class numbering system. Since the individual locomotive running number could only have three digits, the class number 050 was supplemented by 051, 052 and 053. By including the first digit of the individual locomotive number in the class number, each locomotive's original identity remained intact. The resulting series '052' should not be confused with the Class 52 'Kriegslok'. As by 1968 all of the original Class 52 had already been withdrawn by DB, the '052' class number was available for use.

The last Class 50s were withdrawn by DB from Duisburg-Wedau in 1977.

No 051 202-0, built by Wiener Lokomotivfabrik in 1941 as No 50 1202, is seen at Aschaffenburg on 15 September 1970. She was one of 735 members of Class 50 coupled to a tender fitted with a guard's cabin, which entailed a reduction in the coal capacity. In order to maintain the tender water capacity the water tank was extended over the buffer beam. She was renumbered from 50 1202 to 051 202-0 on 1 January 1968 and withdrawn at Ulm on 21 August 1975.
John Worley/Online Transport Archive

No 051 954-6 is also seen at Aschaffenburg on the same date. Built in 1941 by Deutsche Waffen- und Munitionsfabriken AG, she was put in traffic by the Deutsche Reichsbahn as No 50 1954. On 1 January 1968 she became No 051 954-6. Placed in store in April 1975, she was withdrawn at Bayreuth on 2 July 1975.
John Worley/Online Transport Archive

No 052 825-7 is seen at Sauglar in August 1974. Built by Krauss-Maffei in 1942, she entered service in December 1942 as No 50 2825. On 1 January 1968 she became No 052 825-7. Placed in store in April 1975, she was withdrawn at Ulm on 2 July 1975.
Harry Luff/Online Transport Archive

Class 62 was developed by Henschel for the Deutsche Reichsbahn in the 1920s as a two-cylinder superheated 4-6-4T. A total of 15 examples were built. Nos 62 001 and 62 002 operated from Lennep between 1928 and 1932, but although all 15 members of the class had been built in 1928, because of the limited need for the locomotives and their high price the Deutsche Reichsbahn did not accept Nos 62 003-015 until 1932.

Seven members of Class 62 were inherited by the Bundesbahn after the war. By 1956 all of these had been withdrawn by DB. The last example, No 62 003, served as a demonstration locomotive at the drivers' instructional school at Troisdorf between 1956 and 1966, before being scrapped in 1970.

No 62 003 stands at Troisdorf on 2 July 1962.
Les Folkard/Online Transport Archive

The Class 64 2-6-2Ts were built by the Deutsche Reichsbahn between 1928 and 1940 for branch line passenger services.

On the creation of the Deutsche Reichsbahn in 1920 various old Länderbahn classes, which did not reflect the latest developments in locomotive design and which suffered from high running costs, were in use on branch lines. By 1920 designs were already being prepared for a modern, superheated six-coupled tank locomotive, which would also be suitable for lighter loads on main line routes. There were differences of opinion, however, as to whether a tank or tender locomotive was more suitable for branch line passenger services. Eventually the decision went in favour of both alternatives, with orders being placed both for the Class 64 tank locomotive and the related Class 24 tender locomotive.

A total of 520 members of Class 64 were built, of which 393 remained after the war. The Bundesbahn inherited 278, of which the last example was withdrawn in 1975.

No 64 513, built by Jung in 1940 as one of the last of the class, is seen on a freight service in March 1961. Stored in April 1971, she was withdrawn at Heilbronn on 9 September 1971. *Phil Tatt/Online Transport Archive*

No 064 293-4, built by Esslingen in 1934, stands at Weiden on 13 March 1970 with the 13.20 local train to Bayreuth. She was placed in store in February 1969 and withdrawn in July 1969, but was reinstated on 2 November 1969. In June 1972 at Weiden she was placed in store for a second time, and was finally withdrawn on 8 November 1972. *Les Folkard/Online Transport Archive*

After the formation of the Deutsche Reichsbahn more than 50 different classes were in use on branch lines. In addition, there were further classes in use that had been relegated from main line use. For this reason proposals were put forward for new classes for use on branch lines. After various designs had been drafted the choice fell on a 2-8-2T with a 15 tonne axle loading, which would also be suitable for lighter trains on main lines. Class 86 was intended as a standard freight tank locomotive.

The first 16 locomotives were built in 1928 -29. After this, larger orders were placed for serial production, which were delivered between 1931 and 1938. Further orders were placed after the start of the war. From 1942 Class 86 was built in a simplified form, with the most visible alterations being the disappearance of the second cab side window and the use of disk wheels for the pony trucks. The last Class 86 was delivered in May 1943, making a total of 744 supplied to the Reichsbahn.

Alter the war the Deutsche Bundesbahn inherited 386 examples, many of which were based at Nürnberg for use on branch lines in Franconia and at Nürnberg marshalling yard. Hof shed was another well-known centre for Class 86 operations. The DB withdrew its last examples of what by now was Class 086 in 1974.

No 86 576 is seen at Nürnberg Rangierbahn-hof on 12 September 1964. She was placed in store the following year on 1 July 1965, and withdrawn on 1 September of the same year.
Les Folkard/Online Transport Archive

No 86 516, built by Henschel in 1942, is seen at Schweinfurt shed in June 1971 as No 086 516-2. She was placed in store a few months later in October 1971, and was withdrawn from Schweinfurt on 15 December 1971.
Harry Luff/Online Transport Archive

The two examples of Class 10 were built by Krupp in 1957. The new class was intended to replace Classes 01, 03, 18.5 and 39, but their high axle loading restricted their use to a small number of routes, and the rapid roll-out of diesel and electric motive power on the DB meant that no order for further examples was forthcoming.

Initially No 10 001 was coal fired with supplementary oil firing. In contrast, No 10 002 was equipped for full oil firing, which was also later fitted to No 10 001. A distinctive feature of both locomotives was the partially enclosed casing, which was intended to protect the cylinders from excessive cooling and contamination, and also to reduce wind resistance.

Until 1962 both were allocated to Bebra shed, then moving to Kassel, where until March 1967 they operated alongside members of Class 01[10] on express and fast stopping services to and from Gießen. No 10 002 was taken out of service in January 1967 because of major motion damage, and was withdrawn in November 1967. No 10 001 was stored in January 1968, and withdrawn in June of the same year.

For several years No 10 002 was used as a stationary boiler at Ludwigshafen Hauptbahnhof shed, where she is seen in June 1968. She was finally scrapped at Offenburg works in 1972.
Harry Luff/Online Transport Archive

Class 23 was designed to provide powerful locomotives for medium-weight stopping passenger services and for lightweight fast services, and to replace older Länderbahn classes such as the Prussian 'P 8'. The new class very largely fulfilled the DB's expectations. It had a wide route availability and was economical on coal. During trials its boiler outperformed the 'P 8' by 23%, whilst drawbar horsepower was as much as 50% higher. The class had welded plate frames, welded 'Verbrennungskammer'-fitted boilers, and welded tenders. The earlier locomotives had surface feed water heaters and plain bearings. Later examples were equipped with 'Mischvorwärmer' and with roller bearings for the axles and motion. Central lubrication was fitted to inaccessible parts of the running gear. 16 locomotives were fitted with push-pull equipment.

A total of 105 examples of the class were built from 1950 onwards. No 23 105 was taken into stock in December 1959, becoming the last new steam locomotive to enter service in West Germany.

The Class 23s proved equally successful on heavy stopping services and light express services, as well as on freight duties. However, they lasted little longer in service than the Prussian 'P 8s' which they were intended to replace, as the '23s' increasingly lost operational bases due to the relentless modernisation of DB motive power. No 23 058 was withdrawn from Crailsheim in December 1975 as the last example of Class 23.

No 023 029-2 awaits her next duty at Crailsheim, her home shed, in June 1971. She was stored on 12 November 1975 because of a loose tyre, and was withdrawn at Crailsheim shed on 22 December 1975 as one of the last members of Class 023.
Harry Luff/Online Transport Archive

No 23 003 is turned on Trier shed turntable on 11 September 1959. Built by Henschel in 1950, like other members of the first series she had to be taken out of service in early 1952 after barely a year's use and then undergo repairs due to damage to the boiler and distortion around the base of the dome. She was allocated to Trier between June 1958 and January 1963.
John McCann/Online Transport Archive

The term 'Neubaulokomotive' refers to the steam locomotive classes built for the Deutsche Bundesbahn in the 1950s. Significant differences between the Bundesbahn Neubaulokomotiven and the earlier Einheitslokomotiven of the Deutsche Reichsbahn were the use of fully welded plate frames instead of bar frames, and the more efficient, fully welded boilers, mostly featuring a 'Verbrennungskammer'. There were also fully enclosed cabs with sprung and heated floors to provide the locomotive crew with improved working conditions. It is perhaps difficult to appreciate today the impression that the new classes made when they first appeared. They represented not only a leap forward in technology, but also looked very different from the steam locomotive classes that people were used to.

Because of the transition from steam to diesel and electric motive power, however, the new classes often enjoyed only very short working lives, as by the time that the last Neubaulokomotiven were delivered to the DB the fate of steam traction was already sealed. In many cases they were even outlasted by the old classes that they were intended to replace.

No 23 021-9 leaves the turntable at Crailsheim shed on 15 September 1970. She had been allocated to Crailsheim since 14 July 1967. She was placed in store on 22 July 1975 after an accident in which her leading axle had been bent. Withdrawal followed a month later on 21 August.
John Worley/Online Transport Archive

The members of Class 65 were designed for suburban and and Stadtbahn services, where they were intended to replace Classes 78 (Prussian 'T 18') and 93.5 (Prussian 'T 14.1'). Krauss-Maffei delivered 13 examples in 1951 with a further five following between 1955 and 1956. The first casualty, No 65 007, was withdrawn as early as 1966. After some initial problems the locomotives proved themselves to be very reliable, but because they only had a restricted operational range their usefulness was limited. Although the boiler performed well, at first the running characteristics were unsatisfactory, and the running gear was modified at the manufacturer's expense. In 1952, like the early members of Class 23, they were taken out of service due to problems with distortion around the base of the dome, and only reinstated to traffic after a strengthening ring had been fitted to the dome.

No 65 018 was taken out of service at Aschaffenburg shed in 1972 as the last of the class.

Darmstadt was the last shed where members of Class 65 were diagrammed for use on passenger services. No 065 001-0, fitted with a surface feed water heater, is seen on 14 September 1970 outside the shed, where she had been based since March 1951. From 31 December 1970 she moved to Aschaffenburg, where she was placed in store on 5 October 1971 and withdrawn on 15 December. *John Worley/Online Transport Archive*

No 65 015 stands at Limburg in June 1968. She had been based at Essen Hbf shed between February 1956 and May 1966, before moving to Limburg on 19 May 1966. Six months after being photographed at Limburg, No 65 015 was placed in store on 4 December 1968 on the expiry of her boiler certificate. Withdrawal followed on 3 March 1969. *Harry Luff/Online Transport Archive*

Class 66 was designed for fast freight services and for stopping passenger services on both main lines and branch lines, and had a top speed of 100 km/h and an axle loading of just 15 tonnes. They were intended to replace members of the Länderbahn Classes 38[10], 78 and 93. Although they fulfilled all expectations and were considered a successful design, because of the increasing competition from diesel locomotives only two prototype examples were built.

Nos 66 001 and 66 002 were built in 1955, and featured a high performance 'Verbrennungskammer' boiler, roller bearings, a 'Mischvorwärmer' and welded plate frames. Both locomotives were fitted for push-pull operation in the autumn of 1957. Great importance was attached to the working conditions of the driver and fireman, with Class 66 having a fully enclosed cab, heated floor and upholstered seats fitted with seat backs.

No 66 001 was withdrawn at Gießen in 1967 as a result of a broken connecting rod and associated damage to the motion, whilst No 66 002 was withdrawn in 1968 as No 066 002-7.

No 66 001 stands at her home shed of Gießen on 22 May 1965, where she would be placed in store on 3 October 1966 and withdrawn on 24 February 1967. In the background can be seen No 86 381 (also allocated to Gießen). *Les Folkard/Online Transport Archive*

No 66 002 is seen running light at Frankfurt am Main on 6 September 1958. From 29 May 1960 she was allocated to Gießen, where she was placed in store on 15 September 1967, and eventually withdrawn on 12 March 1968. *John McCann/Online Transport Archive*

Class 82 was a superheated 0-8-0T locomotive which was designed for shunting and freight duties. They were intended to replace the 10-coupled Länderbahn classes – especially the Prussian 'T 16.1'. The first examples were built between 1950 and 1951, with another batch following in 1955. The design aimed to produce a locomotive that was equally well suited to shunting and line duties. It featured a welded-construction boiler with a large radiative heating surface, but without a 'Verbrennungskammer'.

To ensure the necessary safe, smooth and track-friendly running characteristics for line duties even at higher speeds, the outer pairs of coupled axles were both combined in articulated Beugniot trucks, which enabled the locomotives to negotiate without difficulty small radius curves such as those to be found in the Hamburg docks network.

The principal places of use were the marshalling yards at Bremen and Hamm, as well as the Emden and Hamburg dock networks. In addition Class 82 could be found operating line duties on the steeply graded lines of the Westerwald and on the Murgtalbahn in the Black Forest.

Withdrawal started in 1966, with the last example being taken out of use at Koblenz Mosel shed in 1972, and Class 82 ended up being outlived by the 'T 16.1s' which they were intended to replace.

In a scene redolent of the last years of steam, No 082 036-5 is seen at Emden depot on 7 March 1969. Based at Emden since May 1951, she was placed in store on 16 February 1970 and withdrawn on 24 June 1970.
Les Folkard/Online Transport Archive

Above: Equally grubby sister locomotive No 82 035 stands on the turntable at Emden on the same date. The cabside numberplate is missing, and the number has instead been applied by hand in a very inexpert manner.
Les Folkard/Online Transport Archive

Below: No 82 038 stands at Koblenz in June 1968 with the empty stock for the 17.26 departure to Limburg. She had been allocated to Koblenz Mosel shed since 22 May 1966, where she was placed in store on 5 May 1971, and withdrawn on 15 December 1971.
Harry Luff/Online Transport Archive

The Nebenbahn Oberschefflenz-Billigheim (length 8.5km) was opened in 1908 to link the Schefflenz valley to the east of Mosbach with the main line. Owner and operator was the Deutsche Eisenbahn-Betriebs-Gesellschaft (DEBG); from 1963 this became the Südwestdeutsche Eisenbahn-Gesellschaft. The level of passenger traffic was always modest, and the railway never fulfilled the hopes that had been placed in it. The principal customer was a brickworks at Billigheim, and when the transport of products from the brickworks was transferred to road transport in 1935, the line's revenue dropped significantly. There remained agricultural products, especially sugar beet, as well as coal for the brickworks. With the introduction of a bus service between Billigheim and Mosbach, passenger traffic shrank significantly as early as the 1920s. Nonetheless this modest railway survived until the 1960s, but eventually the end came on 30 June 1965 for this little piece of 'Kleinbahnromantik'. To the end all services were operated by steam.

Above: The train has arrived with locomotive No 70 at Oberschefflenz in August 1961, where it connects with the main line.
Phil Tatt/Online Transport Archive

Right: No 70 has run round, and waits patiently for the departure time with its train to Billigheim, as she has done so many times before.
Phil Tatt/Online Transport Archive

The minimalist train, consisting of the small locomotive, coach B 20 and a parcels van, stands quietly awaiting departure from Oberschefflenz in the evening sun.
Phil Tatt/Online Transport Archive

Locomotive No 70, a Henschel 0-4-0T built in 1926 as Works No 20693, was originally supplied to the Vorwohle-Emmerthaler Eisenbahn, where she ran as No 10. From the 1930s to the 1950s she was transferred on numerous occasions between DEBG lines – including the Oberschefflenz to Billigheim line – finally returning to the Oberschefflenz to Billigheim line in the 1950s, and remaining there until the end of operations, and her withdrawal, in 1965.
Phil Tatt/Online Transport Archive

The Lokalbahn Deggendorf-Metten was a minor railway in eastern Bavaria with a length of 4.2km, and a 1.1km spur line to the quarries at Metten, which was both built and operated by the Lokalbahn Deggendorf-Metten AG. Its purpose was to provide a rail connection for Metten, and to transport the output of the granite quarries in the region. The line was taken over by the Regentalbahn AG on 1 February 1928, which provided more powerful locomotives that supplemented and eventually replaced the two original Krauss locomotives. The two

0-4-0T Krauss locomotives of 1891 named *Deggendorf* and *Metten* (Works Nos 2451 and 2452), were scrapped in 1965 and 1953 respectively. A diesel railcar was also introduced from 1975 for freight services. Following the end of passenger services in 1983 the Bundesbahn took over responsibility for delivering and collecting wagons.

The last steam-powered train between Deggendorf and Metten ran on 6 November 1975.

Regentalbahn locomotive *Anna* shunting at Deggendorf in August 1961. *Phil Tatt/Online Transport Archive*

Anna with a passenger train at Metten. *Phil Tatt/Online Transport Archive*

Anna, RAGV No 01, a Krauss 0-6-0T built in 1890, Works No 2264, was withdrawn in 1966 after 76 years' service. *Phil Tatt/Online Transport Archive*

The locomotive shed at Metten in August 1961 with RAG locomotive *Anna* standing at the coaling stage. *Phil Tatt/Online Transport Archive*

The line from Cham to Lam was built in two sections. Initially the Königlich Bayerische Staatseisenbanen constructed a branch to Kötzting from the station at Cham on the Schwandorf to Furth im Wald line, with the extension to Lam being built by the AG Lokalbahn Lam-Kötzting in 1891. In 1963 operations on the Lokalbahn section were taken over by the Regentalbahn. In 1973 the Regentalbahn took over the LLK company and wound it up.

Two locomotives of the Lokalbahn Lam-Kötzting, *Hermann Willmann* (left) and *Osser [II]* (right), stand outside the three-road locomotive shed at Lam in August 1961.
Phil Tatt/Online Transport Archive

0-6-0T *Osser [II]* was built by Maffei in 1922 as Works No 5478. In 1966 she was sold to the Regentalbahn, and she was withdrawn in 1970.
Phil Tatt/Online Transport Archive

0-6-2T *Hermann Willmann* was built by Maffei in 1903 as Works No 2299, and entered service as Königlich Bayerische Staatseisenbahn No 2738 of Class D XI. In 1949 she was purchased as Deutsche Bundesbahn No 98 515 for the Lokalbahn Lam-Kötzting. She was withdrawn in 1964
Phil Tatt/Online Transport Archive

The impressive superheated 0-8-0T *Schwarzeck* was built by Maffei in 1928 as Works No 6321. In 1966 she was withdrawn and sold to a scrap dealer, but survived to be preserved, and is now cared for by the Bayerischer Localbahnverein (Bavarian Local Railway Group) along with *Osser*.
Phil Tatt/Online Transport Archive

The Industriebahn (or Kleinbahn) Beuel-Großenbusch on the right bank of the Rhine at Bonn ran from Beuel via Hangelar to Großenbusch, with a short branch from Beuel to Limperich. Its purpose was to serve the various industrial operations in those places. In 1961 there were still 12 separate spur lines in use. The section from Hangelar to Großenbusch was closed on 1 February 1965 and the last locomotives were withdrawn. The residual operation between Beuel and Hangelar (4.7km) was operated by DB locomotives. The Kleinbahn Beuel-Großenbusch owned only steam locomotives – almost exclusively 0-4-0Ts and 0-6-0Ts – and never had any diesels.

A special train with locomotive No 36 operated over the Industriebahn Beuel-Großenbusch system on 5 September 1962 on the occasion of a visit by the Railway Correspondence & Travel Society (RCTS). *Les Folkard/Online Transport Archive*

0-6-0T No 36, built by Henschel in 1919 as Works No 17397, moved to the Industriebahn in 1962 from the Eisenbahn Bremen-Thedinghausen. She was one of the Beuel-Großenbusch line's last three locomotives.
Les Folkard/Online Transport Archive

At the time of the RCTS visit two locomotives – No 36 and 0-6-0T No 38 (Hanomag Works No 23725 of 1938) were still in working order – whilst two others – both also 0-6-0Ts – No 27 (Borsig Works No 8343 of 1911), ex-Eisenbahn Bremen-Thedinghausen, and No 31 (Borsig Works No 5560 of 1905), ex-Teutoburger Wald Eisenbahn – were waiting to be scrapped. The recently withdrawn No 27 awaits its fate at Beuel.
Les Folkard/Online Transport Archive

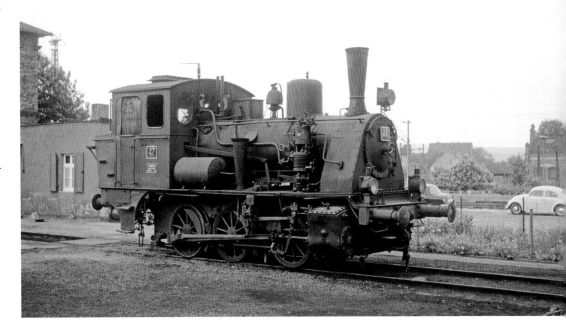

During the visit the other withdrawn locomotive, No 31, was collected by No 36, and propelled by the special train to the end of the branch to Limperich to be scrapped.
Les Folkard/Online Transport Archive

No 36 and the withdrawn No 31 are seen from the balcony of the special train during the journey to Limperich.
Les Folkard/Online Transport Archive

The Frankfurt-Königsteiner Eisenbahn (FKE) began life as the Kleinbahn AG Höchst-Königstein, established in 1901, which later became the Kleinbahn AG Frankfurt-Königstein and finally the Frankfurt-Königsteiner Eisenbahn AG. Services between Frankfurt-Höchst and Königstein (15.9km) started on 24 February 1902. Passenger traffic was the basis of the line's existence; there were only three sidings

for industrial operations, all of which had closed after a few years.

On 1 December 1946 the line was absorbed into the Hessische Landesbahn, with operational responsibility moving to the Deutsche Eisenbahn-Gesellschaft. With effect from the 1959 summer timetable the line largely converted from steam to diesel traction, and 10 years later the last steam locomotive was withdrawn on 30 May 1969.

No 44 of the Frankfurt-Königsteiner Eisenbahn, a 0-6-2T from Henschel (Works No 12478 of 1913) stands outside the locomotive shed at Königstein on 10 September 1959. *John McCann/Online Transport Archive*

No 44 (formerly No 4 until renumbered in 1958) was the last member of a distinctive class, which was almost identical with the Prussian Class T 9.1, and which for many years was characteristic of the FKE. She was taken out of use in 1964 due to a damaged firebox, as one of the last steam locomotives on the FKE. She survived for posterity, being sold two years after withdrawal to Hattersheim municipal council, and for 16 years was displayed in a children's playground. *John McCann/Online Transport Archive*

The Moselbahn, belonging to the former Moselbahn AG, ran on the right bank of the Mosel from Trier to Bullay. Services from Trier to Leiwen began on 2 April 1903. By 29 December 1903 they had reached Andel, which became the operational centre of the line. On 15 March 1904 trains were running as far as Bernkastel, and on 19 August 1905 the last section to Bullay (102.1km) opened to traffic.

From the end of the war in 1945 until April 1947, with the main line 'Moselstrecke' (pages 56-65) unusable due to the destruction of bridges between Trier and Eller, Moselbahn trains ran from Trier Nord the length of the Moselbahn to Bullay, where the Moselbahn connected with the main line, then a further 4km to Neef, where passengers crossed the river by ferry to join a main line train at Eller.

Rising costs combined with very low fares led inevitably to financial difficulties. In addition, great expense was incurred in repairing the line after serious floods in 1955. As early as 1957 an official application was made to close the line, but this was not approved. Instead the Rheinland-Pfalz local government provided short-term financial support, but there was no money available for a necessary thorough modernisation. Instead the line was progressively closed between 1961 and 1968. On 30 September 1961 passenger services were withdrawn over the 23.8km from Bullay to Traben-Trarbach, then on 31 December 1962 the next 38.2km to Niederemmel-Piesport, with freight traffic also being withdrawn between here and Bullay. On 22 May 1966 all traffic ended over a further 4.2km as far as Neumagen-Dhron, and from 1 February 1968 the railcar service was withdrawn from the remaining 35km to Trier. Freight services over the 4.5km between Ruwer West and Trier continued for a few more years.

At its opening the Moselbahn owned two 0-4-4-0T compound Mallets from Hohenzollern (Nos 1 and 2) and four Humboldt 2-4-0Ts (Nos 3-6). Whilst other locomotive made their way to the Moselbahn, both Mallets and two of the Humboldts remained there. From 1936 to 1955 several diesel railcars were acquired, as well as two diesel locomotives in 1953 and 1969.

Moselbahn No 11 stands with a train in the station at Andel. *Les Folkard/Online Transport Archive*

Locomotive No 11 stands on the small turntable in front of the attractive locomotive depot at Andel on 11 September 1959. *John McCann/Online Transport Archive*

No 11 was one of six 2-4-0Ts supplied by Humboldt between 1902 and 1919. By 1959 she was the last survivor of her type on the Moselbahn, and two years later she was withdrawn. *John McCann/Online Transport Archive*

No 11 draws No 226 out of the locomotive shed at Andel on 11 September 1959
John McCann/Online Transport Archive

No 226 stands outside the locomotive shed at Andel on 11 September 1959. Built by Krupp in 1935 as Works No 1500, she first reached the Moselbahn earlier in 1959 from the Braunschweig-Schöninger Eisenbahn. Her stay was relatively short, as just four years later in 1963 she moved on to the Hildesheim-Peiner Kreiseisenbahn, and then in 1964 she returned to the Braunschweig-Schöninger Eisenbahn, where withdrawal came in 1970.
Les Folkard/Online Transport Archive

2-6-2T No 211, seen outside Andel shed on 11 September 1959, was built in 1930 by O&K (Works No 12200) as No 10 of the Elmshorn-Barmstedt-Oldesloer Eisenbahn in Schleswig-Holstein. She moved in 1956 to the Moselbahn, where she was withdrawn in 1966. *Les Folkard/Online Transport Archive*

Also on 11 September 1959, locomotive No 144 is at Andel depot with its coupling and connecting rods removed. No 144 was one of three members of the 2-6-0T 'Elna 2' class on the Moselbahn, which were originally Nos 12-14, and were renumbered as Nos 143-145 in 1952. No 144 (the former No 13) was built by Hohenzollern in 1927 as Works No 4607, was taken out of use at Andel in 1961, and officially withdrawn in 1964 along with her two sisters.

In the background can be seen the out of use No 66 – a 1902-built 0-4-4-0T Mallet from Hohenzollern (Works No 1600), which would be withdrawn the following year. Her two class-mates, Nos 64 and 65 (Hohenzollern Works Nos 1601 and 1602), had already been withdrawn in 1958 and 1956 respectively.
Les Folkard/Online Transport Archive

The Köln-Bonner Eisenbahn AG (KBE) operated an extensive, partially electrified network of lines between Köln and Bonn, the first section of which opened in November 1894. The first line, the Vorgebirgsbahn, was built as a metre-gauge minor railway, but a line linking lignite mines and the new Rhine port at Godorf north of Wesseling, known as the Querbahn, between Vochem and Wesseling, was built as a standard gauge line, with a branch from Godorf to Sürth following. A further standard gauge line between Köln and Bonn – the Rheinuferbahn – was electrified from the outset, and before long was rebuilt as a double track line. A further junction with the main line was provided by the line from Berrenrath to Köln-Sülz with a connection to Köln-Eifeltor freight yard.

In addition to its passenger routes the KBE operated various other lines, for many years the domain of the steam fleet, which were used only for freight, and were not electrified.

In the 1970s it was decided to convert the passenger services on the two principal routes to Stadtbahn (S-Bahn) operation. The conversion took place between 1975 and 1986, with the Rheinuferbahn conversion starting in 1975.

No 95 stands at Hermülheim with a passenger service on 5 September 1959. The first of two rakish-looking 2-6-2T locomotives from Krupp, No 95 (Works No 1469) was delivered to the KBE in 1935, where for a long time she ran as No 90. An identical locomotive followed in 1936, which became KBE No 91. After the arrival of a new No 90 from Krupp in 1952 the original No 90 was renumbered as No 95, and No 91 became No 96. The two locomotives were principally used on passenger services on the Köln Sülz via Hermülheim to Berrenrath line, until they were replaced in 1958/59 by new diesel locomotives. No 95 was withdrawn in 1961, but No 96 became one of the KBE's last three steam locomotives and remained in use until 1964.
Les Folkard/Online Transport Archive

By the end of the 1950s many of the KBE's steam locomotives were already being replaced by diesel locomotives from MaK and Deutz. On 5 September 1959, several locomotives stood out of service, which would officially be withdrawn in the years 1961–64. At the front stand Nos Nr 70 (left) and 71 (right), the only 10-coupled locos on the KBE, supplied by Hohenzollern in 1920, and both taken out of service at the end of the 1950s. Behind No 71 is No 83, the third of nine 2-8-2T locomotives built by Krupp between 1937 and 1942 as KBE Nos 81–89. Beyond No 83 are two further members of this series – Nos 81 (Krupp 1937) and 84 (Krupp 1940). At the end of the row is No 80 – another 2-8-2T, but in this case a one-off from Hanomag, supplied to the KBE in 1929.
Les Folkard/Online Transport Archive

The Kassel-Naumburger Eisenbahn (Kleinbahn Kassel-Naumburg AG) was opened from Kassel-Wilhelmshöhe Kleinbahnhof station to Schauenburg-Elgershausen (13.7km) on 29 October 1903, and to Naumburg (33.4km) on 31 March 1904.

The main purpose of the railway was to provide rail access to three large stone quarries, as well as transporting timber from forest areas. For many years these two loads were the life-blood of the railway, but both disappeared from the 1930s. In 1936 the Henschel aircraft engine works was built at Altenbauna, which brought significant new traffic to the KBE. In 1958 the site was converted into a Volkswagen factory and expanded. The VW factory at Altenbauna would have a great economic importance for the KNE. For many years, however, passenger traffic was dominant on the KNE, but after World War 2 traffic increasingly abandoned the railway for the roads, and the passenger figures dropped dramatically in the 1960s and 1970s, with the result that passenger services ended in September 1977. Freight traffic west of Baunatal-Altenbauna ended in May 1991, but the surviving section continued to enjoy a buoyant freight traffic to the Baunatal VW factory.

Steam traction declined steadily in the 1960s, and in 1973 No 205 was the last steam locomotive to be withdrawn. Since 1972 the line from Wilhelmshöhe to Naumburg has been a well-known preserved railway, operated by the Verein Hessencourrier, notably with original KNE locomotive No 206.

The smartly turned out No 206 of the Kassel-Naumburger Eisenbahn was the last of six 0-10-0Ts, Nos 201-206, supplied by Krauss between 1925 (Nos 201-203) and 1941 (No 206), which were the standard design of the KNE. Withdrawn in 1970, she was purchased by the city of Naumburg and preserved at Naumburg station. She returned to the rails in 1983, being restored to working order over the next two years and named *Naumburg*. Since then she has operated on the 'Hessencourier' preserved operation to Naumburg and other destinations in northern Hessen.
Phil Tatt/Online Transport Archive

No 205, another Krauss 0-10-0T, built in 1938 as Works No 15661, is seen on a passenger service in April 1960. No 205 was taken out of service in 1973 as the KNE's last operational steam locomotive.
Phil Tatt/Online Transport Archive

The Tegernseebahn in Bavaria was opened on 1 August 1883 from Schaftlach to Gmund. On 1 May 1902 services were extended from Gmund to the terminus at Tegernsee (12.3km). The purpose of the line was to connect the Tegernsee area to the main line Staatsbahn for excursion and tourist traffic. Through coaches to and from München operated from 1906.

Tegernseebahn No 7 (TAG 7), a 2-8-2T built by Krauss-Maffei in 1936, remained in active stock as reserve locomotive and for use on excursions until 1975. Since 1975 No 7 has been cared for by the Bayerischer Localbahnverein. For many years she coud be enjoyed in action on her home line, but left the Tegernseebahn in 2000 and since 2008 has stood in the Bayerischer Localbahnverein depot at Landshut with a defective boiler.

Tegernseebahn No 6 was a 0-8-0T, built by Krauss as Works No 8315, which was almost identical with the Bavarian Class Gtl 4/4. On 15 June 1969 she is seen outside the locomotive shed at Tegernsee.
Paul de Beer/Online Transport Archive

Tegernseebahn No 8 was an interesting 2-6-4T, which was supplied to the railway by Krauss-Maffei in 1942 as Works No 16317. A notable feature was that although she had a conventional front pony truck, a Krauss-Lotter truck was used at the rear; this came from Deutsche Reichsbahn electric locomotive No E 79 02, which had been withdrawn in 1940. This combination gave the locomotive especially smooth running properties. No 8 is seen at Tegernsee on 15 June 1969. In 1970 she was sold to a Munich scrap dealer, who rather than scrapping her saved her for preservation. In 1986 she moved to the Bayerisches Eisenbahnmuseum at Nördlingen.
Paul de Beer/Online Transport Archive

The purpose of the Jagsttalbahn was to connect the central Jagst valley with the Staatsbahn line from Bad Friedrichshausen to Osterburken. Construction of the line along the river Jagst from Möckmühl in the district of Heilbronn to Dörzbach started in June 1899. On 18 December 1900 the line was opened to goods traffic, and passenger services began three months later on 13 March 1901. From 1918 the line belonged to the Deutsche Eisenbahn-Betriebsgesellschaft. From 1 January 1963 it was taken over by the Südwestdeutsche Eisenbahn-Gesellschaft (SWEG).

Passenger traffic, which was always insignificant in comparison with goods traffic, finished at the end of 1951, but recommenced on 9 January 1967 in the form of school traffic, which operated until 1979. In 1971 the Deutsche Gesellschaft für Eisenbahngeschichte (DGEG) together with the SWEG began one of the first preserved railway operations in Germany. When two new Gmeinder diesel locomotives, Nos V22.01 and V22.02, arrived in 1965 the last two steam locomotives (No 152 and No 24 II, a 1926 Henschel 0-6-0T) were taken out of use.

Freight traffic, which was operated using 'Rollbock' narrow gauge transporter trucks, continued. In the later years the principal loads were sugar beet and fertiliser for the warehouses in Marlach, Krautheim and Dörzbach. The sugar beet traffic was abandoned at the end of 1986, representing the loss of the Jagsttalbahn's most important freight load. All traffic stopped at the end of 1988 because of the poor state of the track.

Two former Heeresfeldbahn 0-10-0s were acquired in 1949 as Nos 151 and 152. On a sunny morning in August 1961, No 152 is seen shunting near the goods shed at Möckmühl.
Phil Tatt/Online Transport Archive

No 152 was supplied to the military railway authorities by Henschel (Works No 26466) in 1944 but did not enter service, and by 1945 was stored at the Märzfeld area of Nürnberg. She was acquired for the Jagsttalbahn in 1949 together with sister locomotive No 151 (Henschel Works No 26462). No 151 was out of service as early as 1954 due to a broken driving axle crank, and was subsequently used as a source of spare parts for No 152.
Phil Tatt/Online Transport Archive

En route from Möckmühl to Dörzbach No 152 shunts at an intermediate station
Phil Tatt/Online Transport Archive

No 152 pauses with its train at Olnhausen (11.0 km).
Phil Tatt/Online Transport Archive

No 152 rests outside the locomotive shed at Dörzbach in the evening. Although No 151 was already out of service by 1954, and was scrapped in 1960, No 152 performed valuable service until 1965. She hauled her last train through the Jagst valley on 24 October 1965, which was the end of steam traction on the Jagsttalbahn. No 152 was officially withdrawn on 6 November and initially stored at Dörzbach. In 1974 she was sold to the DGEG and in 1976 she was transported to Viernheim.
Phil Tatt/Online Transport Archive

Construction of the metre gauge Brohltalbahn from Brohl am Rhein to Kempenich began in 1898. The section from Brohl via Burgbrohl to Engeln (17.5 km) opened in January 1901, and to Kempenich (23.8 km) in January 1902. The steeply graded 5.5 km section from Oberzissen to Engeln was built as a rack line, but the rack equipment was dismantled in 1934. In 1904 the 1.9 km-long connection to the quay at Brohl was completed, where stone from the quarries could be loaded directly onto barges.

The purpose of the railway was to transport various types of stone and minerals, as well as agricultural products, together with the inbound carriage of coal for local industry. Passenger traffic, in contrast, was relatively insignificant. Standard gauge wagons were initially transported with 'Rollbock' transporter trucks, but from 1928 this changed to 'Rollwagen' transporter wagons. To make the quay section accessible for standard gauge wagons, the section between Brohl

Umladebahnhof and the quay was converted to mixed gauge in 1933. From September 1960 passenger services operated only between Brohl and Oberzissen (11.9km), and these ended on 30 September 1961.

During 1965 and 1966 three new diesels arrived to operate the remaining freight traffic, and during 1967 and 1968 the last three steam locomotives (Nos I, III and IV) were withdrawn. Freight traffic migrated increasingly from rail to road, with the result that the section from Engeln to Kempenich closed on 1 October 1974 and was dismantled in 1976. 'Rollwagen' operations ended in 1978, and by the 1990s the only remaining freight traffic was the transportation of a volcanic rock known as Phonolite.

From March 1977 the 'Vulkan-Expreß' operated the first excursions from Brohl through the Brohl valley to Engeln. From 2015 these featured restored Humboldt Mallet No 11sm, which operated on the Brohltalbahn between 1906 and 1964.

Locomotive No I – a powerful 0-10-0T – was built by Krauss in 1930 as Works No 8488. She was photographed in August 1960.
Phil Tatt/Online Transport Archive

No IV – a 0-8-0T built by Krauss in 1927 as Works No 8399 – arrived in 1937 from the state-operated Waldbahn Ruhpolding – Reit im Winkl, and was withdrawn in 1968. In August 1960 she has charge of a loaded train at the transhipment quay on the Rhine at Brohl.
Phil Tatt/Online Transport Archive

No III – an elegant
0-10-0T – was built
by Jung in 1951, as
Works No 11502,
but only came to the
Brohltalbahn in 1957
from the Nassauische
Kleinbahn, and was
withdrawn 10 years later
in 1967.
*Phil Tatt/Online
Transport Archive*

The Kerkerbachbahn was built to connect the chalk works at Dehrn and Steeden, and the many sites on the southern side of the Weserwald where mineral deposits were mined, with the Staatsbahn and the harbour at Steeden an der Lahn.

The first four kilometre section from Kerkerbach to Dehrn was built as mixed standard and metre gauge line. At first, from 1 May 1886, there were just freight services, with passenger services starting on 1 June 1888. At the same time passenger services began down the Kerkerbach valley to Heckholzhausen. Freight traffic had already started here on 5 November 1887 to Eschenau, and on 10 January 1888 to Heckholzhausen. A few years later the narrow gauge section was extended from Heckholzhausen further into the Westerwald; in October 1905 to Hintermeilingen, in October 1907 to Waldernbach and finally in April 1908 to Mengerskirchen. At this stage the Kerkerbachbahn had reached its full length of 35.1 km.

The always modest passenger traffic ended between Kerkerbach and Dehrn in 1929, but managed to cling on between Kerkerbach and Hintermeilingen until 1 June 1958. Subsequently a single return working ran between Kerkerbach and Schupbach, which itself ended exactly two years later. On 17 December 1960 the remaining freight traffic in the Kerkerbach valley ended, and all narrow gauge rails were removed.

In contrast the transportation of limestone from a quarry at Steeden resulted in continuing high traffic levels on the lower section between Dehrn, Steeden and Kerkerbach. At first the Kerkerbachbahn AG continued to operate this section, until 1 January 1975 when the Deutsche Bundesbahn assumed responsibility for operating it as a feeder spur from 1 January 1975.

On 9 September 1959 the Kerkerbachbahn was visited by the Railway Correspondence & Travel Society, with a special train operating over the line, consisting of locomotive No 16, carriage No 4 and supplementary carriage No 19 (a converted van fitted with benches and windows). The special train ran from Kerkerbach to Dehrn and return, and subsequently from Kerkerbach to Hintermeilingen and return.
John McCann/Online Transport Archive

The RCTS special train pauses at Dehrn.
John McCann/Online Transport Archive

No 16 was originally
built by Jung for the
Heeresfeldbahn in 1942
(Works No 9577) as a
750mm gauge 2-10-2
tender locomotive. She
was rebuilt by the
Kerkerbachbahn to
metre gauge as a
2-10-2T, as was sister
locomotive No 15,
which was built by
Henschel in 1941
(Works No 26169).
*John McCann/Online
Transport Archive*

Passenger services
between Kerkerbach
and Hintermeilingen
ended on 1 June 1958.
The remaining single
return working from
Kerkerbach to
Schupbach ended two
years later on 1 June
1960. On 17 December
1960, just 15 months
after the special train
illustrated, the remaining
freight traffic on the
Kerkerbach valley
section came to an end,
and all narrow gauge
rails were removed.
No 16 was scrapped in
1960, followed two
years in 1962 by No 15.
*John McCann/Online
Transport Archive*

The Bröltalbahn was built to the unusual gauge of 785mm. Originally a horse-drawn line for freight between Hennef (Sieg) and Ruppichteroth, the first steam locomotive was introduced in April 1863. The section to Waldbröl opened in September 1870, and passenger traffic was introduced between Hennef and Ruppichteroth on 1 July 1871.

Work started in 1885 to expand the network. The section from Hennef to Beuel opened in December 1891, followed in January 1892 by Hennef to Buchholz, and in August 1892 by Buchholz to Asbach. By October 1902 the Niederpleis via Oberpleis to Herresbach, Niederpleis to Siegburg and Herresbach to Rostingen sections followed, and the system reached its greatest length of 87.3km. In the years before World War 1 both passenger and freight traffic grew rapidly.

In June 1921 the Bröltaler Eisenbahn-Actien-Gesellschaft was renamed as the Rhein-Sieg-Eisenbahn Aktiengesellschaft (RSE), in part because the line had not run through the Bröl valley for 30 years, and also because there was often confusion with the similarly named Brohltal-Eisenbahn.

In February 1925 the RSE started to introduce bus services on five different routes. From 1929 to 1938 a further six bus routes were opened. To make rail services more attractive, the first railcar was introduced in October 1934, followed by four further units in 1938 and 1939. However, after the war the drift of passengers from rail to bus services continued relentlessly.

In 1951 a phased closure of rail passenger services began. The last passenger train ran on 1 August 1956 between Hennef and Asbach, and the final freight train ran on 17 May 1967 on the remaining section between the quarry at Eudenberg and Beuel. After closure the rails were swiftly removed.

2-8-2T No 52, built by Jung in 1923, stands at the
RSE depot at Hennef on 2 July 1962
Les Folkard/Online Transport Archive

The impressive 2-8-2T No 53, a one-off locomotive from Jung, which was supplied in 1944 as the RSE's final steam locomotive, is also seen at Hennef depot on 2 July 1962. Six years later she was sold to the Deutsche Gesellschaft für Eisenbahngeschichte.
Les Folkard/Online Transport Archive

The Albtalbahn has a rather involved history, of which space permits only a very simplified summary. At its greatest extent the network ran from Karlsruhe via Ettlingen to Busenbach (10.4km), where the line divided in two. One line led in an easterly direction to Pforzheim (34.9km), whilst the other led to the south via Marxzell to Herrenalb (25.8km). The first short section in Ettlingen was opened in 1885. From 1897 the line was extended in stages to Karlsruhe, Herrenalb, Ittersbach and finally in 1901 to Pforzheim. Services were operated by the Badische Local-Eisenbahnen AG (BLEAG), and after its insolvency in 1931 they were taken over by the Deutsche Eisenbahn-Betriebsgesellschaft (DEBG).

The Albtalbahn first introduced electric traction on two short sections in 1898, then during 1910 and 1911 on the Karlsruhe via Ettlingen to Herrenalb main line, and the Busenbach via Ittersbach to Brötzingen branch, but in 1920 the overhead wires were removed between Busenbach and Ittersbach and services reverted to steam haulage. From February 1931 services between Ittersbach and Brötzingen were incorporated into the Pforzheim tramway network. In 1932 the DEBG introduced Rollwagen operations, and in 1936 electric services were reinstated between Busenbach and Ittersbach.

Albtalbahn No 17 was a standard gauge Prussian 'T7' class 0-6-0T, built by Hanomag in 1896 (Works No 2857), which was bought by the BLEAG in 1921 and sent to the Albtalbahn. However, she was frequently hired out to other BLEAG, and later DEBG lines. In 1957 she was transferred to the AVG, but was placed in store in 1958 because she was out of ticket. In April 1961 she is seen in store at Busenbach.
Phil Tatt/Online Transport Archive

On 1 April 1957 the Albtal-Verkehrsgesellschaft (AVG) was founded, which took over operations. In May 1957 conversion from metre to standard gauge began, to integrate the lines into the Karlsruhe tram network. Re-gauging and the introduction of tram services on the main line to Herrenalb took place between May 1957 and August 1961. At first the Busenbach to Ittersbach branch continued to be metre gauge, but here also thoughts turned to conversion to standard gauge. Because the necessary funds were lacking, however, the Langensteinbach to Ittersbach section was closed on 14 November 1964, and only the Busenbach to Langensteinbach section was converted to standard gauge. Demolition of the Langensteinbach to Ittersbach section saw the use of No 99 7203 of the Mosbach to Mudau line, which together with her three sisters had just been made redundant, and was purchased from the DB by the AVG. Subsequently the Langensteinbach to Ittersbach line reopened in 1975 as a standard gauge line on a largely new formation.

Albtalbahn No 7 – a metre gauge compound 0-4-4-0T which was built by Karlsruhe in 1897 – stands at Busenbach in April 1961, stored in working order. No 7 and sister locomotive No 5 were eventually both officially withdrawn by the AVG in 1966. After a long period stored out of use, No 7 was eventually preserved as a 'Denkmallok' at Karlsruhe-Rappenwörth.
Phil Tatt/Online Transport Archive

In spite of the traces of rust on the boiler and firebox cladding, No 050 004-1, seen waiting for the cutting torch in September 1970, still looks fairly presentable. She was one of the first members of Class 50, being delivered to the Deutsche Reichsbahn by Henschel (Works No 24358) in May 1939. Having been placed in store in January 1971, she was withdrawn at Heilbronn on 2 June of the same year. On 14 October 1971 she was sold to scrap merchants Hansa Rohstoffverwertung GmbH of Düsseldorf, and subsequently cut up. *John Worley/Online Transport Archive*

No 39 106 was delivered to the Deutsche Reichsbahn by Borsig in 1924. She was withdrawn at Jünkerath on 20 February 1962, and converted to stationary heating boiler '7007 Saarbrücken' at Nied works. The once proud three-cylinder 2-8-2 awaits scrapping at Trier in July 1967. *John Worley/Online Transport Archive*

Two venerable Prussian 'G 10s', Nos 57 1735 and 57 2559, which spent their last years based at Hagen Güterbahnhof shed, have completed their final duties after a long working life, and await the cutting torch at Hagen Gbf in September 1970. Two years earlier, on 29 September 1968, it had closed as an autonomous depot, and had become a sub-shed of Bestwig. At first not a great deal changed in terms of the supply of motive power, but the final knell for Hagen Gbf shed sounded in the autumn of 1970.
John Worley/Online Transport Archive

A closer view of No 57 2559. Three and a half years earlier on 25 March 1967 a cleaned and polished No 57 2559 had hauled a special train consisting of six 'Donnerbüchse' coaches from Wuppertal Vohwinkel via Wülfrath and Velbert to Heiligenhaus, back to Wülfrath then via Düsseldorf Rath, Gerresheim and back to Vohwinkel, which was organised by the Freundeskreis Eisenbahn Köln (Cologne Railway Enthusiasts Club). Such proud times are now very much in the past. She had been placed in store on 23 February 1970, withdrawal following on 24 June.
John Worley/Online Transport Archive

In September 1970 'P 8' No 38 2212 (Schwartzkopff 1918) is dumped near Bad Friedrichshall Jagstfeld. Her last shed had been Heilbronn, where she was placed in store on 13 June 1968, but not officially withdrawn until 24 June 1970. Three months later she makes a sorry sight.
John Worley/Online Transport Archive

Machine Knitted
BABYWEAR

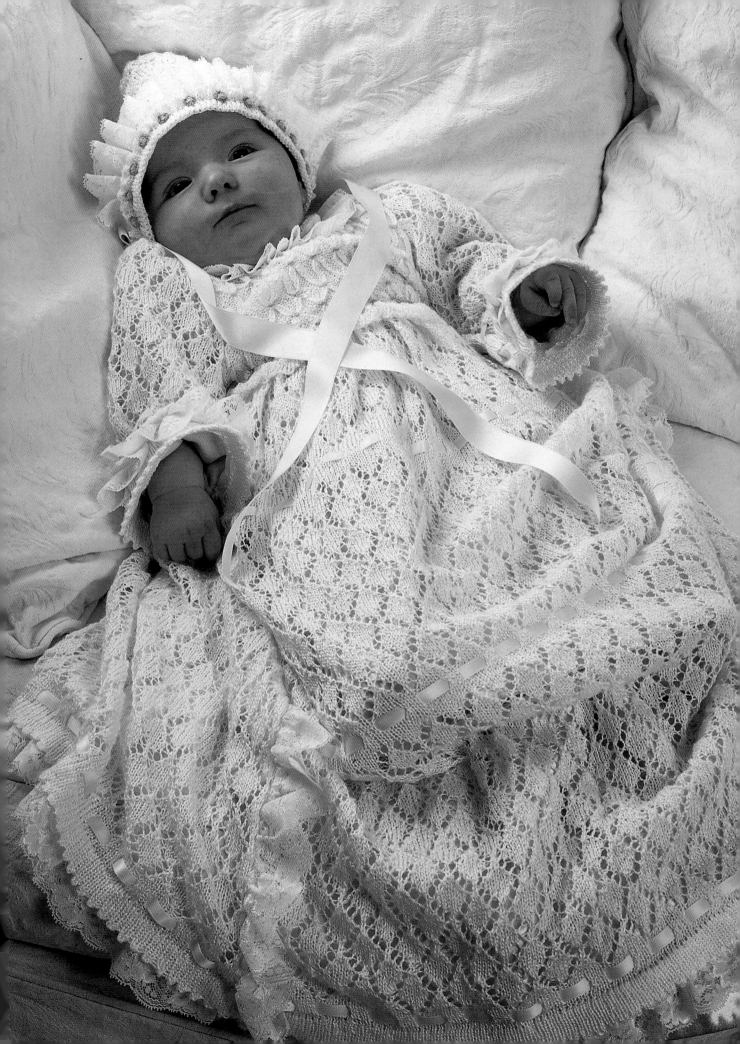

Machine Knitted
BABYWEAR

Christine Eames

GUILD OF MASTER CRAFTSMAN PUBLICATIONS

First published 2003 by
Guild of Master Craftsman Publications Ltd,
166 High Street, Lewes,
East Sussex BN7 1XU

ISBN 1 86108 326 2

Publisher: Paul Richardson
Art Director: Ian Smith
Production Manager: Stuart Poole
Managing Editor: Gerrie Purcell
Commissioning Editor: April McCroskie
Editor: Dominique Page
Pattern Editor: Carol Chambers
Designer: Maggie Aldred
Photographer: Anthony Bailey
Illustrations: Penny Brown
Pattern cards: Carol Chambers
Measurement diagrams: Carol Chambers and John Hawkins

Colour origination by Icon Reproduction, UK
Printed and bound by Stamford Press (Singapore)

DEDICATION

I would like to dedicate this book to my

mother, Mrs Wynne McCarthy, in celebration

of her 90th year.

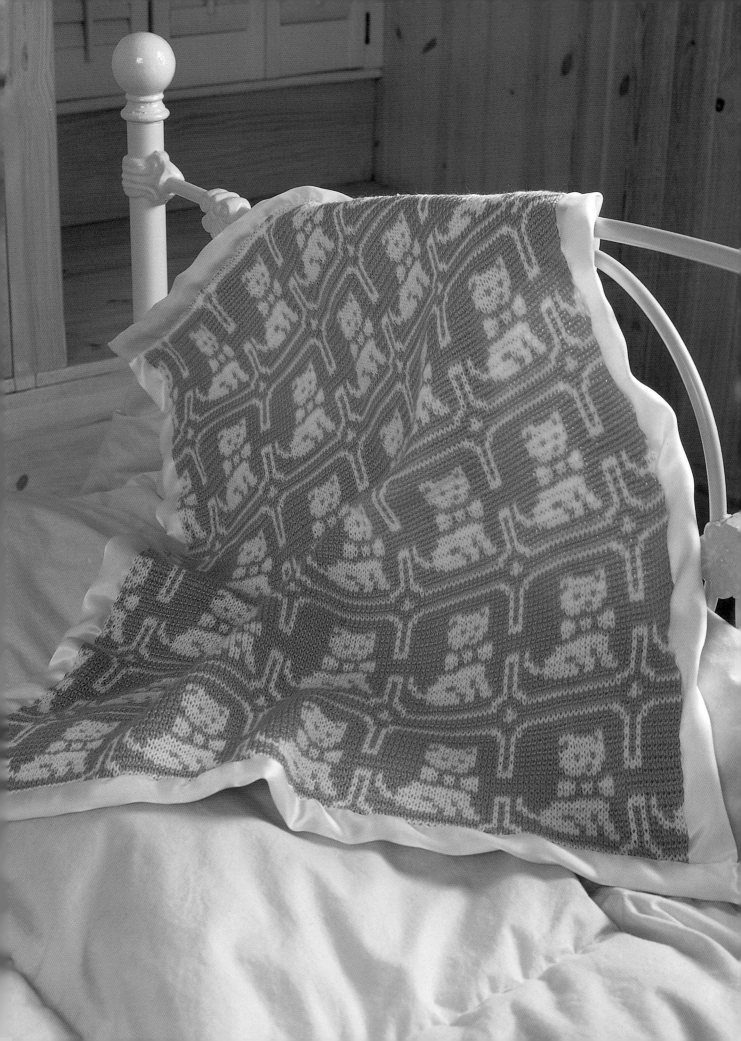

CONTENTS

FOREWORD

Knitting for babies remains as popular as ever, and using a knitting machine to produce the garments simply means you can make a complete outfit in the same time (or less) than you might take to make a matinée coat on two needles! In this beautiful collection of babywear, Christine Eames seeks to encourage your machine knitting skills, and makes this an easy task by providing thorough step-by-step instructions for the techniques that might be new to you. From hints and tips on weighting your work, to knitting spring flowers, and from cables to tuck rib, there's a wealth of information within the pretty and practical patterns. Whatever your level of expertise, these are patterns that will be as delightful to knit as they will be for baby to wear!

Carol Chambers

ACKNOWLEDGEMENTS

I would like to thank my husband, Clive, for his endless faith and encouragement.

I would also like to give special thanks to my daughter, Claire, whose support I have greatly appreciated.

Last, but not least, I would like to thank all the wonderful children that looked effortlessly adorable while modelling my garments.

PUBLISHER'S NOTE
The publisher would like to thank the following people for their time and assistance with the photography: Olivia, Madeleine and Sarah Fitzjohn-Scott, Edward Logan and Emma Stanton, Alfie and Ally Preece, Nicole and Katherine Davies, Maisie Mae and Sally Edmunds.

The publisher would also like to thank The Laurels, Lewes, East Sussex for supplying props, and Silver Reed for giving their permission to use their punch/pattern cards as the basis for the redrawn cards presented within this book, with the exception of pages 36 and 134, which are the author's pattern designs.

ABBREVIATIONS

alt	alternate(ly)
BB	back bed
beg	beginning
CAL	carriage at left
CAR	carriage at right
ch	chain
cm	centimetres
Col 1	colour one
Col 2	colour two
Col 3	colour three
cont	continu(e) (ing)
dc	double crochet
dec	decreas(e) (ing)
FB	front bed
Ff	fully fashioned
FNR	full needle rib
Fig	figure
foll	following
g	grams
HP	holding position
inc	increas(e) (ing)
K	knit
LC	lace carriage
MB	main bed
MC	main colour
mm	millimetres
MT	main tension
MT-1 (2), (3)	one, (two), (three) full sizes tighter than main tension
MT-4 (5), (6)	four, (five), (six) full sizes tighter than main tension
MT+1	one, (two), (three) full sizes looser than main tension
MT+4	four, (five) full sizes looser than main tension
MT+9	nine full sizes looser than main tension
MY	main yarn
N(s)	needles(s)
NRL(s)	needle return lever(s)
NWP	non-working position
0	no stitches or rowsworked
P	purl
Patt	pattern
RB	ribber
RC	row counter
rem	remain(ing)
rep	repeat
sl st	slip stitch
SS	stitch size
st(s)	stitche(es)
st st-	stocking stitch
SYG	second yarn guide
tog	together
T	tension
TD	tension dial
UWP	upper working position
WK	waste knitting
WP	working position
WY	waste yarn
A/B	contrast colours
C & D	colours

INTRODUCTION

Spread across four decades, machine knitting has taken me in many surprising directions: tutor, in-store demonstrator, designer, writer – who could have thought that what started out as a desperate need to clothe a rapidly increasing family would turn into a career that I enjoy to the full! The passion and enthusiasm I have for machine knitting is something I wish to share. For me, the success of machine knitting is all down to sharing: sharing knowledge and expertise so that machine knitters can increase their repertoire of skills and gain satisfaction from creating new and exciting pieces that will delight not just themselves but others too.

This book contains 20 patterns for babies from 0–2 years. It includes some unusual techniques and fresh approaches that should inspire both newcomers to the craft as well as the experienced machine knitter. Enjoy!

MAKING A TENSION SWATCH

The tension swatch is something that most knitters tend to avoid. But, unfortunately, it holds the key to successful knitting: without one it is extremely difficult to create a garment that fits accurately.

Machine knitting without a tension swatch is very much a 'hit and miss' affair. Hand knitters have it easier. They can ask someone, for instance, to 'hold out an arm' for measuring purposes, but when the garment piece is on a knitting machine, this is hardly practical! However, if our sums have been done beforehand, via the tension swatch, the guesswork is taken away, resulting in many more 'hits' and far fewer 'misses'! The step-by-step instructions that follow will help you to create your tension swatch.

Step 1

Using waste yarn, cast on 60 stitches in centre of needlebed and knit several rows. Set row counter to 000. With main yarn and pattern of your choice (providing it is not one for the ribber – they have a section of their own), set the tension dial to one full setting below the recommended one. Knit 30 rows. Put a coloured marker in needles 21 to left and right of the centre 0. It is also good to mark in the centre of the piece the number of stitches that relate to the tension number you are knitting to. If knitting at tension six, mark six stitches. Knit a further 30 rows.

Step 2

Change back to waste yarn and knit several rows, knitting the last few rows in a different colour. Thread up with main yarn again and set your tension dial to the same number that is recommended by the pattern. Repeat the

knitting and marking process as before. When the last row of waste yarn has been knitted, alter the tension dial one full number higher than the pattern states, then repeat the process again. At least one of the three tensions is bound to be correct.

Step 3

Release the knitting from the machine by running the empty carriage across it. Gently tug the work in different directions, as the gauge of the machine needles tends to distort the stitches and some gentle tugging helps to settle them in place. Ideally, the piece should now be pinned (without stretching) to a padded flat surface where a damp cloth is then laid upon it and a hot iron held above, allowing the steam created to permeate the fabric (see Fig 0.1) Allow it to dry thoroughly.

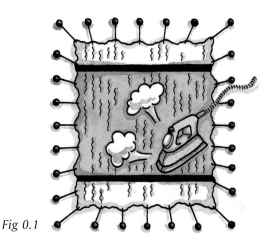

Fig 0.1

Step 4

The green ruler (which should be in your toolbox) is needed now. Place it with the side marked 'R' uppermost, just inside the left edge of the rows of waste knitting. Lay the ruler along the piece until the numbered end just touches the edge of the waste yarn (see Fig 0.2). Read the number it gives and make a note of it. This will be the number of rows you are working to 10cm.

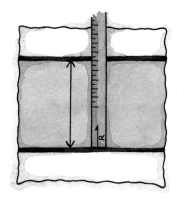

Fig 0.2

Step 5

Now take the green ruler with the 'S' side uppermost, and lay the edge nearest the 'S' on the inside of one of the marked stitches. Lay the numbered end on the inside of the other marked stitch (see Fig 0.3). Make a note of the number it gives, as this is the number of stitches to 10cm that you will be working to. When you get a reading from one of your swatches that gives the same number of stitches and rows as the one suggested on the pattern, then that is the tension setting

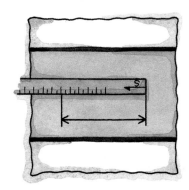

Fig 0.3

for you to work on, and your garment should come out to size. If you want to use this aid to devise your own patterns or alterations, you simply divide the numbers read on the ruler by ten to get the number of stitches to 1cm. You then multiply this figure by the width and length of your finished garment to reach the amount of stitches and rows you need to knit.

Tension swatches for double-bed knitting need to be worked differently. A small piece of knitting is useless here. Cast on at least 50 sts. (Refer to Abbreviations, page X). (This is only for ribber patterns that are reasonably flat and easy to measure – stitch patterns that have plenty of 'stretch' in them need at least 100 sts to measure over.) Stretch the fabric out to get the 'look' you are after, pin to shape, then measure (the back of the fabric is best for this purpose). In stretching the knitting sideways, the piece will lose some of its length, so this must be allowed for.

Creating a tension swatch without a green ruler

Cast on approx. 10–12 sts more than stated tension (e.g. 28 sts to 10cm cast on 38–40 stitches). K approx. 10 rows main yarn, stitch pattern and suggested TD. K2 rows contrast. K half the number of rows to 10cm (e.g. if 28 sts and 40 rows to 10cm, K20 rows). Place a marker either side of number of sts to 10cm. K the same number of rows again. K2 rows contrast. K10–20 rows main yarn and release from machine. After a gentle tug, steaming or pressing and resting (as directed in patterns), measure between st and row markers. Measurements should be 10cm. If incorrect, adjust TD accordingly and swatch again.

DECORATIVE TRIMMINGS

Many high street stores carry a range of knitted babywear that, although basic in design, is perfectly functional, by which I mean the garments provide all the essential requirements for babywear: comfort, warmth, safety and are washable. In such respects, the garments in this book also come under the heading of functional, too. But machine knitters are creative people, so 'functional' is not always sufficient. They strive to give their knitwear a look that is unique – and it is often the small 'additions' to garments that can turn something quite basic into something rather special. It is here that knitting machines can really come into their own – all that knitters require is a little imagination, an open mind, and a willingness to experiment with ideas.

The use of trimmings on babywear is not an original idea, but fresh approaches and exciting fabrics emerge all the time. Take lace edging, for instance. Never out of fashion, it is a traditional trim for baby clothes. However, there is something new on the market – a lace designed especially for knitters. This pretty, double-edged trim is intended to be knitted-in to the knitted stitches (instructions for this technique are provided on page 16).

Flowers can add charm to a baby girl's outfit, and can be embroidered or purchased readymade from haberdashery counters. Machine knitters, however, have another option. They can knit their own flowers in their choice of colours, as shown on the appliqué cardigan and hat, pages 24–31.

Another pretty trim is Swansdown. Used mainly to trim baby bonnets, this delightful, flyaway edging makes the perfect frame for a tiny face.

Fur fabric is not often thought of as a trimming, but is quite versatile and teams particularly well with knitted fabric. It needs a chunky textured-knit fabric to support the extra weight, making tuck patterns ideal for the purpose.

Some knitters may, of course, prefer to work a design without the addition of a trim. Knitters must feel free to utilize their ideas and work on their own initiative wherever possible. It comes down to 'choice' – something that all knitters have.

Finally, it is important not to neglect safety issues when trimming knitwear. Any pearl drops or beads used to trim babywear or childrenswear, must be sewn very firmly in place. Never position them where they can come into direct contact with sensitive skin and cause bruising.

Swansdown trimming, although soft, could cause irritation, and therefore must always be placed well back from a bonnet's brim and sewn securely down.

With regards to necklines, it is illegal to design or sell babywear that has drawstrings threaded around the neck. If a garment needs a ribbon or tape in this area (usually to draw the neckline into shape) it must be constructed in such a way that allows the ribbon or tape to be stitched firmly to the neckline, making it impossible for the neckline to be tightened.

Fleece-lined jacket and hat

A lining of imitation fleece makes this set a must-have for the cold days of winter. With its Peruvian-style cap and toggle-fastening jacket, this outfit is designed to keep your baby snug and fashionable. Because of its outdoor appeal, it was knitted using a yarn containing 50% wool for added warmth.

PATTERN INFORMATION

Sizes
To suit chest 56[61]cm
Finished measurement 62[67]cm
Length 30[36]cm
Sleeve seam 18[20.5]cm
Figures in square brackets refer to larger sizes; where there is only one set of figures this applies to all sizes.

Materials
1 cone 2ply yarn in Oatcake (MC used double)
1 cone 2ply Aran (A used double)
1 cone 4ply Cloud (B)
0.75m cream fur fabric
6 small cream toggles

Garment weight
Approx. 300g for 56cm size (complete with lining)

Main tension
24 sts and 56 rows to 10cm, measured over tuck patt after steaming (TD approx. 7 = MT). Tension must be matched exactly before starting garment.

Note
Knitted side is used as right side. Measurements are those of finished garment and should not be used to measure work on machine.

PATTERN NOTE

Program patt/punch card before starting to knit.
(Pattern is reproduced from card 3A in Silver (Knitmaster) basic pack.)

PATTERN AND COLOUR SEQUENCE

Insert punchcard/program patt on first row. Set carr to select/memorize for patt and K1 row. Release card and set carr for tuck. Work in stripe patt throughout thus: 4 rows Oatcake, 4 rows Aran, 4 rows Cloud.

SPECIAL NOTE

Wind off several balls of the 2ply yarns before starting to knit. Thread one end from 2ply cone and one end from appropriate ball through the same tension mast and into carriage feeder together, treating as though they were the one yarn throughout. Yarns not in use will need to be lifted onto Ns at R edge at each colour change, to prevent 'dragging'.

JACKET BACK

Push 82[88] Ns to WP. Using WY cast on and K a few rows ending CAL. Using MC cast on by hand ('e' wrap) over nylon cord. Weight evenly. Using MT, K3 rows. Insert punchcard/program patt on first row. Set carr to select/memorize for patt and K1 row. Release card and set carr for tuck.

RC000. Start and work in patt (see patt notes) throughout*. K until RC shows 90[112].

Shape armholes Cast off 7 sts beg next 2 rows. 68[74] sts. K until RC shows 72[84].

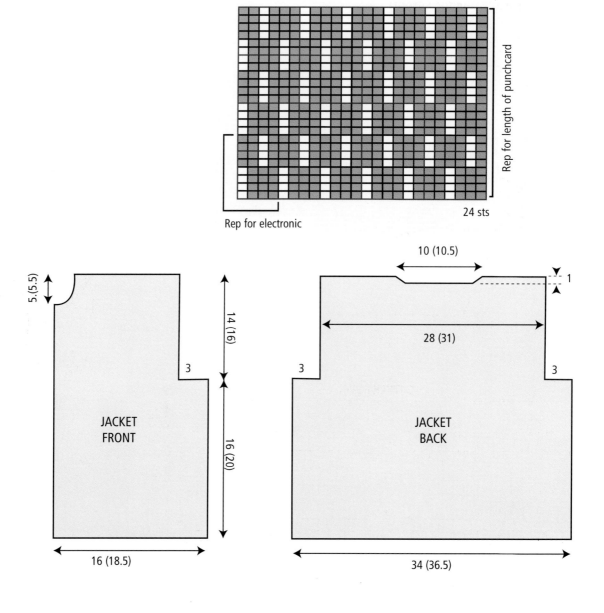

Rep for length of punchcard

24 sts

Rep for electronic

5.(5.5)

14 (16)

16 (20)

JACKET FRONT

3

16 (18.5)

10 (10.5)

1

28 (31)

3   3   3

JACKET BACK

34 (36.5)

Shape neck Note patt row. Using a separate piece of MC, cast off 18[20] sts at centre. Using nylon cord, K22[24] Ns at L by hand, taking Ns down to NWP. Cont over rem 25[27] sts at R for first side and K1 row. Dec 1 st at neck edge on next and every foll alt row 3 times in all. RC shows 79[91]. WK.

CAR. Unravel nylon cord over sts at L bringing Ns down to WP. Reset patt to noted row. Set carr to slip/part/empty and take to L. Reset RC to 72[84]. Release card and working patt from noted position in sequence work L side to correspond with R.

HELPFUL HINT

If you don't have a nylon cord, use any smooth yarn instead.

RIGHT FRONT

Push 38[44] Ns to WP. Work as given for back until RC shows 90[112]. (K1 extra row for L front).

Shape armhole

Cast off 7 sts at beg of next row. 31[37] sts.
RC000 K50[62] rows. CAL. (CAR for L front).

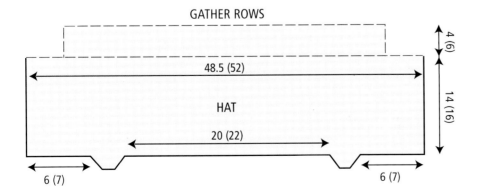

9

. Shape neck

Cast off 3[5] sts at beg of next row, K1 row. Cast off 2[3] sts at beg of next row, K1 row. Cast off 2 sts at beg of next row, K1 row. Dec 1 st at beg of next and every foll alt row 2[3] times in all. 22[24] sts. K until RC shows 79[91] and WK.

LEFT FRONT

Work as given for R front, noting difference in rows to reverse the shaping.

SLEEVES

Push 58[62] Ns to WP. Work as given for back to *. K15[13] rows. Inc 1 st at each end of next and every foll 16[14] rows 5[7] times in all. 68[76] sts. K until RC shows 100[114]. Mark centre st and cast off.

NECKBAND

Push 86[94] Ns to WP. Work as given for back to *. Work 1 patt rep (i.e. 1 col sequence with each yarn – see patt notes). Using MC, work a further 4 rows patt and cast off.

HAT

Push 116[124] Ns to WP. Using WY cast on and K a few rows. Using MC and MT, K1 row. Insert punchcard/program patt on first row. Set carr to select/memorize for patt and K1 row. Release card and set carr for tuck.
RC000. Start and work in patt (see patt notes) throughout and K78[90] rows. WK.

Interim make up Block and steam hat piece to correct measurements. Allow to cool and dry before continuing.

Crown **With wrong side facing pick up sts from below WY of last row worked for hat and hang evenly on to Ns thus:
1 st on first N, *2 sts on next N, 1 st on next N, rep from * to end. Push empty Ns back to NWP. Using MC and MT-1, K6 rows and WK**. Rep from ** to **.
With wrong side facing pick up sts from below WY of last row worked for hat and hang 2 sts on each N, push empty Ns to NWP. Using MC and MT-1, K6 rows and WK.

*** With wrong side facing pick up sts from below WY of last row worked for hat and hang 2 sts on each N, push empty Ns to NWP. Using MC and MT-2, K4 rows*** and WK. Rep from *** to *** once more. Break off yarn leaving approx. 30cm length. Thread yarn through needle or bodkin and thread through each st, then release sts from machine. Pull up thread to gather and fasten off securely.

EARFLAPS AND LOWER EDGES
Push 14[16] Ns to WP. Carefully remove WY from first 14[16] sts and with wrong side facing pick up sts and hang on to Ns. Cast these sts off using MC.

Ear flap Push 20 Ns to WP. Remove WY from next 20 sts and with wrong side facing hang on to Ns. Using MC and MT, K4 rows. Dec 1 st at each end of next and every foll alt row 4 times in all, K1 row. Cast off rem 12 sts.

Front edge Push 48[52] Ns to WP. Remove WY from next 48[52] sts and hang them on to Ns and cast them off using MC.

Ear flap Remove WY from next 20 sts and work second ear flap as given for first. Remove WY from last 14[16] sts and hang on to Ns. Cast off using MC.

JACKET LOOPS
Make three, plus an extra smaller one for hat (optional).
Push 3 Ns to WP. Using WY, cast on. Using MC and MT K2 rows.
Set carr for slip/part/empty in one direction (i.e. set carr for cord

knitting). K until cord is approx. 16cm long.
Pick up the first row of MC sts and place on
corr Ns. Cast off (2 sts tog along the row).

TO MAKE UP

Jacket Join side seams. Block and steam
jacket section, also sleeves and neckband.
Allow to dry.

To attach fur fabric

STEP 1: The fur fabric lining for the jacket is
cut in one piece (apart from the sleeves) to
reduce bulk. Lay fur on a flat surface, smooth
side uppermost. Keeping measurements
correct, pin onto it the joined jacket section
– sleeves, neckband and hat. (Leave the hat
crown for the moment.) Mark with pencil
around the outlines, leaving a seam allowance
of approx. 1.5cm *except* along lower edge of

jacket and lower edge of sleeves. On these, leave an allowance of
approx. 6cm for hem.

From the fabric, mark and cut two facings for the jacket fronts,
25[31]cm long and approx. 8cm wide.

For the hat crown, take a circular object, such as a small saucer, that
is approx. 17cm circumference and lay it on the fabric. Mark around
it, leaving a seam allowance of 1.5cm.

STEP 2: Remove knitted sections from fabric. Cut out the marked
shapes. Prepare fur for sewing by 'shaving' the seam allowances. You
will need a pair of sharp, pointed scissors, and care must be taken at
this stage to avoid snipping the fur backing. It is a good idea (if this
is a new procedure for you), to practise 'shaving' on a spare piece of
fur until you feel confident to continue.

Normally, scissors are held upright when we cut, but for this they
must be laid flat and only the fur pile is cut away, as close to the
fabric as possible. This will give you nice flat seams when you come
to sew pieces together. Shave along all the edges.

STEP 3: Take the jacket and join the shoulder seams (by sewing
machine, or firmly by hand). Sew sleeve seams together and sew
sleeves into armholes. Sew the back seam of hat. Join the fur

HELPFUL HINT

Basting before sewing – especially if using a machine to sew – is a worthwhile task, and well recommended.

If you don't get it right the first time, unpicking is much easier from basting stitches than from machine stitches. Be aware that when unpicking stitches there is a risk of inadvertently snipping the fabric and not the stitch, so care must be taken.

shoulder seams and sleeves. With the fur pile as the right side, line the jacket and baste into place. When satisfied with 'fit', fold over the fur allowance at lower edge, to cover the knitted cast on edge, and sew down.

With the wrong sides of fabric facing you lay the front facings in place along the front edges of the jacket leaving approx. 1cm at bottom edge (for turning under). Stitch firmly through knitted and fur fabrics. Fold the facings in half, (fur should be uppermost) and turn under to meet the fur lining. Sew down. Close the small gap created by the 1cm allowances, at facings lower edges.

STEP 4: Lay the knitted neckband (right side facing you) onto the smooth side of the fur neckband and baste the two together. Fold the fur fabric at top edge, over the cast-off edge of knitted piece and leaving a fur edge showing, turn under the seam allowance (in between the knitted piece and the lining) and slip stitch down. Sew the lining and the knitted edges of the neckbands fronts together, turning only the lining to the inside. Baste together the knitted jacket and fur lining around the neck. Baste the neckband in place, bringing the front edges to meet and enclose the front edges of jacket. Join the neckband to the jacket by carefully unravelling a few at a time the stitches held on WY, gently easing them around the neck shaping and sewing them down with backstitch.

On the inside, turn the neckband's fur allowance under and sew to the lining around neck. Fold to right side the fur allowance at lower edge of sleeves and sew down.

STEP 5: With the seam at the back of the hat joined, run with double thread, a row of small stitches around the hat's seam allowance, and gather slightly. Take the crown section and place it inside the circle of the gathered top. Adjust the gathers to fit crown. Baste, then sew around seam allowance. Turn the seam allowance around the hat's edges under and sew together with the knitted fabric. Stitch knitted cord into a loop and secure to centre of crown.

Cord loop Neaten ends of yarn. Lay the loop flat and sew down its centre, sewing the two 'cords' and leaving a small loop at both ends. Sew the joined cord onto jacket. Sew on toggles to correspond with open loops.

Coat, bonnet and bootees with knitted-in lace

The patterning sequence and differing thickness of yarns are what gives this design its dainty shell edging. Knitted-in lace is shown to good effect on all three items, and the use of Swansdown around the bonnet adds to the overall look of baby femininity. The tuck stitch adds warmth to the jacket fabric without extra weight.

PATTERN INFORMATION

Sizes
To suit chest 41[46:51]cm
Finished measurement 46[46:52]cm
Length 28[28:31]cm
Sleeve seam 12[14.5:15.5]cm
Figures in square brackets refer to larger sizes; where there is only one set of figures this applies to all sizes.

Materials
1 cone of 4ply 100% acrylic in white (MC)
1 cone of industrial 100% acrylic single-strand yarn in white (C)
Lace trim
Approx. 5m of knitted-in lace
3m of narrow white baby ribbon
1m of 2.5cm wide white satin ribbon
30[32:36]cm of Swansdown

Garment weight
For set in first size approx. 250g

Main tension
22 sts and 60 rows to 10cm, measured over tuck patt (TD approx. 9 = MT).
28 sts and 40 rows to 10cm, measured over st-st (TD approx. 7 = MT). Tension must be matched exactly before starting garment.

Note
Purl (tuck) side is used as right side for most pieces except for yokes and picot edgings where knitted side is used as right side. Measurements are those of finished garment and should not be used to measure work on machine.

PATTERN NOTE
Program patt/punch card before starting to knit.
(Pattern is reproduced from card 2 in Silver (Knitmaster) basic set.)

PATTERN AND COLOUR SEQUENCE
Insert punchcard and lock/program patt on first row. Set carr to select/memorize for patt and K1 row. Release card and set carr for tuck. Using MC and T9, K14[14:18] rows. Set carr for st st and using C, K4 rows. Rep this 18[18:22] row sequence throughout.

SPECIAL NOTES
Do not be tempted to guess the amount of lace needed for any garment section and pre-cut. Always work from the long length. Because of the 'panel' widths, there will be long floats of the

single-strand yarn along the right edges, especially when increasing for sleeve shaping. To prevent these threads from getting caught up or from pulling tight, lift them onto the first needle before starting tuck stitch, and let them knit in.

EASY STEPS TO ATTACHING KNIT-IN LACE

STEP 1: Push 60 Ns to WP, and using MC cast on and K20–30 plain rows.

STEP 2: Fold the lace in half, lengthways – short amounts at a time – and you will see what looks like a 'dip' and a 'block' of lace. Hold this folded edge against the first few needles.

STEP 3: Using your single-transfer tool, slide it under the first 'block' of lace and lift it onto the first needle, giving you one stitch and one 'block' on this needle. Repeat this procedure with the second needle and the second 'block'.

STEP 4: Only work in sets of two or three stitches until you feel more confident.

Because the lace has a springy texture, you'll find it has a tendency to jump off the needles. To prevent this, lay your index finger directly below the needles you are working on, pressing against them and their stitches.

STEP 5: When all the lace has been placed on the needles (one 'block' for each needle) take the length of spare, MC and proceed to hand knit the row. If in doubt, this is done by pushing the first needle forward until both its stitch and its block have slipped behind the needle's latch. Now lay your spare yarn across the empty needle and pull the needle back to working position, knitting a new stitch and, at the same time, knitting-in your lace. Make sure you take this stage slowly. You will find that confidence and success will increase with practice.

KNITTING TIPS

I have described above the method known as 'hand knitting', and this manual working of the stitches has many uses. The garment you are planning to knit is worked using a tuck pattern, which, because of its construction, gives two or more loops on some needles.

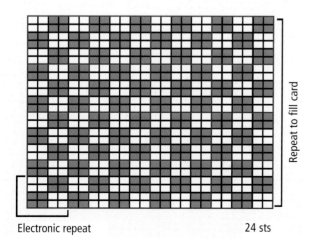

Electronic repeat   Repeat to fill card   24 sts

When casting-off stitches, the side stitches on the bonnet for instance, you will find it much easier if the required number of stitches have been 'hand knitted' in, losing the loops (no longer required) and leaving only a single stitch on each 'cast-off' needle. With 'tuck knitting', it is important that some weights are used, evenly spaced along the width of the work. This will help to hold the knitting down and assist in keeping the loops in place. Sometimes, a fine knitting needle (or two) can be used to balance the weights. Simply weave the knitting needle in and out of the work, then suspend the weights – the small square claw weights that came with your machine or perhaps the small ribber weights – evenly along the knitting needle(s). This method prevents the 'claws' from damaging your yarn.

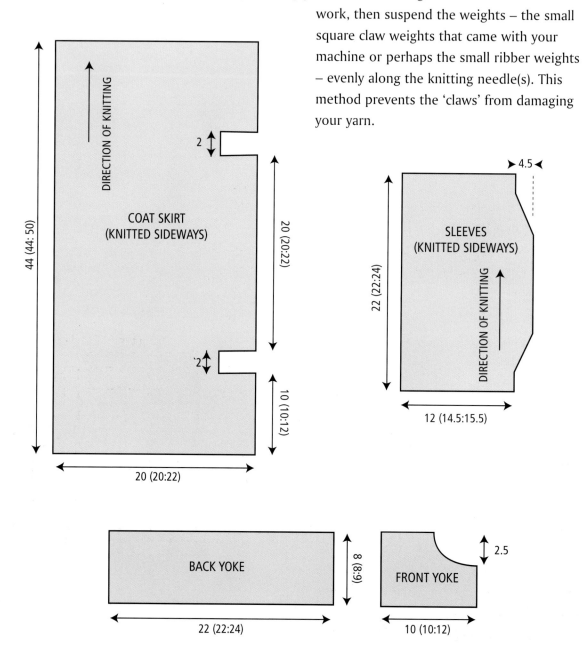

Because you will be holding your work against the knitting machine (e.g. while you pick up the front and neck edges, and when picking up skirt sections of coat to attach yokes) you'll find it useful to cover your ribbing attachment with a sheet of plastic or purchased ribber covers. This will help to prevent those annoying specks of black oil from getting onto your work.

With regards to the punchcard: once it is released to start patterning, there is no need to stop and start it every time the carriage is set to stocking stitch. Let it keep turning – you're less likely to forget to restart it!

These instructions are written for standard gauge punchcard or electronic machines.

COAT SKIRT

Push 40[44:48] Ns to WP. Using WY cast on and K a few rows. Hang weights evenly across the row.

Using MC and MT, start and work in patt and col sequence as given. Keeping patt sequence correct throughout, work two full panels ending on second row of st st section. Attach the knit-in lace (see instructions, page 16) leaving approx. 2–3cm of spare lace at the bottom edge. Work a further two panels ending on row 4 of next tuck stitch panel.

> ### HELPFUL HINT
> *Knit one row of nylon cord, after ending your waste yarn cast on knitting at left. It will be clearer and easier to pick up stitches.*

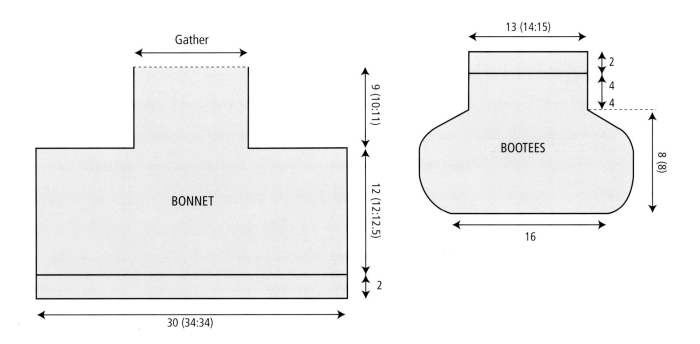

Shape R armhole *Break off C. CAR. Cont with MC and patt, cast off 6[6:8] sts at beg of next row. K to last 2 rows of tuck sequence. CAR, cast on 6[6:8] sts. K2 rows. Rejoin C.* Cont working in panels until you have completed eight further panels for back skirt.

Shape L armhole On the ninth panel, K2 rows of tuck patt, and rep shaping as for first armhole (from *to*)
Work two further panels. Attach knit-in lace as before, leaving 2–3cm spare at bottom edge.
Work two final panels then WK.

RIGHT YOKE

Push 28[30:34] Ns to WP. With wrong (K) side of work facing you, hold the R front skirt section against the Ns. Lift the sts along the top edge onto the Ns. If, as sometimes happens during this procedure, a small 'hole' appears, rectify this by picking up the heel of an adj st. As the first K row will be tight, it is suggested that this row is K by 'hand'.
RC000. CAR. Using MC and MT, K17[17:21] rows. (K1 extra row for L yoke).

Shape neck RC000. CAL. Cast off 5 sts at beg of next row, K1row. Cast off 2[2:3] sts at beg of next row, K1 row. Cast off 2 sts at beg of next and foll alt row, K1 row. Dec 1 st at beg of next and foll alt row. 17[17:20] sts K until RC shows 16 and WK.

LEFT YOKE

Work as given for R yoke noting difference in rows and reading L for R and vice versa to reverse shapings.

BACK YOKE

Push 56[60:66] Ns to WP. With wrong side of work facing you, pick up sts from top edge of back skirt. K the first row by hand as for front yokes.
RC000. Using MC and MT (in st st) K32[32:36] rows.

Shape shoulders and back neck CAR. WK the first 17[17:20] sts (for L shoulder). With a contrast WY, WK the next 22[26:26] sts (for back neck) WK over rem 17[17:20] sts (for R shoulder).

RIGHT FRONT PICOT EDGING

Push 53[56:59] Ns to WP. With wrong side of work facing you, pick up sts of R front from below WY tog with sts from R yoke front. Using MC and MT, K6 rows. Transfer second and every foll alt st to its adj N, leaving empty Ns in WP. MT+1 K1 row. MT K5 rows. Cast off loosely.

LEFT FRONT PICOT EDGING

Work as given for R front edging.

NECKBAND

Join the back and front shoulders by picking up the first row of MC sts from below WY and hanging them on Ns (you should have 2 sts on each N: a back shoulder st and a front shoulder st). Cast off all sts. It is also a good idea to sew down the picot edge at this stage. With wrong side of work

facing you, pick up sts evenly from around L neck front (including the picot edge) then the 22[26:26] sts held on WY for the back neck, and finally the sts for the R front neck. Knit a picot hem as for front edges, but on this occasion, WK instead of casting off (because you'll find that when it comes to sewing down the hem it will be on a curve, and sewing into held sts while releasing the WY, will give the curve more flexibility).

SLEEVES

Push 26[32:34] Ns to WP. Using WY, cast on and K a few rows. Work select/memorize row for patt (see patt notes). Hang weights evenly. RC000. Using MC and MT start and work in patt thus: 14[14:16] rows tuck MC. 4 rows st st in C. K5 rows. Inc 1 st at R edge on next and every foll 6 rows 3 times in all.

Knitting tip: As the sts are inc for the armhole shaping, there will be long threads of single-strand yarn. To prevent these from pulling the knitting tight, it is recommended that you lift the threads up into the end N every few rows. It is also advisable to add edge-weights to the inc sts, moving them up every few rows.

K4 rows. Inc 1st at R edge on next and every foll 5 rows until 36[42:44] sts. RC shows 55. K8 rows. K1 row st st. Add knit-in lace on next row. With carr set for tuck, K until RC shows 74. Dec 1 st at R edge on next and every foll 5 rows, until 29[35:37] sts. K5 rows. Dec 1 st at beg of next and every foll 6 rows, 3 times in all. K6 rows. K1 row st st.

Join the sleeve seam by bringing up the sts held on WY, and transfer the first row of MC sts to the corresponding sts on the N bed. K1 row at highest tension. Cast off loosely.

BONNET

Push 66[70:74] Ns to WP. Using WY, cast on and K a few rows (enough to hang weights evenly). Using MC and MT, K6 rows. Transfer second and every foll alt st to its adj N, leaving empty Ns in WP. T10 K1 row. CAL, using MT-1, K7 rows. Turn up a hem, leaving WY in place holding weights. K2 rows. Attach lace on next row, leaving none spare at edges. Set carr to tuck and release patt card. Using MT, work three tuck panels (see patt notes).

Shape back RC000. CAR. Cast off (loosely) 20[22:24] sts at beg of next 2 rows. 26 sts rem. Work in tuck (without panels) until RC shows 54[60:66]. K1 row st st and WK.

Joining back of bonnet to bottom edge Push 16 Ns to WP. With right side of bonnet facing you, pick up sts from below WY, spreading them evenly, but at the same time gathering the row, e.g. with 1 st only on the first and last two Ns, but 2 sts on all other Ns.

Now pick up 22[24:28] sts from the R bottom edge. Rep the process at the L side. 60[64:72] sts. Using MC and T7, K6 rows (st st). MT+1, K1 row. T7, K7 rows. Cast off loosely.

BOOTEES
(Not worked in panel patt)

Push 36[40:44] Ns to WP. Using WY, cast on and K a few rows. Hang weights evenly.

Using MC and MT-2, K6[6:8] rows. Using MT start and work in tuck patt and *at the same time,* inc 1 st at beg of next 4 rows. K3 rows. CAL. K1 row st st. Attach knit-in lace on next row, leaving approx. 2–3cm spare at *both* ends. (This row not counted on RC.) Set carr to tuck and K8[8:10] rows. Dec 1 st at beg of next 8 rows. K2[2:4] rows. 32[36:38] sts. Set carr for st st. K2 rows. Transfer every third st to adj N, leaving empty Ns in WP (for eyelets). K2 rows. Set carr for tuck. RC000. K20[24:26] rows. Set carr for st st. MT-1, K6 rows. T10+ K1 row. MT, K5 rows. Cast off loosely.

TO MAKE UP

Coat Having joined the shoulders and worked the neck hem, sew down the loose hem sts on the inside of the yoke, curving them to fit. Set in sleeves, easing top of cap to fit and centralizing lace trim with shoulder 'seam'. Neaten spare lace at bottom edge, turning it under and sewing in place. Thread ribbons through the 'ladder' effect at the bottom edges of sleeves, drawing them to fit and tying with bows. Sew ribbons at front edge of yoke and also at neck edge, slipping the ends inside the hem before stitching securely into place.

Bonnet Sew the two open sides together. Stitch Swansdown securely, sewing from the inside of bonnet, and being sure to insert needle through the central 'core' of Swansdown. Fold hem at lower edge, enclosing raw edges of Swansdown and lace then slip stitch into place. Attach satin ribbons at bonnet sides.

Bootees Fold bootee in half. Sew two spare ends of lace, turning them under. Sew along bottom foot (sole), catching stitches held on WY. Sew along toes and instep, then up the front leg.
Finally, fold down picot hem and sew. Thread ribbons through eyelets at ankles.

HELPFUL HINT

An adjustable transfer tool makes transferring every third stitch quick and easy.

Appliqué cardigan and hat

Drifts of bluebell, wild rose, calendula and primrose trim this eye-catching twosome. Basic in design and construction, this cardigan and hat is an ideal starter project for inexperienced knitters as it is worked entirely in stocking stitch and does not need the facility of a ribbing attachment.

PATTERN INFORMATION

Sizes
To suit chest 51[56:61]cm
Finished measurement 55[59:65]cm
Length 30[36:39]cm
Sleeve seam 18[20:23]cm
Figures in square brackets refer to larger sizes; where there is only one set of figures this applies to all sizes.

Materials
1 cone 4ply acrylic in white (MC)
Oddments of industrial single strand (bright acrylic) in blue, gold, pink, white, green and pale yellow
6 white buttons.
1 packet small white pearls.

Garment weight
For set in size 56cm approx. 240g

Main tension
32 sts and 40 rows to 10cm, measured over st st, after light steaming (TD approx. 7 = MT). Tension must be matched exactly before starting garment.

Note
Knitted side is used as right side. Measurements are those of finished garment and should not be used to measure work on machine.

SPECIAL NOTE
The knitted cords for the hat are worked thus:
Push 4 Ns to WP. Using MC, cast on by hand ('e' wrap). Set carr to slip/part/empty in one direction and K in the other. Add a claw weight as the cord progresses. Knit to approx. 35cm (measured without claw weight). Make two.

EASY STEPS TO KNITTING FLOWERS AND LEAVES
Making flowers and leaves on your knitting machine is simple. Follow these easy steps to get you started.
STEP 1: Familiarize yourself with your transfer tools, as you will need them to complete the flowers and leaves for this design, and while experienced knitters can use them with dexterity, beginners can feel all 'fingers and thumbs'. Practise using the single-transfer tool first, moving just one stitch at a time, taking it from the needle until it slides onto the tool, leaving you able to complete the transfer by placing the stitch onto the needle of your choice. Only when these movements come easily to you, progress to the next step.

STEP 2: With your double-transfer tool, transfer the two end stitches simultaneously, moving them to adjacent needles. When you can do that with ease, move on to the next step.

STEP 3: Now try using your treble-transfer tool. You will come across this transferring technique in many machine-knitting patterns. It is used mainly for shaping – especially raglan armholes and anywhere else that might require a special effect – and is known as 'fully-fashioned' (Ff). Before long, when using your knitting machine, you will come to feel that these transfer tools are simply an extension of your fingers.

CARDIGAN BACK

Push 86[92:102] Ns to WP. Using WY cast on and K a few rows, ending CAR. Using MC and MT-1 K11 rows. T10 K1 row. MT K12 rows. Turn up hem by picking up loops from first row worked in MC and hang evenly along the row**.

RC000. MT K 52[68:76] rows*. Place a marker at each edge.

Reset RC to 000. K52[60:64] rows.

Back neck and shoulders Using a separate piece of MC cast off 32[36:44] sts at centre. Set carr for HP and push 27[27:29] Ns at L to HP. WK across rem 27[27:29] sts at R.

Push Ns at L to UWP and WK.

RIGHT FRONT

Push 44[46:52] Ns to WP. Work as given for back to *. Place a marker at R edge.

RC000. K31[33:37] rows. (K1 less row for L front). CAL.

Shape neck Cast off 3[4:4] sts at beg of next and foll alt row. K1 row. Cast off 3 sts at beg of next and foll alt row, K1 row. Cast off 2[2:3] sts beg next row. K1 row. Cast off 2 sts at beg of next row, K1 row.

Dec 1[1:2] sts at beg of next row. K1 row. Dec 0[0:1] st at beg of next and foll alt row. 27[27:29] sts. K11[13:13] rows and WK.

LEFT FRONT

Work as given for R front, noting difference in rows and reading L for R and vice versa to reverse shaping.

SLEEVES

Push 50[54:58] Ns to WP. Work as given for back to **. CAR.
RC000. Using MT, K0[0:2] rows. *Inc 1 st beg next 4 rows, K2 rows.*
Rep the sequence from *to* until 82[94:100] sts K until RC shows
56[64:76]. Cast off loosely.

BUTTONHOLE BAND

Push 60[72:80] Ns to WP. With wrong side of work facing you, pick
up sts evenly along front edge and hang evenly on to Ns. Using MC
and MT, K1 row. MT-1, K5 rows. Work six evenly spaced buttonholes

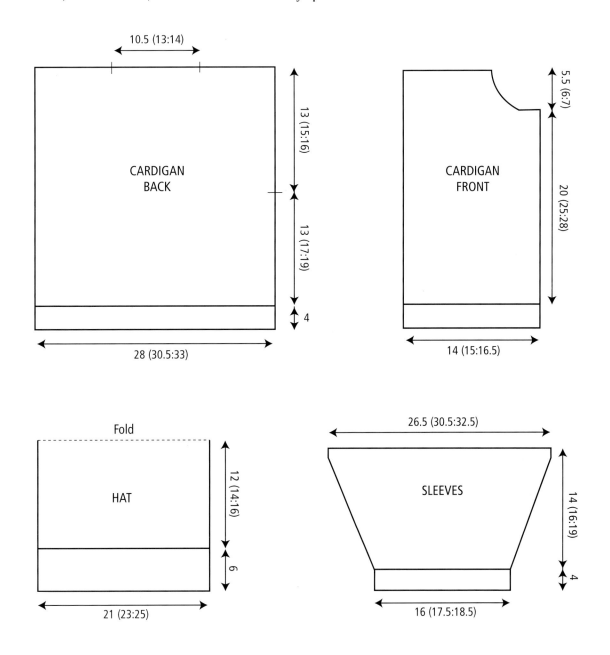

along the row. K5 rows. T10, K1 row. MT-1 K5 rows. Work
buttonholes as before. K5 rows. Cast off loosely. Fold the band
to wrong side and slip st down.

BUTTON BAND
Work as given for buttonhole band omitting buttonholes.

INTERIM MAKE UP
Block and steam jacket sections to correct measurements. Allow to
cool and dry. With right side facing, pick up sts from back shoulder
and hang evenly on to same number of Ns. With wrong side facing
pick up appropriate front shoulder and hang evenly on to same Ns.
Using MC and MT+1 K2 rows. T10, K1 row and cast off loosely.
Join second shoulder seam in the same manner.

NECKBAND
With wrong side of work facing you, and with shoulder seams
joined, pick up the sts from R front neck (including the sts of the
front band – on the second size, 22 sts were picked up at this point).
Cont to pick up sts from below WY of back neck, before going
down the L front – matching the same number as for the R front
 – and including the sts of the band. CAR. Using MC and MT, K4
rows. At the beg of next row, work a buttonhole over Ns 4 and 5.
K5 rows. MT-1, K2 rows. CAR. MT, K4 rows Work a buttonhole over
same Ns as before. K4 rows. WK.

HAT
The hat is made in a single piece and folded in half.
Push 64[72:78] Ns to WP and arrange for 1 x 1 mock rib. Using WY
cast on and K a few rows, ending CAR. Using MC and MT-1, K36
rows. Push empty Ns to WP. Turn a hem by picking up loops from
first row worked in MC and hang evenly along the row. Using MT
K96[120:128] rows. Set for 1 x 1 mock rib. MT-1 K36 rows. WK.

FLOWERS
Wild roses Push 42 Ns to WP. Using WY cast on and K a few rows
ending CAR. Using double-stranded industrial yarn and T approx. 3
K6 rows. Set carr for HP and push Ns 7, 14, 21, and 28 to HP. K6
rows. Using contrast yarn (white), and MT+4 set carr so HP Ns will K

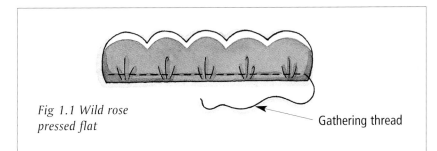

Fig 1.1 Wild rose pressed flat

Gathering thread

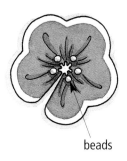

beads

Fig 1.2 Wild rose gathered

and K4 rows. Using MC and MT, set carr for HP and push the same Ns as before to HP and K6 rows. Turn a hem by picking up loops of first row of main yarns from below WY and hang evenly along the row. K1 row. Break off yarn, leaving approx. 15cm. Thread this yarn into a darning N (or your double-eyed bodkin) and run it along the row of sts, lifting them from the machine and onto the yarn. With a moderate iron, press flat (on the wrong side), pressing the 'petals' out (see Fig 1.1). When cool, draw up the loose yarn end, gathering the flower at its centre. Sew the side seams together and trim with a circle of pearl beads (optional – see Fig 1.2).

Bluebells Push 22 Ns to WP. Using WY cast on and K a few rows. Using 2–3 strands of industrial yarn (blue) K6 rows. Using white, K2 rows. Leaving empty Ns in WP, transfer alt sts onto adj Ns on next row. K1 row. Using MC, K6 rows. Pick up the sts from first row knitted in MC and place onto Ns (2 sts on every N). T10, K one row. Break off yarn, leaving approx. 30cm to be threaded into a darning N or your double-eyed bodkin. Transfer the sts from the needle-bed onto the darning N and gather up tightly, sewing the sides together and securing the gather (see Figs 1.3 and 1.4). Sew a pearl drop at the lower edge of the flower if desired.

When attaching the bluebells to the hat's knitted cords, push the ends of the cords inside the bluebells before gathering then stitch the cords firmly in place as you gather.

Calendula Push 2 Ns to WP. Using fine, gold or orange yarn cast on by hand ('e' wrap). Using approx. MT3-4, K6 rows, pulling down firmly. Pick up the 2 cast on sts and place them onto the Ns, thus forming a loop, or 'petal'. K6 rows, pull down firmly, then lift 2 sts from the first of the preceding 6 rows. Rep until you have five loops. Cast off and sew into a circle (see Fig 1.5, page 30).

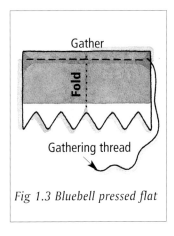

Gather

Fold

Gathering thread

Fig 1.3 Bluebell pressed flat

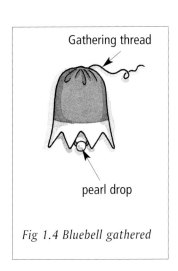

Gathering thread

pearl drop

Fig 1.4 Bluebell gathered

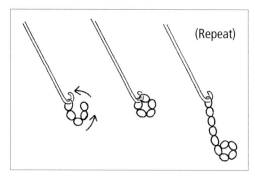

Fig 1.5

Primroses Push 20 Ns to WP. Using fine pale yellow yarn cast on by hand ('e' wrap). Using approx. MT3-4, K8 rows. Using white and MT-2, K4 rows. MC and MT, K8 rows. Pick up sts from cast on row, giving you 2 sts on each N. Break off yarn but thread a length into darning N and run through all sts, removing them from machine and at the same time gathering tightly. Sew side seam. Press white centre inwards.

Leaves Using three strands of green industrial yarn and TD approx. 3, cast on 3 sts and K2 rows. Inc 1 st at both ends by transferring the end sts to their adj empty Ns and K3 rows. Inc 1 st at both ends by trans 2 sts at either side, out onto their adj empty Ns. K3 rows. Rep, only this time move 3 sts out at the sides (see Fig 1.6, below) K3 rows. On the next rep move 4 sts out each side. K5 rows. (Dec 1 st each end of next row, pushing empty Ns to NWP, K3 rows) 5 times in all. Cast off rem st.

The flowers and leaves can be enlarged by using extra strands of yarn and by adding extra sts and rows. They can also be made smaller by using fewer yarn strands and less sts and rows.

Fig 1.6

1 SQUARE = 1 STITCH & 1 ROW

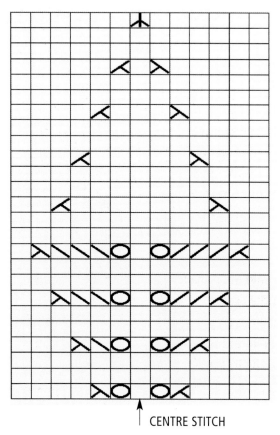

CENTRE STITCH

St transferred to L to R

St transferred to L or R and empty N pushed to NWP

St transferred to L to R and onto centre stitch

Empty N leave in WP

TO MAKE UP

Cardigan Join side seams. Fold neckband to wrong side and catching the loose sts held on WY, gently curve them round the neck shaping, slip stitching them down. Join sleeve seams. Set in sleeves. Sew on buttons to correspond with buttonholes. Align buttonholes, sewing them together. Neaten loose ends of flowers and trim the jacket's lower edge, saving four bluebells to trim the hat.

Fig 1.7

Hat Stitch the mock rib (held on WY) into place, and fold hat in half. Join side seams. If not already done, push the ends of the cords inside a bluebell, gather tightly and stitch securely into place. Fashion the cords into mock 'bows' (real ones would be too bulky) and sew onto the corners of the hat (see Fig 1.7). Trim the lower edge of hat with flowers and leaves.

HANDTOOLING

Handtooling is best described as a partnership between machine and knitter. Despite the extensive technology that has gone into creating the knitting machine and the admirable tasks of which it is capable, it still has its limitations. Knitters, on the other hand, are limited solely by their imagination and what they are prepared to bring to the craft.

Learning how to hand-manipulate your needles, yarn, and transfer tools is an important step in furthering your machine knitting skills. You may ask 'why?' Why go to the trouble of doing things by hand when automatic machines do such an excellent job of patterning? This is a reasonable question, and one for which there are many answers.

Firstly, not all machines will create patterns automatically. If you possess such a machine and you wish to knit anything other than stripes, handtooling is your only option. Secondly, while the ability to turn out beautifully patterned garments in next to no time is a tremendous boon to busy people, machine knitting as a craft is not always about 'speed'; therefore, it is sometimes beneficial to take time out from a hectic schedule to experiment and 'play' with yarns and accessories, and, in doing so, discover the hidden potential within yourself and your knitting machine.

Handling transfer tools with confidence is an essential part of machine knitting. They sometimes seem to have a life of their own, and go in any direction but the one you would like. However, it is a joy when you master them, making the transferral of stitches from one needle to another, so essential to the job of decreasing and casting-off stitches, much easier.

Once you know how to manipulate yarns and needles by hand, there is seemingly no end to the stitch formations you can arrange. Take crochet, for instance. There are many much-admired crochet stitches, but a firm favourite seems to be the pretty, openwork of Diamond Mesh. It is an intricate-looking arrangement of chains and loops that can easily be worked on knitting machines. The selected yarns will make all

the difference to the finished result, too. For example, if a fine, single thread is used, your fabric will come off the machine with all the texture of a cobweb, but if a thicker, woolly yarn is employed, then the openwork of the stitch will be closer and fluffier.

'Loopy Knitting' is another unusual and interesting technique to experiment with. It is not often associated with machine knitting, but it can be done. The size of the loop is dependent upon the 'gadget' chosen to wind the yarn around. I found a 15cm plastic ruler was suitable when it came to working the loops on the red bonnet and hand-muff on pages 51–58).

Once again, yarn plays an important role in the finished result. A soft, baby yarn of, say, 3 or 4 ply would result in a rather more dense fabric, while one of the bouclé-type yarns would result in loops with a 'crinkly' appearance. I chose a yarn with a 'velvety' finish to knit the loops on the bonnet and hand-muff. It comes with a strand of silver filament running through it, which catches the light and sparkles, giving an effect of

frost on snow that is both seasonal and attractive. Mohair, however, is another popular choice for this type of knitting, especially for older children. When 'brushed' it looks lovely, doubling its density and warmth potential, and making it an ideal choice for cold weather garments.

A more traditional stitch arrangement, and one that has been around for many years, comes in the form of cabling. For the experienced knitter it lends itself to many interesting variations. It is worked by crossing groups of stitches over one another, and patterns of immense originality can be created, including the wonderful and popular Aran knitting. For the winter outfit on pages 42–50, the cabling was kept simple with beginners in mind. Bobbles were introduced for added colour and stitch interest.

Finally, it must be said that although the techniques used to produce the garments within this chapter are not difficult, they will require a little patience and practice. I can assure you, though, that the end results will be garments to be proud of.

Crochet-effect sundress and hat

When the temperature climbs, cool, white cotton is the perfect choice for a sundress and matching, sun hat, and is delightfully easy to knit. After steaming it keeps its shape and crisp appearance, while retaining its soft texture. 'Mock' crochet frills around the armholes and hat brim provide a lovely trim to the set.

PATTERN INFORMATION

Sizes
To suit chest 51[56:61]cm
Finished measurement before gathering 75[82:90]cm
Length 35.5[37.5:40]cm
Figures in square brackets refer to larger sizes; where there is only one set of figures this applies to all sizes.

Materials
I cone Yeoman's Canelle in white (MC) and navy (C)
3 snap fasteners

Garment weight
For size 51cm set approx. 250g

Main tension
32 sts and 41 rows to 10cm, measured over st st, after steaming (TD approx. 6 = MT). Tension must be matched exactly before starting garment.

Note
Knitted side is used as right side. Measurements are those of finished garment and should not be used to measure work on machine.

PATTERN NOTE
Program patt/punch card before starting to knit.

PATTERN AND COLOUR SEQUENCE
Insert punchcard/program patt on first row. Set carr to select/memorize for patt and K1 row. Release card and set carr for Fair Isle using MC in feeder 1/a and C in feeder 2/b throughout K20 rows. Set carr for st st and cont in MC throughout.

SPECIAL NOTE
Owing to the pattern, long threads (floats) may appear at the back of the garment pieces. These can be eliminated (or lessened) after the fabric leaves the machine by taking a long float in the latch tool and chaining the float into the other threads before sewing neatly down.

These instructions are written for standard gauge punchcard or electronic machines.

The Fair Isle bands within this set leave what are know as 'floats' on the back of the work, but neatening them is not difficult. The long strands of loose yarn can be picked up in your latch tool and latched up to a point where they can be neatly sewn-in (on the wrong side of your work). Or, if you prefer, they can be sewn down in situ, making it impossible for tiny fingers (or toys) to be caught up in them.

FRONT SKIRT

Push 128[140:152] Ns to WP. Using WY cast on and K a few rows ending CAL. Using nylon cord, K1 row.

RC000. Using MC and MT-1, K9 rows. T10, K1 row. MT-1, K10 rows. Pick up loops from first row worked in MC and hang evenly along the row. Remove WY.

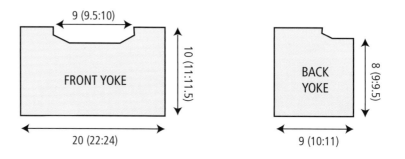

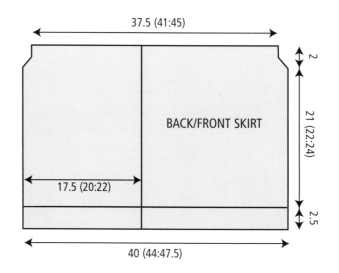

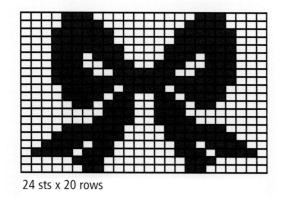

24 sts x 20 rows

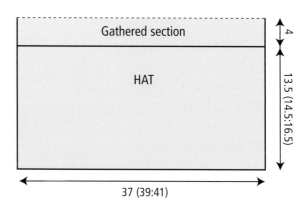

RC000. Using MT K5 rows. Start and work border patt (see patt note). K until RC shows 86[90:98].

Shape armholes Cast off 3 sts at beg of next 2 rows. K2 rows. Dec 1 st at each end of next 2 rows. WK over rem 120[132:144] sts.

RIGHT BACK SKIRT
Push 56[64:70] Ns to WP. Work as given for front until RC shows 86[90:98]. K1 extra for L back. CAR.

Shape armholes Cast off 3 sts at beg of next row, K3 rows. Dec 1 st at armhole end of next row. WK over rem 52[60:66] sts.

LEFT BACK SKIRT

Work as given for R back skirt noting difference in rows and reading L for R and vice versa to reverse shapings.

FRONT YOKE

Push 64[70:76] Ns to WP. Using WY, cast on and K a few rows. Hang weights evenly. Insert punchcard and lock/program patt on row 5 and lock.

RC000. Using MC and MT K3 rows. Set carr to select/memorize for patt and K1 row. Release card and set carr for Fair Isle using MC in feeder 1/a and C in feeder 2/b, K16 rows of patt. Set carr for st st and using MT cont in st st throughout. K until RC shows 24[28:28].

Shape neck Using a separate piece of MC cast off 10[10:12] sts at centre. Using nylon cord K27[30:32] sts at L by hand taking Ns down to NWP. Cont over rem 27[30:32] sts at R for first side. Dec 1 st at neck edge on next 5 rows, K1 row. Dec 1 st at neck edge on next and every foll alt row 4[5:6] times in all. 18[20:21] sts. K1[2:2] rows and WK.
Reset RC at 24[28:28]. CAL. Unravel nylon cord bringing Ns back to WP and work L side to correspond with R.

RIGHT BACK YOKE
Push 28[32:35] Ns to WP. Work as given for front yoke (ignoring neck shaping) until RC shows 34[40:42]. (K1 extra row for L back yoke.) CAR.

Shape neck Cast off 6[6:7] sts at beg of next row, K1 row. Cast off 2[3:4] sts at beg of next row, K1 row. Cast off 2[3:3] sts at beg of next row. WK rem 18[20:21] sts.

LEFT BACK YOKE
Work as given for R back yoke noting difference in rows and reading L for R and vice versa to reverse shapings.

HAT
Push 118[124:130] Ns to WP. Using WY, cast on and K a few rows ending CAR. Hang weights. Using nylon cord, K1 row. Using MC cast on ('e' wrap) over nylon cord and WY sts. CAR. Insert punchcard and lock/program patt on row 5 and lock.
RC000. Using MC and MT K5 rows. Set carr to select/memorize for patt and K1 row. Release card and set carr for Fair Isle using MC in feeder 1/a and C in feeder 2/b, K16 rows of patt. Set carr for st st and using MT cont in st st throughout. K until RC shows 56[60:68]. WK. With wrong side of work facing you, rehang sts from WK onto Ns, placing 1 st on first N, then 2 sts on 2nd N. Rep this sequence to end. MC and MT-2 full dots, K10 rows. WK.
*Rep the re-hanging process as before *but* now place 2 sts on every N to end*. MC and MT-1 K6 rows. WK. Rep from *to*. K4 rows. Break yarn leaving long length which needs to be threaded into darning N (or double-eyed bodkin) and taken through rem sts on machine, lifting them off and gathering them tightly before securing yarn.

JOIN SHOULDERS

Push 18[20:21] Ns to WP. With right side facing, pick up sts from below WY on one front yoke shoulder and hang on to Ns. With wrong side facing pick up sts from below WY on appropriate back yoke shoulder and hang evenly on to same Ns. Using MT, cast off. Rep with second shoulder.

TO MAKE UP

Block and steam pieces to correct measurements. Allow all pieces to dry. With right side of front yoke facing you, pick up the sts from WY and replace on Ns. With wrong side of work facing you, replace the sts held on WY from the front skirt, placing them on corr Ns, thus: Hang 1 st of skirt on first and last 3 Ns, (of yoke) rem sts hang 2 sts tog along the row. Using MC, cast off. Join back skirt sections to back yokes in same way.

Pick up the sts from around (joined) front and back armhole. Using MC and MT-1, K5 rows. T10, K1 row. MT-1, K5 rows. Cast off loosely. Work second armhole and neckband in the same manner.

Mock crochet frills

STEP 1: With the armhole edges encased in a band, there is a more solid area to start working on. You may find it helpful to stand the cone of yarn on the floor beside you, letting the yarn run through your fingers as you work. Hold the armhole edge against the N bed, and using the single transfer tool, pick up the first st of the armband and place on a N (see Fig 2.1). Hand knit (as described on pages 16–19) one st, 5 times. Pick up another st from the armband (3 sts on) and lift it onto an empty N.

STEP 2: Take the last stitch of the 5 st chain you have just knitted and place that also on the same N, forming a 'loop' (see Fig 2.2).

Fig 2.1 First stitch of five-chain sequence being picked up

Fig 2.2 Five chains being knitted onto a single needle

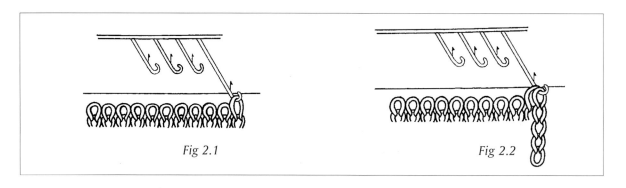

Fig 2.1

Fig 2.2

(K this st manually through the first st, leaving only one st in place.) Take this st and hand knit it 5 times, as before. Pick up a stitch from the armband – about 3 sts further on – and lift it onto an N (see Fig 2.3). Place the last st of the hand knit '5 sts' on the same N and K it through, just as before. Rep this sequence of hand knitting and 'looping' to the end of the armband. At the last stitch, turn the work around with the stitch still on the N, so that you will be working in the opposite direction.

STEP 3: Into the st, hand knit 5 rows (or chains). With the single-transfer tool, move this st now into the centre of the first loop (see Fig 2.4) lifting both the loop and the st onto a N. Hand knit the st through the loop. With the st remaining, cont in same sequence along the row of loops until you have a second row of loops. Work a third row of loops, but replace the '5-chain sequence' with 6 chains. On a fourth row of loops, work 7 chains. Break off yarn. When both armholes have been worked, pin out and steam the looped frills. When dry, sew side and back seams of dress. Attach snap fasteners on back yokes.

Fig 2.3 Row of chain stitches being placed on their next needle – three edge stitches along the row

Fig 2.4 Chain loops formed during transfer

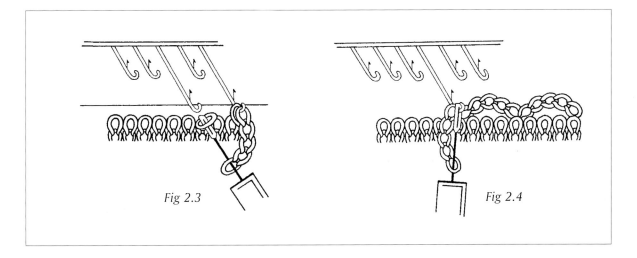

Fig 2.3 *Fig 2.4*

Hat frill

Unravel WY from the lower edge of hat. The closed-edge cast on gives a loose edge, which is needed around the base of the hat, making it more flexible. Working into the 'closed-edge' sts, work the '5-chain (6-chain) loops' as for the dress frills. Block out and steam frill before sewing back seam of hat.

To block and steam hat, turn inside out and place over suitable size basin. Cover with damp cloth and steam as for dress.

Cable and bobble winter outfit

With beginners in mind, cabling in its simplest form and colourful bobbles are employed to create this suit. It is knitted using a soft-handle acrylic 4ply in white, but can also be worked in other shades. You can incorporate as many bobbles as you wish, and in colours of your choosing.

PATTERN INFORMATION

Sizes
To suit chest 31[36:41:46:51]cm
Finished measurement
36[40:48:50:56]cm
Length 20[25:30:34:37]cm
Sleeve seam 14[15:17.5:20.5:23]cm
Figures in square brackets refer to larger sizes; where there is only one set of figures this applies to all sizes.

Materials
1 cone acrylic 4ply in white (MC)
Oddments of contrast yarns for bobbles
3[3:3:4:4] small white buttons
Approx. 60cm white elastic

Garment weight
For size 31cm approx. 275g

Main tension
35 sts and 36 rows to 10cm, measured over cable patt, after light steaming (TD approx. 6 = MT).
Tension must be matched exactly before starting garment.

Note
Knitted side is used as right side. Measurements are those of finished garment and should not be used to measure work on machine.

EASY STEPS FOR KNITTING BOBBLES

STEP 1: Note which Ns are required for working the bobbles over. If following a chart, it is usually the central Ns that are worked and counted from. Decide also on colour sequence desired and wind off a small ball of each colour.

It is helpful to place a claw weight immediately beneath the group of sts being used for making a bobble, as it holds them down from the needle bed.

STEP 2: Select your first set of Ns, but push the Ns (L and R) immediately adj, to HP (see Fig 2.5). Always winding yarn around the HP N nearest to the start of each row, hand knit 8 rows, *but* on last row, knit-in the needles in HP, returning them to normal WP.

Fig 2.5 Positioning of cables and bobbles

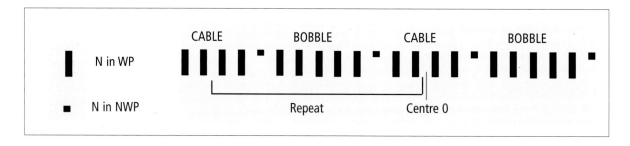

HELPFUL HINTS

*Write the six-row
sequence for cables on a
sheet of paper and keep
it with the pattern. If
you are interrupted you
can check it to continue
the sequence.*

*If you have difficulty in
getting the cabled
stitches to knit cleanly
from the needles, push
the needles to holding
position before knitting
the row.*

Cut yarn and tie both ends securely or, alternatively, cut yarn and sew ends in later. Cont along the row, alternating colours. When row is complete, pass carriage steadily across, checking before the next row that stray sts or threads have not caught on the front rail of N bed.

STEP 3: This step serves to demonstrate an 'alternative' way of knitting bobbles.

Using a contrast colour (or CC), cast on 3 sts and using MT, K8 rows. Pick up sts from first row and put on Ns, knitting them in so that 3 sts still rem on Ns. Trans both end sts to central N and knit in. Cast off single stitch leaving sufficient yarn for sewing bobble to garment. Work as many bobbles as required. Bobbles can be enlarged or made smaller, according to preference. For larger bobbles, knit them over more Ns and work extra rows. For smaller ones, reverse the process.

CABLES

Cables in knitting are made by the crossing over of designated sts, and many different patterns and effects can be obtained by strategically placed cables. The ever-popular Aran knitting consists chiefly of variations of this stitch, many of which are suitable for adaptation to machine knitting patterns. The number of sts that are crossed, varies, but six (three over three) appears to be the most popular, especially on single-bed knitting where there is not as much leeway for 'give' between the stitches. Cable knitting, where a given number of sts are worked on the MB while another set are worked on the RB, has the advantage of producing a fabric with more elasticity and scope for patterning, and there is nothing to stop anyone from experimenting. However, for the benefit of knitters without a ribbing facility, and also for simplicity, this design uses only four crossover stitches (two over two) and is worked on every sixth row on the single bed only. To make the cable panel stand out, separate from the st-st panels, a stitch at either side of the cable section is put out of work. However, these sts are counted as 'sts' throughout.

To work a simple cable, rows of st st are knitted (five in this instance). Taking two double-ended transfer tools, insert first, one set into the first two sts to be 'crossed', transferring them onto the tool and holding them while the second pair of sts are transferred to the second tool. Carefully cross (always work in the same direction sequence unless otherwise directed) your two tools R over L, and place the crossed sts onto the empty Ns. Cable complete, K the row.

These instructions are written for standard gauge machines with or without ribber.

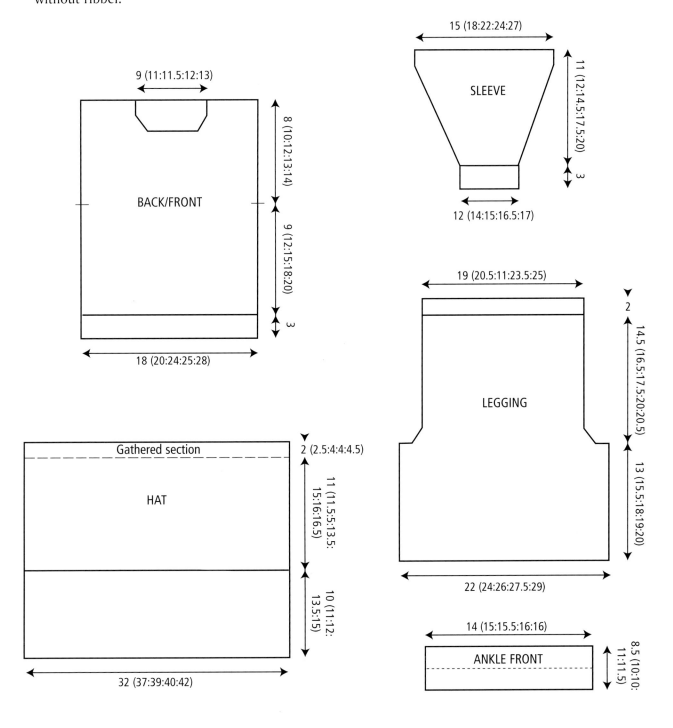

9 (11:11.5:12:13)

8 (10:12:13:14)

BACK/FRONT

9 (12:15:18:20)

3

18 (20:24:25:28)

15 (18:22:24:27)

SLEEVE

11 (12:14.5:17.5:20)

3

12 (14:15:16.5:17)

Gathered section

2 (2.5:4:4:4.5)

HAT

11 (11.5:5:13.5:
15:16:16.5)

10 (11:12:
13.5:15)

32 (37:39:40:42)

19 (20.5:11:23.5:25)

2

14.5 (16.5:17.5:20:20.5)

LEGGING

13 (15.5:18:19:20)

22 (24:26:27.5:29)

14 (15:15.5:16:16)

ANKLE FRONT

8.5 (10:10:
11:11.5)

HELPFUL HINT

To avoid confusion when knitting sleeves and counting row increases, have to hand a list of row numbers on which the 'sixth-row cable crossover' occurs.

SWEATER BACK

RIBBER: With RB in position set machine for 1 x 1 rib. Push 62[70:84:88:98] Ns on MB and corr Ns on RB to WP. Arrange Ns for 1 x 1 rib. Using MC, cast on and K3 tubular rows.
Using MT-3/MT-3, K20 rows. Transfer sts to MB.

SINGLE BED: Push 62[70:84:88:98] Ns to WP. Arrange Ns for mock 1 x 1 rib. Using WY, cast on and K a few rows ending CAR. Using MC and MT-3, K30 rows. Push empty Ns to WP. Turn a hem by picking up loops from first row worked in MC and hang evenly on to empty Ns.

ALL MACHINES: RC000**. Using MT K4 rows. Work 1 row of bobbles as chart (see patt notes). K2 rows. CAR.
RC000. Transfer sts and arrange Ns for cable patt as chart (see patt notes) and K5 rows. Work cable on next and every foll 6 rows throughout and K until RC shows 32[44:54:64:72]. (Lengthen or shorten here approx. 4 rows per cm.) Place a marker at each edge. Work 1 row of bobbles following same colour sequence and over same Ns as before, but if a cable row coincides with a bobble row, omit the cables until next sixth row count.*
RC000. K28[36:44:46:50] rows. T10+, K1 row and cast off.

FRONT

Work as given for back to*. RC000. K14[18:26:24:28] rows.

Shape neck Using a separate piece of MC, cast off 12[14:14:14:16] sts at centre. Using nylon cord K25[28:35:37:41] sts at L by hand taking Ns back to NWP. Cont on 25[28:35:37:41] sts at R for first side. Dec 1 st at neck edge on next 6[7:8:8:8] rows, K1 row. Dec 1 st at neck edge on next and every foll alt row 4[5:5:6:7] times in all. K0[1:0:2:0] rows. Cast off rem 15[16:22:23:26] sts.
CAL. Reset RC at 14[18:26:24:28]. Unravel nylon cord over sts at L bringing Ns down to WP. Work L side to corr with R.

SLEEVES

RIBBER: With RB in position set machine for 1 x 1 rib. Push 42[48:52:58:60] Ns on MB and corr Ns on RB to WP. Work as given for back to **.

SINGLE BED: Push 42[48:52:58:60] Ns to WP. Work as given for back to **.

ALL MACHINES: Using MT, Inc 1 st at each end of next row, K3 rows.

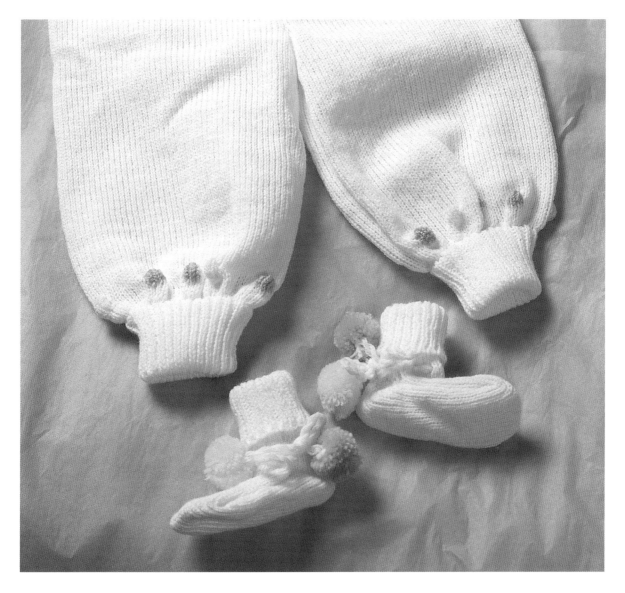

CAR. Work 1 row of bobbles, K2 rows. Trans third st at L and of R of centre '0' onto its adj N, pushing the empty Ns to NWP. Remembering the cabling sequence (K5 rows and sixth row cable), work with the 4 centre cable sts and *at the same time,* inc 1 st at each end of every foll 6[5:4:4:4] rows, 5[8:12:13:17] times in all *but* when RC shows 36[38:46:58:66], work 1 row of bobbles. Cont without cables until RC shows 40[44:52:64:72] and cast off rem 52[64:76:84:94] sts loosely.

NECKBAND

Sew L back and front shoulder seam. With purl side facing, pick up sts evenly down R front, across centre and up L front, continuing across back neck. Using MC and MT-1, K2 rows.

RIBBER: Push RB to WP and transfer sts for 1 x 1 rib. MT-2/MT-2, K6[8:10:10:12] rows. MT-3/MT-3, K6[8:10:10:12] rows. MT K1 row and cast off loosely.

SINGLE BED: Transfer sts for 1 x 1 rib. MT-2, K6[8:10:10:12] rows. MT-3, K6[8:10:10:12] rows. Push empty Ns to WP and using MT-1, K1 row and cast off loosely.

TO MAKE UP

Fold neckband in half and sew down, easing the cast-off row round the neck curve. Join rem shoulder seam for approx. 2cm, starting at the armhole edge. Sew body and sleeve seams. Set in sleeves noting the markers and placing the centre of cables against the centre of shoulder seams. Thread darning N with MC and work a row of blanket st along back shoulder opening. Rep along front shoulder opening. Now work 3[3:3:4:4] buttonholes into this row. Sew buttons on back to correspond with buttonholes. Check at this stage that all bobble stitches have knitted in. If any are loose, sew them in at back of work.

LEGGINGS

Push 76[84:90:96:102] Ns to WP. Using WY cast on and K a few rows ending CAR.

RC000. Using MC and MT K48[56:64:68:72] rows.

Shape crotch RC000. Cast off 3[4:4:5:5] sts at beg of next 2 rows. K1 row. Dec 1 st at each end of next and every foll alt row 2 times in all. 66[72:78:82:88] sts. K until RC shows 52[59:63:69:72].

Shape waist band MT-1, K8 rows. MT-2, K1 row. MT-1, K9 rows and cast off.

ANKLE CUFF

RIBBER: With RB in position set machine for 1 x 1 rib. Push 48 [52:54:56:56] Ns to WP on MB and corr Ns on RB to WP. Arrange Ns for 1 x 1 rib. Using MC cast on and K3 tubular rows.

RC000 T3/3, K31[35:37:39:41] rows. CAL. Transfer sts to MB.

SINGLE BED: Push 48[52:54:56:56] Ns to WP. Arrange Ns for 1 x 1 rib. Using WY, cast on and K a few rows ending CAR. Using MC and T3,

K31[35:37:39:41] rows. CAL. Push empty Ns to WP. Turn a hem by picking up loops from first row worked In MC and hanging evenly on to empty Ns.

ALL MACHINES: MT, K1 row. T10+ K1 row. Cast off.

TO MAKE UP

Join front and back seams as far as crotch. Fold leg seams in half and sew to crotch. Turn under ribber ankle cuffs and slip stitch down. Sew down hem at waist and thread with soft elastic.

HAT

RIBBER: With RB in position set machine for 1 x 1 rib. Push 112[118:124:128:134] Ns on MB and corr Ns on RB to WP. Using MC cast on and K3 tubular rows. T3/3, K36[40:44:48:54] rows. Transfer sts to MB.

SINGLE BED: Push 112[118:124:128:134] Ns to WP. Arrange Ns for 1 x 1 mock rib. Using WY, cast on and K a few rows ending CAR. Using MC and T3, K 56[60:64:68:74] rows. Push empty Ns to WP. Turn a hem by picking up loops from first row worked In MC and hang evenly on to empty Ns.

ALL MACHINES: RC000. Arrange Ns for cable panels. Using MC and MT K40[42:48:54:60] rows. Work a bobble row. MT-1, K6 rows and WK. Push 56[59:62:64:67] Ns to WP. With wrong side facing pick up sts from below WY, placing 2 sts on each N. MT-2, K8[10:14:14:16] rows. Break off yarn. Thread darning N with MC and run through sts, lifting them from machine and gathering tightly. Secure thread.

Crochet or knit cords thus: 1 x 4cm, 1 x 5cm, and 1 x 6cm long. Make pom-poms and attach to cords.

SOCKS

RIBBER: With RB in position set machine for 1 x 1 rib. Push 32[34:38:40:42] Ns on MB and corr Ns on RB to WP. Arrange Ns for 1 x 1 rib. Using MC, cast on and K3 tubular rows. RC000. T3/3 K36[40:44:48:50] rows. Transfer sts to MB.

SINGLE BED: Push 32[34:38:40:42] Ns Arrange Ns for 1 x 1 mock rib. Using WY, cast on and K a few rows ending CAR. Using MC and T3, K36[40:44:48:50] rows. Push empty Ns to WP. Turn a hem by picking up loops from first row worked In MC and hang evenly on to empty Ns.

ALL MACHINES: Using MT K2 rows. Transfer second and every foll alt st to its adj N, leaving empty Ns in WP. K2 rows. CAR. (K1 extra row for second sock). RC000. Cast off 14[16:18:19:20] sts at beg of next row. Cont over rem sts, K20[24:26:26:28] rows.

Shape toe Set carr for HP and always taking yarn round first inside N in HP, push first N at opposite end of carr to HP on next 10[10:10:12:12] rows. Push 1 N at opposite side to carr to UWP on next 10[10:10:12:12] rows. K20[24:26:26:28] rows.

Shape heel Work as given for shape toe, *but*, after HP shaping, K only 4 rows. Cast off. Work second sock as first noting difference in rows to reverse shaping.

To make up Fold foot section in half at toe. Sew the foot and leg seam. Join heel cast-off sections. Thread ribbons or twisted cords through eyelets. Using the 'alternative' method of making bobbles, as patt notes, work three for each bootee and sew in place.

Coat with loopy-knitted bonnet and hand-muff

The warmth of wool is always a good idea for winter clothing, and this red coat, with its matching loopy-trimmed bonnet and hand-muff, was made in just such a yarn. Loops produced during knitting gives an interesting texture to garments, but it is often thought of as a hand knitters' skill. As you will see, machine knitters can work Loopy-knitting to good effect, too.

PATTERN INFORMATION

Sizes
To suit chest 56[61:66]cm
Finished measurement 58[63:69]cm
Length 43.5[47.5:51]cm
Sleeve seam 19[20:21]cm
Figures in square brackets refer to larger sizes; where there is only one set of figures this applies to all sizes.

Materials
1 x 500g cone 4ply pure wool in MC
200g in C
Buttons to match MC
Trimmings for bonnet and muff
16cm plastic ruler

Garment Weight
Approx. 450g for 61cm size

Main tension
30 sts and 40 rows to 10cm, measured over st st, after steam pressing (TD approx. 7 = MT).
Loopy Knitting: 28 sts and 48 rows to 10cm.
Tension must be matched exactly before starting garment.

Note
Knitted side is used as right side. Measurements are those of finished garment and should not be used to measure work on machine.

SPECIAL NOTE

Yarn used for the loops in this design, is Sirdar's 'Snowflake' (Chunky). This yarn is unsuitable for small babies, due to the yarn's filament content. A substitute yarn of your choice can be used (mohair can look very pretty). To avoid disappointment, please check when using pure wool that the colour does not 'bleed' when washed and is shrink-resistant. A test sample knitted and washed beforehand is recommended.

EASY STEPS TO LOOPY-KNITTING

STEP 1: Choose the yarn that is going to be 'looped' and place it in a container on the floor beside you. Anchor the end firmly in the 'clasp' at the R end of the needle bed. Wind off a ball of main yarn for the hand knitted rows. Working on only a few Ns at a time, take the ruler in your R hand, and hold it close to the sinker pegs.
STEP 2: Taking hold of the 'loopy' yarn in your left fingers, proceed to wind it once around the ruler, but not too tightly

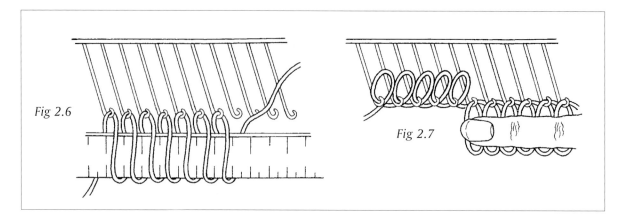

Fig 2.6

Fig 2.7

Fig 2.6 Wind yarn around ruler and then needle
Fig 2.7 Keep your finger against the loops when removing the ruler

(see Fig 2.6, above). Pull the first N forward and wind the yarn up from the ruler and over the N before drawing the N back again (taking the yarn with it). Now rep the process with the next N and another loop.

STEP 3: Continue in this manner until there are four or five loops of yarn around the ruler and over Ns. Carefully slide the ruler from the loops, but press your right index finger against the newly released loops, holding them against the N bed, (so that they don't get up onto the sinker posts (see Fig 2.7, above). Commence with the next batch of loops and Ns, working eventually to the last stitch.

STEP 4: Let the loopy yarn hang loose, but take up the loose ball of main yarn and hand knit it into every N for the first row, from R to L. Using MC, K2 rows. Take up 'loopy' yarn and ruler, and working from L to R rep the 'looping' and laying in N' process as before, until end of row. Hand knit the row, taking the ball of wool from L to R. K2

These instructions are written for all standard gauge machines with ribber.

BACK BODICE
Push 90[96:102] Ns to WP. Using WY cast on and K a few rows ending CAR*.
RC000. Using MC and MT K36[40:44] rows.

Shape armholes RC000. Cast off 4 sts at beg of next 2 rows. Cast off 2 sts at beg of next 2 rows. Dec 1 st at beg of next 2 rows. 76[82:88] sts. K until RC shows 44[48:50].

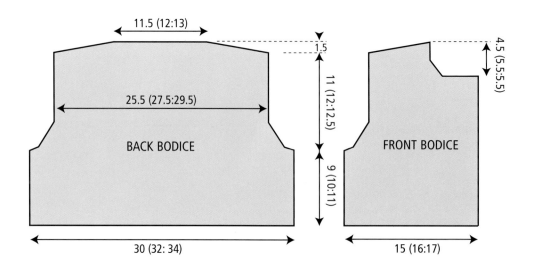

11.5 (12:13)

1.5

4.5 (5.5:5.5)

25.5 (27.5:29.5)

11 (12:12.5)

BACK BODICE

FRONT BODICE

9 (10:11)

30 (32: 34)

15 (16:17)

Edge to be gathered back on machine when joining

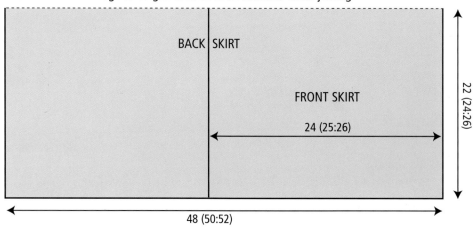

BACK SKIRT

FRONT SKIRT

22 (24:26)

24 (25:26)

48 (50:52)

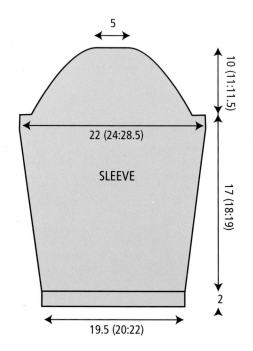

5

10 (11:11.5)

22 (24:28.5)

SLEEVE

17 (18:19)

2

19.5 (20:22)

Shape shoulders Cast off 7[7:8] sts at beg of next 6 rows.
Cast off rem 34[40:40] sts.

RIGHT FRONT BODICE
Push 45[48:51] Ns to WP and work as given for back until RC shows
36[40:44]. (K1 extra row for L front bodice.)

Shape armhole RC000. Cast off 4 sts at beg of next row, K1 row.
Cast off 2 sts at beg of next row, K1 row. Dec 1 st at beg of next row,
K1 row. 38[41:44] sts. K until RC shows 33[33:41].
CAL. (CAR for L front).

Shape neck Cast off 7[7:8] sts at beg of next row, K1 row. Dec 1 st
at neck edge on next 3[4:4] rows. Dec 1 st at neck edge on next and
every foll alt row 6[7:7] times in all. At the same time when RC
shows 44[48:56] CAR. CAL for L front.

Shape shoulder Cast off 7[7:8] sts at beg of next and every foll alt
row 3 times in all.

LEFT FRONT BODICE
Work as given for right front bodice, noting difference in rows to
reverse shapings.

SLEEVES
Push 54[58:60] Ns to WP. Work as given for bodice back to *.
Using MC and MT-1 K9 rows. T10+, K1 row. MT, K12 rows.
Turn a hem by picking up loops from first row worked in MC and
hang evenly along the row**.

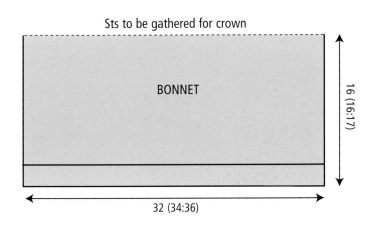

Sts to be gathered for crown

BONNET

16 (16:17)

32 (34:36)

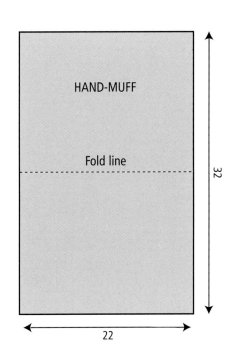

HAND-MUFF

Fold line

32

22

HELPFUL HINT

Knit one row of nylon cord before waste knitting. This will make the waste yarn easier to remove.

RC000. Inc 1 st at both ends of next and every foll 10[9:8] rows, 6[7:8] times. 66[72:76] sts. K until RC shows 68[72:76].

Shape top

RC000. Cast off 4 sts at beg of next 2 rows. Cast off 2 sts at beg of next 2 rows, K2 rows. Dec 1 st at both ends of next and every foll 3 rows, 8[10:10] times in all. Dec 1 st at both ends of next 11[12:13] rows. Cast off rem 16[16:18] sts.

BACK SKIRT

Push 150[154:158] Ns to WP and work as given for sleeve to **.
RC000. K88[96:104] rows. WK.

FRONT SKIRT

Work two pieces alike.
Push 75[75:77] Ns to WP. Work as given for back skirt.

TO MAKE UP

Block and steam press pieces to correct measurements. When dry, join front and back shoulders. With right side of back bodice facing, pick up sts from first row worked in MC and hang on Ns.

Join back skirt section to back bodice: With wrong side facing, unravel WY from top edge, a few sts at a time, and hang MC sts – 1 st on each of first 2 Ns, foll by 2 sts on every 3rd N to end, finishing with 1 st on each of the last 2 Ns. Using MC and MT+1, K1 row and cast off. Join front bodices to front skirts in same manner as for back. Join side and sleeve seams. Set in sleeve, easing to fit and gathering slightly on shoulders.

Front bands With wrong side of garment facing, pick up sts along R front edge (from hem to neckline). Using MC and MT, K4 rows. Make five evenly spaced buttonholes, from front neck to just below the waistline. K5 rows. T10+ K1 row. MT-1, K5 rows. Work buttonholes to correspond with first set. K4 rows. Cast off loosely. Work button band as for buttonhole band omitting buttonholes.

Collar With right side of work facing, pick up 25 sts along left front neck, 35 sts along back neck, and 25 sts along right front. (If the sts

have pulled tight while being lifted on to the Ns, it might be wise
to hand knit the first row). Using MC and MT, K4 rows.
Push RB to WP and transfer sts for 1 x 1 rib. Weight evenly. T 4/4 K2
rows. Inc 1 st at each end of next and foll 4th row, K3 rows. T5 Inc 1
st at each end of next row, K2 rows. T6, inc 1 st at each end of next
row, K4 rows. Cast off loosely.

BONNET
Push 96[102:108] Ns to WP and work as given for sleeve to **.
RC000. K6 rows. Start and work loopy patt (see patt notes).
Work 11[11:13] rows of loops. Using MC only, K10 rows and WK.
Turn work so plain side of work facing you and pick up sts from
below WY and hang evenly on to Ns. Using MC and MT K20[22:26]
rows and WK.

Push 72[77:81] Ns to WP. With wrong side facing, pick up sts from below WY, putting 2 sts on every third N along the row. Unravel WY. Using MC and MT-1 K10[12:14] rows and WK. Push 36[39:41] Ns to WP. With wrong side facing, pick up sts from below WY, putting 2 sts on every N to 0[last:last] N, 1 st on last 0[1:1] N. Using MC and MT K8[8:10] rows. Break yarn, threading end through darning N or bodkin. Run N and yarn

through sts, lifting them from machine and drawing tight to form bonnet's crown. Secure end of yarn.

TO MAKE UP

Sew together approx. 6[6:7]cm of bonnet's back seam. With wrong side of work facing, pick up sts around bottom edge of bonnet. Using MC and MT-1, K6 rows. MT-2, K2 rows. MT-1 K7 rows. Cast off loosely. Fold hem to inside and slip-st down. Make two twisted cords, or two knitted cords. Make two pom-poms with loopy knit yarn, and sew to ends of cords. Attach free ends of cords to bonnet sides. Add a 'seasonal' motif if desired.

HAND-MUFF

Push 50[60:60] Ns to WP and work as bodice back to *. Using MC and MT K4 rows. Leaving the first and last 4 Ns, start loopy patt (see patt notes) over the rem Ns, but when it comes to the hand knitted row, K over these end Ns. Work until fabric is approx. 32cm in length. (In this instance, it is safe to measure while still on the machine.) Pick up first row of sts worked in MC. T10+ K1 row and cast off loosely.

TO MAKE UP

Turn muff to wrong side. Turn over the edge made by the end 4 sts, and slip st down both sides. Make a cord approx. 66cm long sewing loose ends inside of muff. Add decorative motif as for bonnet.

RIBBING TECHNIQUES

The primary reason ribbers are added to single-bed machines is so that garments can be knitted with neater, more 'professional-looking' ribs. But right from the outset, using this technique introduces an intriguing new concept of patterning. Added depth and textures begin to emerge, even as one starts to learn how to operate 400 needles, instead of the more usual 200.

In this chapter, patterning has, on all three garments, been kept simple in the interests of the beginner. But for the knitter who wants to delve further into this promising stitch technique, there are plenty of articles in knitting magazines and books that focus solely on the subject of ribbing.

One of the most popular stitch combinations with the ribber is 'tuck patterning'. It works the same as on single-bed knitting with needles designated by the pattern card 'tucking' or 'holding' a given number of stitches on the main bed. With the ribber, the patterning is more

pronounced, the fabric has more elasticity, and we can, at the flick of a switch, alter the pattern completely if it takes our fancy. The plain rib pattern of the over-bodice of the christening gown, featured on pages 70–79, is just one example. Only one in four stitches is worked on the ribber, presenting a series of vertical lines, but what can be done with them is quite outstanding – they can be manipulated and joined together to form an attractive honeycomb design.

Yarns play a huge role in this area of patterning. Fancy yarns and ultra-fine yarns that one may have looked askance at in pre-ribber days, now come under the spotlight as it is discovered that quite magical effects can be created with single-ply industrials and cobweb-like mohairs.

Finally, with regards to tuck rib, there are endless variations of this type of patterning. And, depending on the use of yarn, a vast range of fabrics – from fine lace, right across the range to chunky 'Aran-effect' knitting.

Cosy bodywarmer

Quilting on the knitting machine involves the use of a ribbing attachment. This method is ideal for outdoor garments like this bodywarmer, especially if the chosen yarn contains a high percentage of wool.

PATTERN INFORMATION

Sizes
To suit chest 51–61cm
Finished measurement 68cm
Length 30.5cm
Figures in square brackets refer to larger sizes; where there is only one set of figures this applies to all sizes.

Materials
1 cone 2ply 50% wool, 50% acrylic yarn in MC
0.5m Terylene wadding
1 x 25cm nylon zip fastener

Garment weight
Approx. 145g (inc wadding)

Main tension
Use T4/5 as MT, provided it knits comfortably. An accurate swatch is difficult because pockets can be stuffed in varying degrees, which would affect overall stitch and row count.

Note
Knitted side is used as right side. Measurements are those of finished garment and should not be used to measure work on machine.

PATTERN NOTE
Program patt/punchcard before starting to knit.

QUILTED POCKETS
Set machine for FNR tubular knitting. You may need to consult your instruction manual for this, but most, if not all, machines work tubular rib on the principal that only the MB Ns, K in one direction, while the only RB Ns K in the other direction.

Silver Reed (Knitmaster) machines are set with the R side lever back, and the L one brought forward. The carr is set to slip. On the RB carr, the L set lever is on 0, and the R one is set at 1. For plain tubular knitting this setting works fine – but when the card is inserted and locked on the appropriate row, the setting is disrupted! By altering the textbook setting, I was able to knit the pockets I wanted. As the book says: L set lever (on the RB) is on 0. The R set lever -1. Main carriage: L side lever brought forward (not back), R side lever is put back. * Insert punchcard/program patt and lock (all the time) on first row. Set carr to select/memorize for patt and K1 row. Set MB carr to slip as above and K42 rows circular. Move carr to

PUNCH CARD/ELECTRONIC PATTERN

Note: Only 1 row required. Card is locked throughout.

the R with cam lever on stockinet but on bringing the carr back to the L, put the cam lever to slip*. Working from *to* knits pocket pattern.

SPECIAL NOTE

A piece of strong plastic approx. 7cm long and 4–5cm wide, cut in a U-shape at the lower end and without any sharp edges (see Fig 3.1, below) assists with the insertion of the wadding sections into the knitted pockets. The wadding simply slides down the plastic 'shute' and lessens the possibility of wadding fibres becoming attached to the sinker gates. It is also beneficial to pre-cut a selection of wadding pieces approx. 4 x 4cm in size.

These instructions are written for standard gauge punchcard or electronic machines with ribber.

BACK

With RB in position set machine for FNR. Push 38 Ns at L of centre '0' and 64 Ns to R on MB and corr Ns on RB to WP. Using MC cast on and K3 tubular rows. T1/1, K30 rows.

RC000. Using MT, insert punchcard and lock/program patt on first row. K2 rows.

Start and work pocket patt (see patt notes) until 3 rows of pockets have been made (RC132) ending on first st st row of pocket closure**.

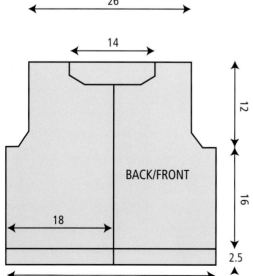

4

Plastic strip cut-out

7

Fig 3.1

Shape armholes Cast off 8 sts at beg of next 2 rows (if required, transfer sts to be cast off MB and cast off together). Cont in pockets patt and work 2 more rows of pockets and at the same time cast off 2 sts at beg of next 2 rows. Dec 1 st at beg of next 4 rows. Transfer sts to MB. MT+1, K1 row. At each end, run 26 sts onto WY. Cast off rem centre sts.

FRONTS

Work two pieces alike (quilting is reversible so no need to K a L and a R front).

With RB in position set machine for FNR. Push 42 Ns

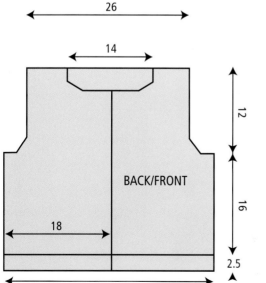

26

14

BACK/FRONT

18

34

12

16

2.5

L of centre '0' and 15 at R on MB and corr Ns on RB to WP. Using MC cast on and work rib as given for back to **. CAR.

Shape armhole Cast off 8 sts at beg of next row, K1 row. Keeping pockets patt correct throughout, cast off 2 sts at beg next row and foll alt row. Complete one more set of pockets, ending on a st st row. (CAR for L front).

Shape neck Cast off 14 sts at beg of next row, K1 row. Cast off 2 sts at beg of next and foll alt row, K1 row. Dec 1 st at neck edge on next 6 rows. Complete a second pocket. K4 rows stockinet. Transfer sts to MB. MT+1 K1 row and WK.

ARMBANDS

With RB in position set machine for 1 x 1 rib. Push 90 Ns on MB and corr Ns on RB to WP. Arrange Ns for 1 x 1 rib. Using MC cast on and K3 tubular rows. Using T1/1, K16 rows. Transfer sts from to MB. T3 K2 rows and cast off.

NECKBAND

With RB in position set machine for 1 x 1 rib. Push 114 Ns on MB and corr Ns on RB to WP. Arrange Ns for 1 x 1 rib. Using MC cast on and K3 tubular rows. Using T1/1, K16 rows. Transfer sts from to MB. T3 K4 rows and cast off.

TO MAKE UP

Push 26 Ns to WP and pick up sts from below WY on back shoulder. Hang front shoulder on to same Ns. T10+ using MT, K1 row and cast off. Rep with second shoulder.

Join side seams, folding the ribbed hems in half and sewing down on the inside. Sew zip fastener to front edges. Sew the cast on edge of rib bands to the inside of armholes and neck. Fold in half, sewing the cast-off edges onto the right sides of garment using backstitch, and enclosing the zip ends.

Tuck-stitch dungarees, sweater and hat

Tuck stitch is not only one of the most versatile types of patterning, it can also be one of the easiest to master, which is why it has been chosen, in its simplest form, for this snug and modern dungaree set.

Measurements include the sizing for premature babies, as the garments are suitable, both in yarn content and design, for very small babies.

PATTERN INFORMATION

Sizes
To suit chest 31[36:41:46]cm

Sweater
Finished measurement
36[40:44:48]cm
Length 23[27:29:31]cm
Sleeve seam 14[16:18:20]cm

Dungarees
Leg seam (exc cuff) 12[14:16:18]cm
Figures in square brackets refer to larger sizes; where there is only one set of figures this applies to all sizes.

Materials
1 cone acrylic 3ply in white (MC)
3 small white buttons
Approx. 60cm white elastic

Garment weight
For size 31cm approx. 160g

Main tension
42 sts and 42 rows to 10cm, measured over tuck rib (TD approx. 4/5 = MT).
Tension must be matched exactly before starting garment.

Note
Knitted side is used as right side. Measurements are those of finished garment and should not be used to measure work on machine.

PATTERN NOTE

Program patt/punch card before starting to knit.

Arrange Ns as shown below. Cancel any end N selection (Brother models may need to adjust pink cams under carr – see your manual). Before casting on, lock punchcard/program patt on first row and set carr for tuck. Run empty carr across Ns a couple of times, to check if the pattern has been picked up by the memory drums/selected. The Ns should come forward in formation as in the pattern and it is fine

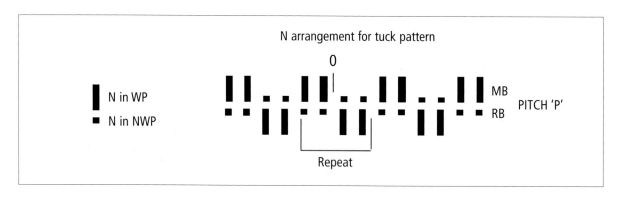

N arrangement for tuck pattern

N in WP
N in NWP

0

MB
RB

PITCH 'P'

Repeat

for you to proceed. However, if the Ns come forward but stay in a straight line, then your N arrangement is not correct.

SPECIAL NOTE

Side weights need to be hung on shaped sections of the knitting, e.g. sleeves, and moved up as the work progresses.

These instructions are written for standard gauge punchcard or electronic machines with ribber.

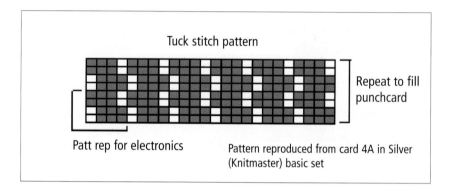

Tuck stitch pattern

Repeat to fill punchcard

Patt rep for electronics

Pattern reproduced from card 4A in Silver (Knitmaster) basic set

SWEATER

Back and Front Work two pieces alike. With RB in position set machine for 1 x 1 rib. Push 76[84:92:100] Ns on MB and corr Ns on RB to WP. Arrange Ns for 1 x 1 rib. Using MC cast on and K3 tubular rows. T2/2 K9[9:11:13] rows. Transfer sts as N arrangement. Insert punchcard and lock/program patt on first row. Set carr to select/memorize for patt and K1 row. Release card and set MB carr for tuck.

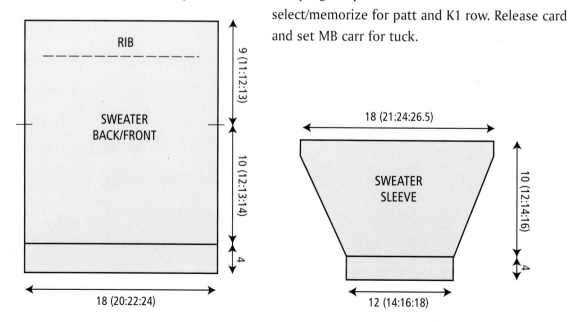

RIB

SWEATER
BACK/FRONT

9 (11:12:13)

10 (12:13:14)

4

18 (20:22:24)

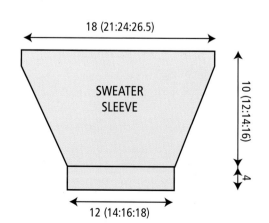

18 (21:24:26.5)

SWEATER
SLEEVE

10 (12:14:16)

4

12 (14:16:18)

RC000. Using MT K42[50:54:58] rows. Place a marker at each edge.
RC000. K30[38:34:38] rows. Set carr to K and using T2/2,
K10[10:12:14] rows. Transfer sts to MB and cast off.

SLEEVES

With RB in position set machine for 1 x 1 rib. Push 50[58:68:76]
Ns to WP on MB and corr Ns on RB to WP. Arrange Ns for 1 x 1
rib. Using MC cast on and K3 tubular rows. T2/2 K9[9:11:13] rows.
Insert punchcard and lock/program patt on first row. Arrange Ns
as N arrangement. Set carr to select/memorize for patt and K1 row.
Release card and set MB carr for tuck.
RC000. Using MT K1[2:2:1] rows. Inc 1 st at each end of next and
every foll 3[3:3:7] rows 13[16:12:8] times in all, K0[0:3:6] rows. Inc
1 st at each end of next and every foll 0[0:4:0] rows 0[0:4:1] times
in all. 76[90:100:112] sts. K until RC shows 41[50:58:68]. Mark centre
st and cast off.

TO MAKE UP

Lightly steam pieces to correct measurements. Join 4[5:6:7]cm
from armhole edge for shoulder seam. Matching centre marker
to shoulder seam. Set in sleeves. Join side and sleeve seams.

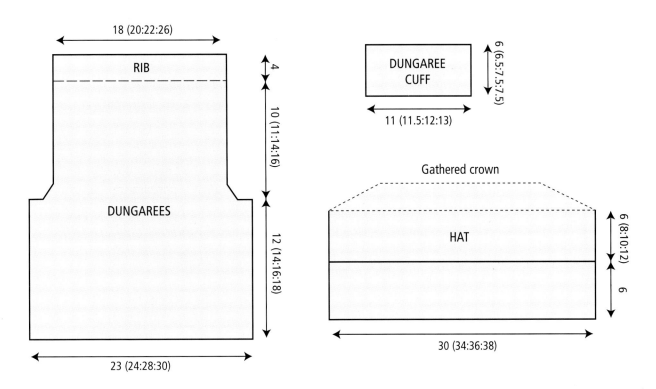

RIB

18 (20:22:26)

DUNGAREES

4

10 (11:14:16)

12 (14:16:18)

23 (24:28:30)

DUNGAREE CUFF

6 (6.5:7.5:7.5)

11 (11.5:12:13)

Gathered crown

HAT

6 (8:10:12)

6

30 (34:36:38)

HELPFUL HINT

Move edge of claw weight up regularly as work progresses.

DUNGAREES

Legs Work 2 pieces alike. With RB in position set machine for 1 x 1 rib. Push 96[101:118:126] Ns on MB and corr Ns on RB to WP. Arrange Ns for 1 x 1 rib. Using MC cast on and K2 tubular rows. Insert punchcard and lock/program patt on first row. Arrange Ns as N arrangement. Set carr to select/memorize for patt and K1 row. Release card and set MB carr for tuck.
RC000. Using MT K 50[58:68:76] rows. CAR.

Shape crotch RC000. Cast off 4[4:5:5] sts at beg of next 2 rows. K1 row. Dec 1 st at each end of next and every foll alt row 4 times in all, K2 rows. Dec 1 st at each end of next and every foll alt rows 3 times in all. K until RC shows 42[46:58:67]. Set carr to 'knit' T2/2, K18[20:24:24] rows. Transfer sts to MB (not in empty needles). T10+, K1 row and cast off.

ANKLE BAND

Push 46[48:50:54] Ns to WP. With wrong side of work facing pick up loops from first cast on edge, gathering them evenly across the Ns. Using MC and T2, K2 rows. Push RB to WP. Transfer sts for 1 x 1 rib. Add comb and weights (or knitting needle if preferred) T2/2, K26[28:32:32] rows. Trans sts to MB (filling empty Ns). T10+ K1 row. Cast off.

STRAPS

Work two alike.
With RB in position set machine for 1 x 1 rib. Push 15 Ns on MB and corr Ns on RB to WP. Arrange Ns for 1 x 1 rib. Using MC, cast on and K3 tubular rows.
RC000. T2/2 K to approx. 22[24:26:28]cm. Remove the weights and measure while on machine. Make a note of RC number, so as to get exact length for second strap. Any surplus length can be disposed of when the straps are sewn into place. (If more length is required, simply return to machine and K extra rows.)

TO MAKE UP

Sew front and back body seams of dungarees as far as crotch. Sew inner leg seam and ankle ribs. Turn ankle ribs to inside and sew down. Measure straps for length and sew either side of back seam.

On front ends of straps, thread a darning N with yarn, and work a loop buttonhole. Sew buttons on front of dungarees – one at either side of centre seam.

HAT

With RB in position set machine for 1 x 1 rib. Push 126[144:150:159] Ns on MB and corr Ns on RB to WP. Arrange Ns for 1 x 1 rib. Using MC cast on and K3 tubular rows.

RC000. Using T2/2, K 29[35:39:45] rows. Arrange Ns as N arrangement. Insert punchcard and lock/program patt on first row. Set carr to select/memorize for patt and K1 row. Release card and set MB carr for tuck.

RC000. Using MT K28[32:40:46] rows. Reset carr to 'knit' T2/2 K16[20:24:28] rows. Transfer sts to MB Ns (those are holding sts). K1 row and WK. Push 42[48:50:53] Ns to WP. With wrong side facing, pick up sts from below WY and hang on to Ns, placing 3 sts on each N. Using MC and T1/1, K4 rows. Thread a darning N or double-eyed bodkin, run yarn through all sts, removing them from machine, except for the 7 centre sts. K16 rows. Dec 1 st at each end of next and every foll alt row until 2 sts rem. Cast off. Pull knitted strip lengthways. Tie in a knot.

TO MAKE UP

Sew back seam. Turn brim under, or over if preferred.

Smocked christening gown

This is a beautiful christening gown for a baby's first special occasion. Only the over-bodice is worked in rib, where one in every four stitches is knitted on the front bed, showing a way in which the vertical rib stitches can be rearranged to form a smocked effect. The embroidery on the smocking is optional, as one or two small stitches drawing the rib stitches into a honeycomb design would work equally well.

PATTERN INFORMATION

Sizes
To suit approx. 3–5 months
Finished measurement 49cm
Length 42cm
Sleeve seam 14cm
Figures in square brackets refer to larger sizes; where there is only one set of figures this applies to all sizes.

Materials
1 x 500g cone Yeoman Yarns Janeiro (viscose/linen/acrylic) in cream (MC)
1.5m peach satin fabric
7m cream lace edging
7m narrow cream satin ribbon
1m cream satin ribbon, approx. 3cm wide
5 small cream buttons
3 small clear snap fasteners
Embroidery silks to tone

Garment weight
Approx. 425g (without satin or knitted underskirt)

Main tension
22 sts and 48 rows to 10cm, measured over lace patt after light steaming (TD approx. 4 = MT for lace).
32 sts and 52 rows to 10cm measured over st st after light steaming (TD approx. 3 = MT for st st).
Tension must be matched exactly before starting garment.

Note
Knitted side is used as right side. Measurements are those of finished garment and should not be used to measure work on machine.

PATTERN NOTE
Program patt/punch card before starting to knit.
Patt is reproduced from card L–1 in Silver Reed's (Knitmaster's) basic lace pack. This patt can also be used by Toyota models with lace carriages that can transfer and K in the same row. Other models and Brother machines can substitute an alternative lace pattern in the format suited for their machine.

SPECIAL NOTE
SKIRT LENGTH: This can be a matter of preference for the knitter. Given the tension and row numbers, this gown had a skirt length of 62cm, but it can be shortened by subtracting rows or increasing them if a longer skirt is preferred. The only thing to remember is that all three skirt panels must have the same number of rows.

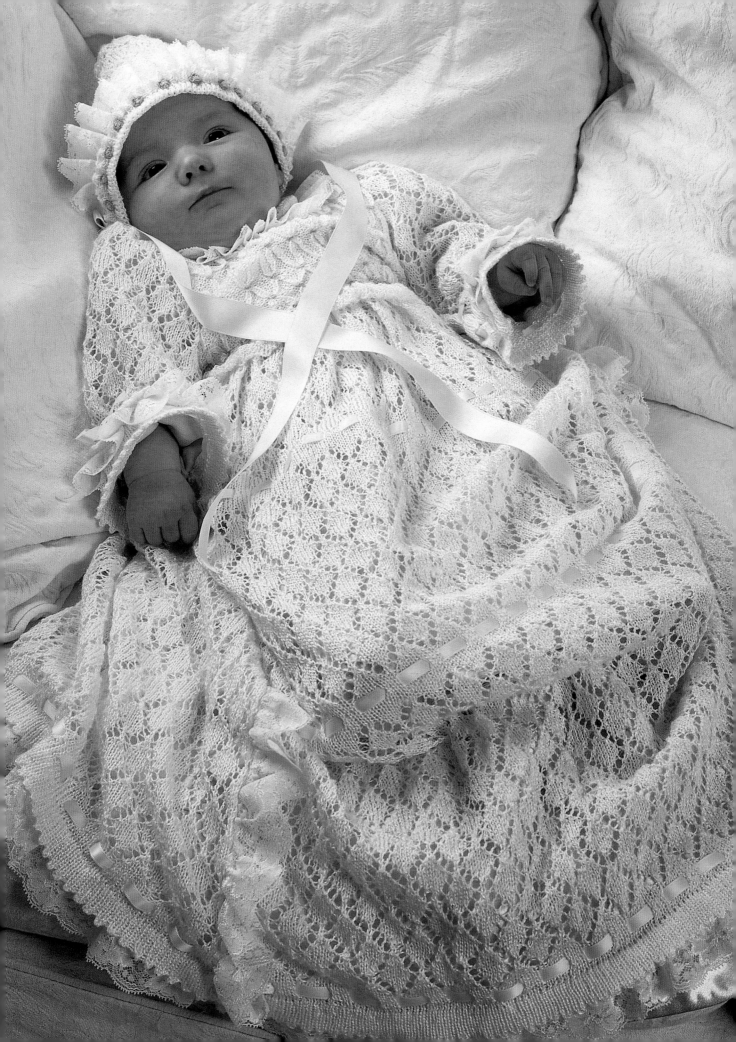

> **HELPFUL HINT**
>
> *Because of the silky texture of this yarn, it is advisable to catch immediately any stitch that drops!*

These instructions are written for standard gauge punchcard or electronic Silver Reed machines with lace carriage and ribber (see pattern notes for alternatives for other machines).

FRONT SKIRT PANEL

Push 180 Ns to WP. Using WY cast on and K a few rows ending CAR. Using MC and MT, K10 rows. Transfer second and every foll alt st onto its adj N, leaving empty Ns in WP. MT+4, K1 row. MT, K11 rows. Turn a hem by picking up loops from first row worked in MC and hang evenly along the row. K2 rows. Insert punchcard and lock/program patt on first row and place LC on N-bed. K2 rows. Release card, set carr for lace knitting, and add weights evenly across WY.

RC000. K112 rows.

RC000 Lock patt card, set carr to knit st-st. K4 rows. Make a row of eyelets by transferring every fourth st to adj N all along the row, then K the row. K4 rows. Release patt card, reset carr to K lace K until RC shows 70. Rep from *to*. K until RC shows 42. Rep from *to* once more. Set carr to K st-st. K6 rows. Place marker thread in centre st and WK.

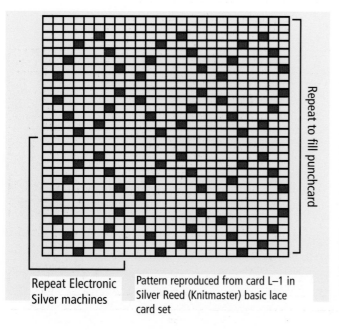

Repeat Electronic Silver machines

Pattern reproduced from card L–1 in Silver Reed (Knitmaster) basic lace card set

Repeat to fill punchcard

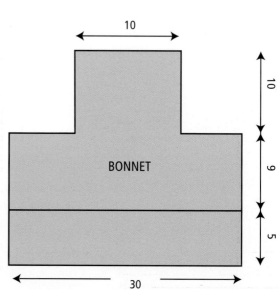

10

10

9

5

BONNET

30

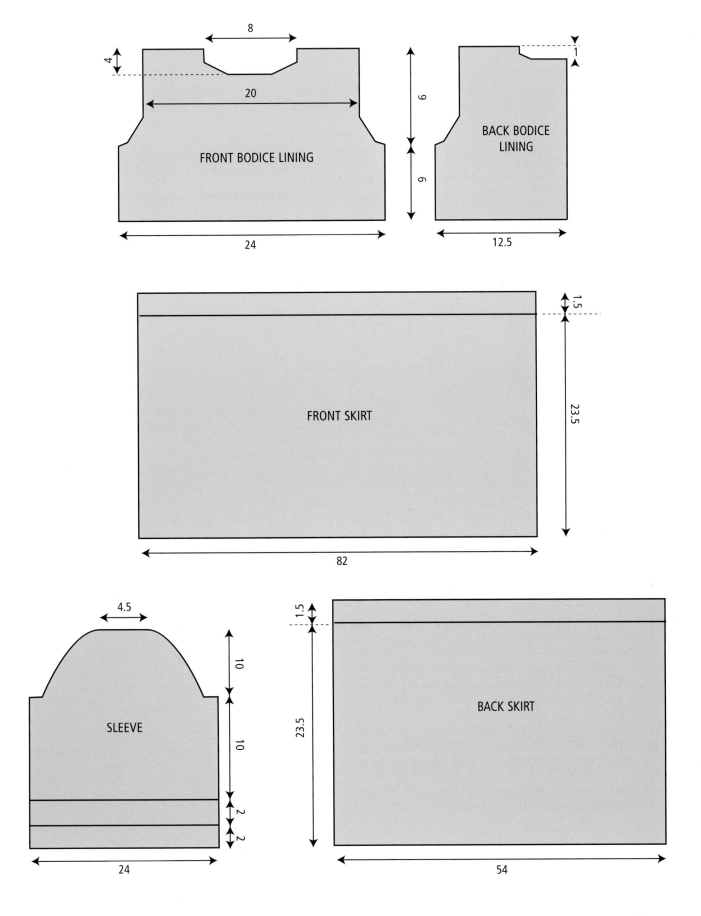

BACK PANELS

Work two alike.

As these panels are used to allow the front skirt to have extra width, a portion of their width is later joined to the front bodice.

Push 120 Ns to WP and work as given for front panel.

OVER-BODICE FRONT

With RB in position set machine for FNR. Push 110 Ns on MB and corr Ns on RB to WP. Arrange Ns for FNR. Using MC cast on and K3 tubular rows.

RC000 T3/4, K4 rows. CAR Arrange Ns as in Fig 3.2 and K until RC shows 42.

Shape armholes RC000. Cast off 4 sts at beg of next 2 rows. Cast off 2 sts at beg of next 2 rows. Dec 1 st at both ends of next and foll alt row. 94 sts. K until RC shows 34.

Shape neck Using a separate piece of MC, cast off 20 sts at centre. Set carr for HP and push Ns at L to HP. K1 row. Dec 1st at neck edge on next 5 rows, K1 row. Dec 1 st at neck edge on next and every foll alt row 5 times in all. 27 sts. K until RC shows 62. Transfer sts to MB and cast off.

CAL. Reset RC at 34. Set carr so HP Ns will K and work L side to correspond with R.

LEFT OVER-BODICE BACK

With RB in position set machine for FNR. Push 56 Ns on MB and corr Ns on RB to WP. Work as given for bodice front until RC show 42. CAR. (K1 extra row for R back).

Fig 3.2 Needle arrangement for yokes

Shape armhole RC000. Cast off 4 sts at beg of next row, K1 row. Cast off 2 sts at beg of next row, K1 row. Cast off 2 sts at beg of next row. K until RC shows 57. CAL (CAR for R back).

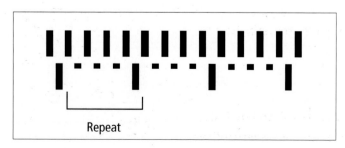

Repeat

Shape neck Cast off 12 sts at beg of next row, K1 row. Cast off 5 sts at beg of next row, K1 row. Cast off 4 sts at beg of next row. Cast off rem 27 sts.

RIGHT OVER-BODICE BACK

Work as given for L back, noting difference in rows to reverse the shaping.

FRONT BODICE LINING

Worked on MB.

Push 74 Ns to WP. Using WY, cast on and K a few rows ending CAR. Using MC and T3, K32 rows. CAR.

Shape armholes RC000. Cast off 3 sts at beg of next 2 rows. Cast off 2 sts at beg of next 2 rows. Dec 1 st at beg of next 2 rows. 62 sts. K until RC shows 26.

Shape neck Using a separate piece of MC cast off 8 sts at centre. Set carr for HP and push Ns at L to HP. Cont over rem sts at R. K1 row. Dec 1 st at neck edge on next 3 rows. Dec 1 st neck edge on next and every foll alt row 4 times in all. K until RC shows 46. Cast off rem 20 sts.

CAL. Reset RC at 26. Set carr so HP Ns will K and work as given for R side.

RIGHT BACK BODICE LINING

Push 38 Ns to WP and work as given for front bodice lining until RC shows 37. CAL (K1 extra row for L back lining – CAR.)

Shape armhole RC000. Cast off 3 sts at beg of next row, K1 row. Cast off 2 sts at beg of next row, K1 row. Dec 1 st at beg of next row. 32 sts K until RC shows 42.

Shape neck Cast off 10 sts at beg of next row, K1 row. Cast off 2 sts at beg of next row, K1 row. Cast off rem 20 sts.

LEFT BACK BODICE LINING

Work as given for R back bodice lining, noting difference in rows to reverse shapings.

SLEEVES

Push 52 Ns to WP. Using WY cast on and K a few rows ending CAR. Using MC and MT (for lace), K9 rows. *Transfer 2nd and every foll alt

> ### HELPFUL HINT
>
> *When choosing the lining fabric, pick one that is crease-resistant. A simple test is to take a corner of fabric (while still on the roll) and fold it tightly between finger and thumb. If it creases, choose another!*

st onto its adj N, leaving empty Ns in WP. T10+, K1 row. MT, K8 rows. Turn a hem by picking up loops from first row worked in MC and hang evenly along the row*. K11 rows. On next row, run a fine but strong contrast yarn through feeder with MC. MC only, K9 rows. Work from *to* of picot hem, picking up the MC sts from the row carrying the contrast yarn. K4 rows. Work a row of eyelets, by trans every fourth st to adj N and leaving empty Ns in WP. Insert punchcard/program patt on first row and change to LC. RC000. K2 rows. Release card and set carr for lace. K until RC shows 48. CAR.

Shape top RC000. Cast off 4 sts at beg of next 2 rows. Cast off 2 sts at beg of next 2 rows. Dec 1 st at each end of next and every foll 5 rows, 5 times, K2 rows. Dec 1 st at each end of next and every foll 3 rows, 4 times in all. Dec 1 st at each end of next 6 rows. K until RC shows 48 and cast off rem 10 sts.

TO MAKE UP

Block and steam sleeves to correct measurements. When dry, pin to paper and draw around shape. Cut out, adding a seam allowance of approx. 2cm all round. Pin paper pattern to satin fabric and cut out. Sew knitted sleeve seams. Sew on lace edging and thread ribbons at wrists. Machine or hand-sew satin sleeve linings (working a French seam, owing to fraying nature of satin). Put sleeve linings inside sleeves. Turn a hem under at wrists, and baste around the sleeve caps. Trim away any surplus satin.

Skirt panels Sew lace edging, gathering slightly, along the sides of front panel. Sew tog with the sides of back panels. Block and steam the bodice lining sections to correct measurements and allow to dry.

Fig 3.3 Smocking sequence

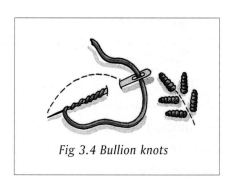

Fig 3.4 Bullion knots

Pin knitted lining pieces onto paper and mark the outline, adding a seam allowance as before. Pin the paper pattern onto satin fabric. Cut out the satin lining of front and back bodices and lay to one side. Take the ribbed over-bodice, and, following Fig 3.3 on facing page, stitch the ribbed sts in the smocking design, starting 2cm from the bottom edge and using 2 strands of embroidery thread (pale peach). On the first row of smocking, use bullion stitch to work rosebuds in dark peach (see Fig 3.4 on facing page and Fig 3.5, right). Finish with pale green leaves (see Fig 3.6). With the smocking complete, the over-bodice will have been made narrower but flexible. Lay the smocked sections upon the knitted linings and ease them together until they fit. Sew them lightly together around the armholes and neck.

With right side of work facing, rehang the first row of MC sts at the bottom edge of front bodice lining. Matching the marker threads at centre, and with wrong side facing, pick up the sts of front panel and approx. 1cm at each side of back panels, gathering sts evenly across the row. Using MC and MT, K2 rows. T10+ K1 row. Rep this step with the back bodices and rem sts of back skirt panels, thus joining the skirt sections to the bodice. Bring the fluted bottom edge of the over-bodice, over the waist join, and stitch in place. Sew shoulder and side seams of both bodices. Set sleeves in position, sewing them to both bodices, and binding the seams afterwards with satin bias ribbon (to prevent satin edge from fraying), gathering around top of cap, easing to fit.

Sew back seam, leaving approx. 7cm open from waist. Thread ribbons in eyelets and add lace under the hem and around neckline, gathering it as you work. Bring neckband to right side and sew it to cover the gathered edge of the lace. On the back opening, work a row of buttonhole st, followed by five evenly spaced buttonholes on the right side. Sew buttons to correspond on the L side.

Satin underskirt Take the length measurement of the knitted gown and mark it lightly on the satin, adding 1–2cm at the waist (for seaming), and 3cm at the bottom edge (for hem). Measure the gown's width and mark that, also adding a back seam allowance. Cut to size. Gather at the waist and sew to the satin bodice. Neaten at neck and armholes. Sew back seam (French seam), leaving a 7cm opening. Sew small seams on back openings. Attach snap fasteners. Turn up hem at bottom edge.

Fig 3.5 Three stages to forming a rosebud using bullion knots

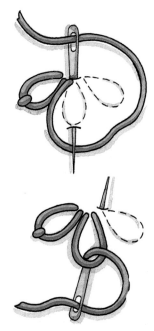

Fig 3.6 Formation of Lazy-Daisy stitch for leaves

Alternative knitted underskirt Knitted with two strands of bright acrylic.

TENSION: 36 sts and 50 rows to 10cm after light steaming TD approx. 2.

To obtain the necessary fullness in the skirt, there will have to be a centre panel and two back panels, where part of them forms a part of the front panel during the making-up process (as in the lace skirt). To obtain the same skirt length as the lace overskirt, you will need to knit 310 rows for each skirt section. The full width of the machine (200 sts) will be required for the width of the front panel, and 170 sts for each of the back panels.

Start with WY, followed by a hem in the double stranded yarn – a picot hem like on the top skirt. When the main skirt is attached (on the machine) to the bodice lining, simply add the sts from the knitted underskirt or, if this seems too bulky, cast off the underskirt sts, gather them by hand, then sew the skirt section to the inside waistline of the finished gown.

BONNET

Push 96 Ns to WP. Using WY cast on and K a few rows. Using MC and MT (for lace) K10 rows. Work a row of eyelets for picot hem (as on sleeves) MT+4 K1 row. MT, K11 rows. Turn a hem by picking up loops from first row worked in MC and hang evenly along the row. K18 rows. On next row, run a nylon cord (or strand of fine but strong contrasting yarn) through the same feeder as MC. K10 rows. Work eyelets for picot hem as before, then K11 rows and turn up hem (picking up sts from marked row below). K2 rows. Remove contrast yarn. Insert punchcard/program patt on first row. K6 rows. Weight work evenly and change to LC.

RC000. Release card and set carr for lace. K until RC shows 44. Set carr for st st and K4 rows.

Shape top

Cast off 32 sts at beg of next 2 rows. 32 sts. K52 rows and cast off.

TO MAKE UP

Pin piece to correct measurements and steam lightly. When dry, pin to sheet of plain paper and draw around the bonnet's outline. Cut out the paper shape, adding a seam allowance of approx. 2cm around the edges. Pin the paper shape to satin. Cut out. Sew (hand

or machine) the satin side seams.
Sew the knitted side seams.
Turn bonnet inside out and lay the
lining over it. Baste into place. Turn
under front edge of lining and slip
st down, approx. 2–3cm from the
front hem. Trim away any excess
satin from bottom edge. Turn over
knitted hem around bottom edge of
bonnet, and sew in place, enclosing
the raw satin edges. Attach ribbons
at sides. Add lace edging and
embroidered rosebuds.

SLIPPERS

With RB in position set machine for
FNR. Push 60 Ns on MB and corr Ns
on RB to WP. Using MC cast on and K3 tubular rows. T5/5, transfer sts
for rib patt as on bodice, and K12 rows. Transfer sts to MB. T3, K2
rows and WK. Push 42 Ns to WP. Pick up sts from below WY and hang
on to Ns dec 18 sts evenly along the row. WK by hand 21 sts at R and
cont working on rem 21 sts. K24 rows.

Shape toe Set carr for HP. *Always taking yarn under the first inside N
in HP, push 1 N at opp end to carr, to HP on next 12 rows. Push 1 inside
N at opp end to carr to UWP on next 12 rows. All Ns in WP* K24 rows.

Shape heel Work as for toe shaping from *to*. K2 rows and WK.
Work a second slipper to match, but reverse the shaping by running the
21 sts onto WY at the L instead of the R side.

TO MAKE UP

Rehang the heel sts (top and bottom) from WK, with right side facing
inside. T10+ K1 row and cast off. Fold foot section in half at toe and
seam along sides. Sew up ribbed ankle section, letting ribbed area
'frill' out. Under the frill, where ribbing ends and st-st begins, run a
double thread of shirring elastic, knotting it securely. Sew lace edging
under frill, and add small satin bow at one side, embroidering a
rosebud in centre.

SLIP STITCH AND JACQUARD

Slip stitch

Machine knitters are often disappointed by the rather flat and unimaginative fabrics that slip stitch can produce. However, there is much more to this stitch if you explore its potential further. For example, if you look at the texture of the sweater on page 89 you may find it hard to believe it was knitted in a fine 3ply. The sleeves are knitted in plain stockinet, albeit in double-stranded yarn to match the thick body of the sweater, to set off the body's slip-stitch patterning.

There are similarities between slip stitch and tuck stitch, but the difference is in the patterning cams. With the machine set to 'slip', the chosen needles do not move and the yarn actually passes over the needles, leaving a strand of yarn on what becomes the 'purl' side. As this side is usually considered to be the right side in slip-stitch

patterning, the effects are not always clear. It depends on the yarn chosen and also the stitch tension. Sometimes it helps to use a higher than usual tension, or an unusual yarn to create an interesting and pleasing fabric. Experiment with yarns and tensions, and keep an open mind.

Jacquard

Jacquard knitting produces some highly unusual fabrics. The patterning resembles Fair Isle, but there are several differences, although both techniques employ two different colour yarns. With jacquard, a much denser fabric is produced because of the full needle rib structure. With main carriage set to slip, two rows of knitting produce one colour row, while on the ribber side with carriages set to K, two rows are knitted in each colour. This means there are

four rows of 'backing' to every two rows of colour pattern, and therefore the backing is striped and dense. On the 'knitted' side of the fabric, we see the pattern, while on the back there are stripes of colour. The colours are changed every two rows, and the addition of a colour changer, while not absolutely essential, does make knitting jacquard less time-consuming.

The downside to knitting jacquard is the problem of remembering which colour needs to be changed. Over a few rows, the problem does not exist – but over 400? When knitting the pram blanket (see pages 90–92) I used 2/30s yarn double-stranded in both colours to get the weight I wanted, but on their journey through the colour changer, both yarns occasionally 'split' and came out of the feeder, and it was difficult to remember which colour belonged where!

I have since discovered that to avoid this you simply need to place your chair at whichever end of the machine your colour changer is situated and watch intently as the yarns are changed. If they separate, you can act immediately, replacing them before they 'knit' and cause tangles.

To know which colour needs changing, always stop with your carriage at the right side of the bed if you have to leave the machine for any length of time. As the colour changer is on the left side, when you come back to knit you will be able to see instantly which colour row you are on. (Knitters with colour changers situated on the right side of their machine, sit at the left side.)

Apart from those very minor 'hiccups' jacquard knitting is relatively straightforward. More information, if required, can be found in knitters' instruction manuals.

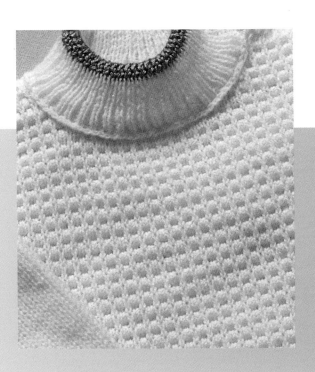

Slip-stitch matinée jacket

This matinée jacket, with its two-colour slip-stitch yoke, has a simplicity that will appeal to knitters who do not like anything too fussy. The teaming of white with navy is both smart and fashionable, as many of today's knitters are moving away from the more classic baby shades and instead favouring strong colour schemes.

PATTERN INFORMATION

Sizes
To suit chest 31[36:41:46:51]cm
Finished measurement (before gathering on to yoke)
44[48:52:56]cm
Length 27[29:31:32]cm
Sleeve seam 16[17:17:18]cm
Figures in square brackets refer to larger sizes; where there is only one set of figures this applies to all sizes.

Materials
1 cone acrylic 3ply in white (MC) and small amount in navy (C)
1m narrow white ribbon

Garment weight
For size 41cm approx. 75g

Main tension
32 sts and 42 rows to 10cm, measured over st st, (TD approx. 5 = MT).
36 sts and 54 rows to 10cm measured over slip-stitch patt (TD approx. 6 = MT+1)
Tension must be matched exactly before starting garment.

Note
Knitted side is used as right side. Measurements are those of finished garment and should not be used to measure work on machine.

PATTERN NOTE
Program patt/punch card before starting to knit.
(Pattern is reproduced from card 3A in Silver (Knitmaster) basic pack.)

PATTERN AND COLOUR SEQUENCE
Insert punchcard and lock/program patt on first row. Set carr to select/memorize for patt and K1 row.
Release card and set carr for slip/part/empty. MC, K2 row; C, K2 rows. Rep these 4 rows throughout.

These instructions are written for standard gauge punchcard or electronic machines.

BACK SKIRT
Push 84[90:96:102] Ns to WP. Using WY cast on and K a few rows ending CAR.
RC000. Using MT-1, K8 rows. Transfer second and every foll alt st to adj N, leaving empty Ns in WP. MT+1, K2 rows. MT-1, K8 rows. Pick

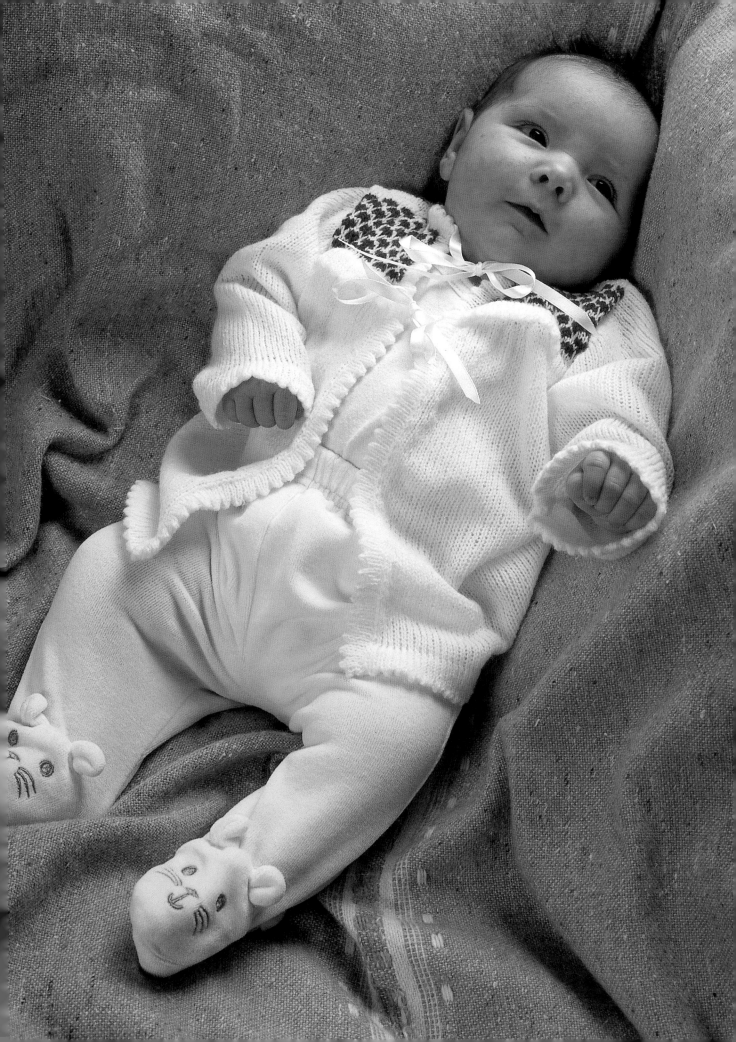

up loops from first row worked in MC and hang evenly along the row. Remove WY**.
RC000. Using MT, K 76[84:88:92] rows*.

Shape armholes Cast off 4 sts at beg of next 2 rows. Dec 1 st at beg of next 6 rows. 70[76:82:88] sts. WK.

RIGHT FRONT SKIRT

Work as given for back to *. K1 extra row for L front skirt.

Shape armhole Cast off 4 sts at beg of next row, K1 row. Dec 1 st at beg of next and every foll alt row 3 times in all. 35[37:41:45] sts. WK.

LEFT FRONT SKIRT

Work as given for R front skirt noting difference in rows to reverse shaping.

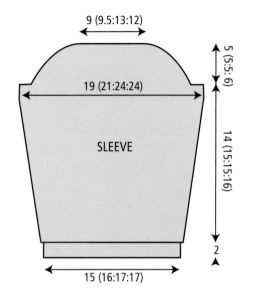

9 (9.5:13:12)

19 (21:24:24)

SLEEVE

5 (5:5:6)

14 (15:15:16)

2

15 (16:17:17)

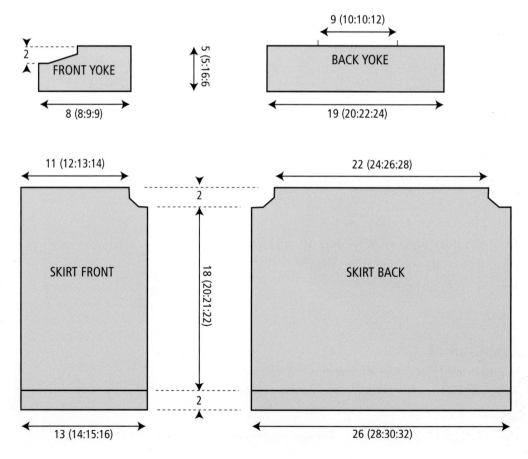

2

FRONT YOKE

8 (8:9:9)

5 (5:16:6)

9 (10:10:12)

BACK YOKE

19 (20:22:24)

11 (12:13:14)

2

SKIRT FRONT

18 (20:21:22)

13 (14:15:16)

22 (24:26:28)

2

SKIRT BACK

2

26 (28:30:32)

BACK YOKE

Push 68[72:80:86] Ns to WP. With wrong side facing pick up sts from below WY of back skirt and hang on to Ns dec evenly along the row as required. Remove WY. Using MC and MT, K1 row. CAL. K next row with fine contrast thread in with MC. MT-1, K8 rows. Transfer second and every foll alt st to adj N, leaving empty Ns in WP. MT+1, K2 rows. MT-1, K8 rows. Turn a hem by picking up loops from row marked with contrast thread below and hang evenly along the row. Remove contrast thread.

RC000. Using MC, K1 row. MT+1, start and work patt (see patt note – commencing with memorize row) throughout**. K until RC shows 24[30:30:34]. Set carr for st st and using MT, K2 rows and WK.

RIGHT FRONT YOKE

Push 28[28:34:34] Ns to WP. Work as given for back yoke to **. K until RC shows 13[19:19:23]. CAL (K1 extra row for L front yoke CAR).

Shape neck Cast off 6[7:7:8] sts at beg of next row, K1 row. Cast off 2 sts at beg of next and foll alt row. Dec 1 st at neck edge on next 3 rows. WK over rem 15[15:20:20] sts.

LEFT FRONT YOKE

Work as given for R front yoke, noting difference in rows to reverse shaping.

INTERIM MAKE UP

Push 15[15:20:20] Ns to WP. With right side facing pick up sts from below WY on one back shoulder. With wrong side facing pick up sts from below WY on matching front shoulder. Remove WY. Using MC and MT K2 rows. T10+, K1 row and cast off. Rep for second shoulder.

FRONT BANDS

Work two alike.

With wrong side facing, pick up sts evenly from front edge, (from bottom of picot hem to neckline inc yoke picot hem) and hang evenly on to Ns. Using MC and MT-1, K6 rows. Transfer second and

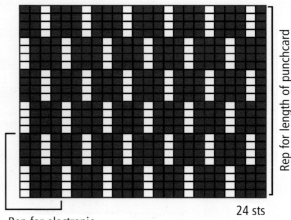

Rep for electronic

Rep for length of punchcard

24 sts

every foll alt st to adj N, leaving empty Ns in WP. MT+1, K2 rows. MT-1, K6. Cast off loosely. Turn to inside and slip stitch down.

NECKBAND

With wrong side facing, pick up sts evenly from front, back and front neck edges (inc sts from picot hems). Work as given for front bands.

SLEEVES

Push 48[52:54:54] Ns to WP. Work as given for back skirt to **.
RC000. Using MT, K5[5:4:4] rows. Inc 1 st at each end of next and every foll 6[6:5:5] rows 4[5:12:8] times in all. 56[62:78:70] sts.
K7[7:0:5] rows. Inc 1 st at each end of next and every foll 8[8:0:6] rows 2[2:0:4] times in all. 60[66:78:78] sts. K until RC shows 58[63:63:68].

Shape top Cast off 4 sts at beg of next 2 rows. 52[58:70:70] sts.
Dec 1 st at each end of next and every foll alt row 6 times in all.
40[46:58:58] sts. Dec 1 st at each end of next 6[8:8:10] rows.
Cast off rem 28[30:42:38] sts.

TO MAKE UP

With wrong side facing block and lightly steam pieces to correct measurements. Ensure picot hems of yokes are flat and turned downwards. Sew in sleeves easing any gathering in to top. Join side and sleeve seams. Sew ribbons to neck and front yoke edges.

Patterned slip-stitch sweater

This classic white sweater shows a version of slip stitch to its best advantage. Worked in a fine 3ply, this stitch turns what would have been a soft but limp fabric, into something more chunky. To offset the deeply patterned 'body' of the sweater, the sleeves have been knitted in plain stockinet, using the 3ply yarn doubled to match the 'body' in weight.

PATTERN INFORMATION

Sizes
To suit chest 51[56:61]cm
Finished measurement 56[60:64]cm
Length 32[34:36]cm
Sleeve seam 27[29:31]cm
Figures in square brackets refer to larger sizes; where there is only one set of figures this applies to all sizes.

Materials
1 cone acrylic 3ply in white (MC)
Small amount in contrast

Garment weight
For size 51cm approx. 400g

Main tension
30 sts and 12 'ripple' to 10cm, measured over slip st, (TD approx. 5 = MT).
28 sts and 36 rows to 10cm measured over st st using MC double (TD approx. 9)
Tension must be matched exactly before starting garment.

Note
Purl side is used as right side. Measurements are those of finished garment and should not be used to measure work on machine.

PATTERN NOTE
Program patt/punch card before starting to knit.

SPECIAL NOTE
Sleeves are worked using MC double. Wind off a ball of yarn and thread one end from ball and one from cone through tension mast and into feeder together – treating as though they were the one yarn – only for double sections.

These instructions are written for standard gauge punchcard or electronic machines with ribber.

BACK
With RB in position set machine for 1 x 1 rib. Push 84[90:96] Ns on MB and corr Ns on RB to WP. Arrange Ns for 1 x 1 rib. Using MC cast on and K3 tubular rows. T2/2, K46 rows. Transfer sts to MB. RC000. Insert punchcard and lock/program patt on first row. Using MT, K3 rows. Set carr to select/memorize for patt and K1 row. Release card and set carr for slip/part/empty. K until RC shows 164[184:204].

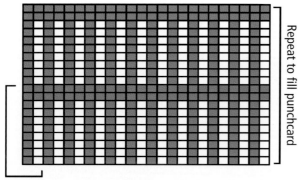

Repeat to fill punchcard

Repeat for electronic machines

Shape armholes RC000. Cast off 6 sts at beg of next 2 rows. 72[78:84] sts. K until RC shows 180[210:220] and WK.

FRONT

Work as given for back until RC shows 110[130:150] after armhole shaping.

Shape neck Note patt row. Using a separate piece of MC cast off 12 sts at centre. Using nylon cord, K30[33:36] sts at L by hand taking Ns down to NWP. Cont over rem 30[33:36] sts at R for first side. K1 row. Dec 1 st at neck edge on next 6 rows, K1 row. Dec 1 st at neck edge on next and every foll alt row 6 times in all. 18[21:24] sts. K until RC shows 180[210:220] and WK. CAR. Unravel nylon cord over sts at L bringing Ns down to WP. Turn punchcard and lock/program patt on noted row. Set carr to slip/part empty and take to L. Set card to rotate and reset RC at 110[130:150]. Work as given for R side.

SLEEVES

Push 62[68:72] Ns to WP. Using WY, cast on and K a few rows ending CAR.

RC000. Using MC double (see special notes) and T9, work in st st throughout and K10[12:16] rows. Inc 1 st at each end of next and every foll 10[11:10] rows 8[8:9] times in all. 78[84:90] sts. K until RC shows 90[98:106] and cast off loosely.

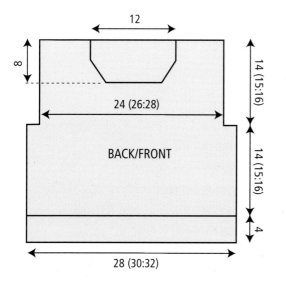

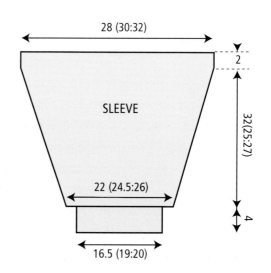

CUFF

With RB in position set machine for 1 x 1 rib. Push 50[56:60] Ns to WP. Using MC (single) cast on and K3 tubular rows. Using T2/2, K20 rows. K4 rows contrast, MC, K20 rows. Transfer sts to MB. With wrong side of sleeve facing, pick up sts from below WY and hang on to Ns dec 12 sts evenly along the row. T5, K2 rows. T10+ K1 row and cast off.

NECKBAND

Join R shoulder seam. With RB in position set machine for 1 x 1 rib. Push 88[94:100] Ns to WP. Using MC (single) cast on and K3 tubular rows. Using T2/2 K10[14:16] rows. Using contrast, K4 rows. Using MC, K10[14:16] rows. Transfer sts to MB. T10+ K1 row and cast off.

TO MAKE UP

With wrong side facing block and very lightly steam pieces to correct measurements. Join L shoulder seam starting at armhole edge for approx. 3cm. Turn ribbed hem to inside forming a double hem and sew down. Set in sleeves. Turn cuffs in half to inside and slip stitch down. Join side and sleeve seams. Fold neckband in half and baste to neck edge sewing one side of neckband to inner edge and the other to outer edge. Neaten all loose threads. Embroider a row of blanket stitch along both edges of neck opening. On the front opening work three evenly spaced loop buttonholes. Sew buttons on other side to correspond with buttonholes. Sew in sleeves. Give a final press.

Jacquard blanket

This lovely blanket, suitable for use in a pram, cot or for simply wrapping around a sleepy baby, incorporates a wonderful cat pattern. I have knitted it with pink as the main colour, but you can, of course, choose an alternative colour scheme. The satin ribbon edging gives it a luxurious touch.

PATTERN INFORMATION

Sizes
Finished measurement 50 x 66cm

Materials
1 cone acrylic 2/30s in pink (MC) and white (C)
1 cone bright acrylic in white
1m narrow white ribbon

Garment weight
Approx. 215g

Main tension
30 sts and 56 rows to 10cm, measured over double jacquard, using 3 strands of each yarn together throughout (TD approx. 5/6 = MT).
Tension must be matched exactly before starting garment.

Note
Knitted side is used as right side. Measurements are those of finished garment and should not be used to measure work on machine.

PATTERN NOTE
Program patt/punch card before starting to knit.
(Pattern is reproduced from card 20R in Silver Reed/Knitmaster basic ribber/colour changer pack.)

PATTERN AND COLOUR SEQUENCE
Insert punchcard and lock/program patt on first row. Put double-bed colour changer in position at L of machine and thread up second feeder with C. Depress colour change button 1 (where MC will go). CAR. Set carr to select/memorize for patt and K1 row. Release card and set carr for slip/part/empty. C, K2 rows; MC, K2 rows Rep these 4 rows throughout.

SPECIAL NOTES
Weights on the knitting will need to be lifted up the fabric at regular intervals.
Positioning your chair nearest the colour changer (if you are using one) is helpful. It enables you to spot – and often prevent – a possible yarn mix-up during the yarn changes. Sometimes your index finger laid over the yarn changer makes for a smoother changeover. Should you have cause to leave your machine for a while, let the

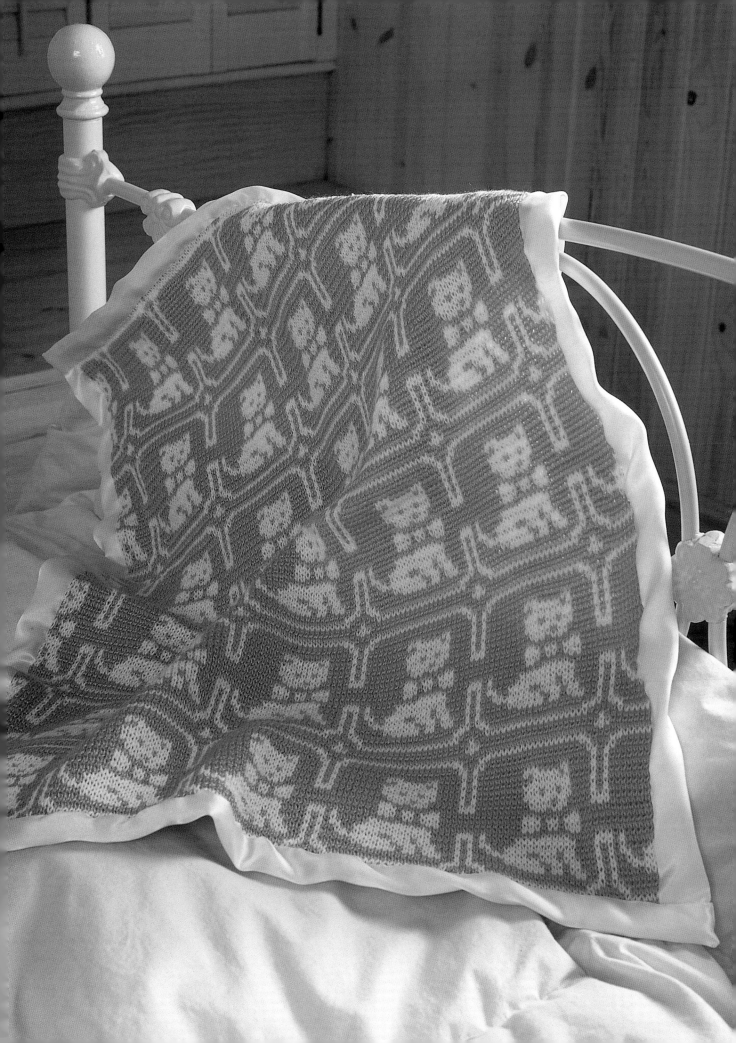

carriage remain at the side of the bed, opposite the colour changer – that way, you will be able to see at a glance which colour should be changed next.

To see what is happening behind the knitting (almost impossible on double-bed work) a long-handled mirror makes a useful tool.

These instructions are written for standard gauge punchcard or electronic machines with ribber. A colour changer makes this easier to knit but is not essential if colours are changed manually.

BLANKET

With RB in position set machine for FNR. Push 150 Ns on MB and corr Ns on RB to WP. Arrange Ns for FNR.

RC000. Using MC cast on and T2/3 K4 tubular rows. Insert punchcard and lock/program patt on first row. K10 rows. CAR. Set up and start patt (see patt notes). Using MT, work in patt throughout and K until RC shows 420. (Adjust rows for longer or shorter blanket.) Set both carr to K and using MC, K10 rows. Transfer sts to MB and cast off loosely.

TO MAKE UP

Lightly steam piece on completion and darn-in all ends. Bind edges with satin ribbon as shown.

24 sts x 60 rows

Pattern is reproduced from card 20R in Silver Reed (Knitmaster) basic ribber set.

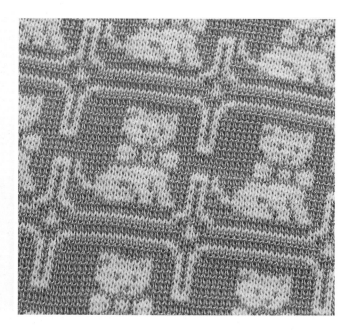

PILE AND PLATING

To many knitters, pile and plating may seem to belong to an entirely different craft. In fact, they both hold a well-deserved place within the realms of machine knitting, although, sadly, neither are well-known or used. Perhaps owners of automatic machines have become so comfortable and delighted by the speed and simplicity of the more usual patterns, such as Fair Isle and lace, that they do not see the need to look any further. If so, they are missing out. In not trying to extend their range of capabilities, how can they know what they and their machines can achieve? Machine knitters should not be afraid to experiment, for they have nothing to lose, and everything to gain.

Pile and plating techniques have several things in common, which is why they share a chapter. They both make use of a little device known as the 'auxiliary yarn feeder'; they both use two different yarns that are knitted simultaneously; the techniques both involve use of the double bed; and they both produce attractive and unique fabrics that are unobtainable by any other method. But there the similarities end, for the fabric finishes are vastly different.

Pile

Silver Reed knitting machines have an in-built pile-knitting facility and pile-levers, situated at the sides of the ribber bed. Toyota (901 model) machine owners will find that their facility for knitting pile comes as an optional extra, and will need to be purchased from their knitting machine stockist. Brother machines, to the best of my knowledge, do not have the facility at all.

So, what is pile knitting? It is a method of knitting using yarns of different thicknesses. The thicker yarn is fed through a special feeder at the back of the ribber (the auxiliary yarn feeder). Both yarns are knitted together with the main carriage set on 'slip'. The ribber knits the stitches and the main bed forms the loops on every alternate row. The loops are then dropped from the needles on the next row by using a gadget known as the P-carriage (it comes as an accessory with Silver Reed ribbers). The following two rows pick up the stitches again and the process is then repeated.

The knitting produces tactile, regulated tufts or loops, resembling the texture of towelling, and quite unlike the longer loops featured on the hand-muff and bonnet on pages 51–52. The choice of yarns plays an important role in the resulting fabric that comes off the machine, giving the knitter a wide range of possibilities with this stitch. Too thick a yarn combination and a fabric that is stiff as carpet is the result. Yarns that are too fine, can produce something a bit too flimsy. By using lightweight yarns – two strands of 2/30s wound together in the main feeder and a single strand in the auxiliary feeder on the ribber – one is able to produce a fabric that is perfect for a baby's garment.

Punchcard patterns can be used with this technique and, while 'ordinary' pile knitting provides neat, regular lines of small loops, the use of patterning, especially where two colours are used, gives the added interest of plain knitting as a background and raised, colourful loops on top. Special patterns for this type of effect can be found in Silver Reed instruction manuals.

Plating
Plating, unlike pile, can be worked either as a single- or a double-bed project, which offers

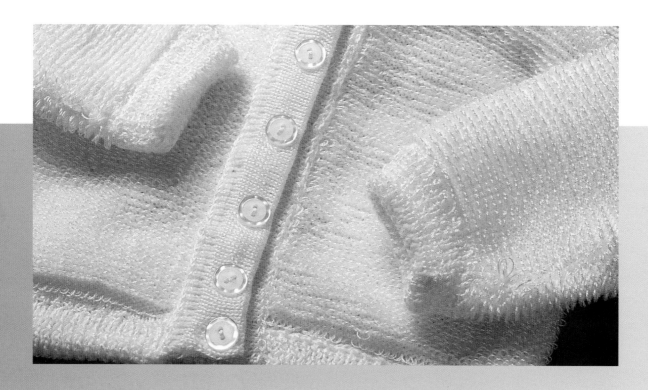

the adventurous knitter a wider scope of patterning. Fortunately, most modern machines come with plating feeders, but a quick glance through an instruction manual will tell a knitter if their own machine comes under that category. It will also inform the knitter of how to recognize and fit it.

Plating is most often worked using two yarns and, when working it on the ribber, the close-knit bar can also be used. As with most knitting techniques, it pays to experiment when it comes to yarn choices. Different yarns and favourite stitch patterns receive an immediate 'make-over' when the plating technique is tried. For thicker yarns, the close-knit bar will not be needed.

The way that plating works is as follows: one yarn goes behind a small wire barrier, while the other yarn slots into a little open 'mouth'. Care must be taken, though, not to twist the two yarns while threading. Fine yarns, which the plating method favours,

have many benefits for the knitter. Apart from being economical in use, you can incorporate an expensive or luxury yarn together with a cheaper yarn and still achieve a stunning effect.

Colour combinations play a large part in plating. The use of two yarns allows for a wider spectrum of colour, whether it is subtle and muted, or bright for maximum impact. Knitters are often astounded by the way colours react to plating, as one of its main features is that it can make a fabric completely reversible: one colour shows through on one side, while the contrast shade appears on the other. Whether the two colours are entirely different or shades of the same is entirely up to you and the expanse of your imagination.

Plating provides a multitude of creative possiblities and is therefore an extremely worthwhile technique to add to your repertoire of skills.

Pile-knitted hooded jacket

The little 'ears' on the hood of this jacket definitely gives it the 'ah' factor, making it an absolute must-have. If you wish, the pink yarn that has been used for inside the ears and to trim the jacket can be replaced with traditional blue to make it suitable for a baby boy.

PATTERN INFORMATION

Sizes
To suit chest 46[51:56]cm
Finished measurement 48[56:60]cm
Length 24[26:28]cm
Sleeve seam 16[18:20]cm
Figures in square brackets refer to larger sizes; where there is only one set of figures this applies to all sizes.

Materials
1 cone bright acrylic 3ply in white (MC)
1 cone 2/30s industrial acrylic in white (C)
Oddment of contrast yarn (A)
Buttons

Garment weight
For size 41cm approx. 265g

Main tension
30 sts and 50 rows to 10cm, measured over pile knitting using 2 ends of bright acrylic (MC) together with one end of 2/30s (C), (TD approx. 3/4 = MT). Tension must be matched exactly before starting garment.

Note
Loop side is used as right side. Measurements are those of finished garment and should not be used to measure work on machine.

SPECIAL NOTES
Wind off several balls of MC before starting to knit. Thread one end MC from cone and one from ball through the same tension mast (see 'Easy Steps to Pile Knitting', below and pages 98–99).
The knitting needs to be weighted at all stages, preferably with the knitting N method, (see Glossary, page 140) with the Ns taking the weights 'claws' and not the pile fabric, which is easily damaged. Practise moving the p-carr smoothly across Ns. Jerky movements can bring Ns out of line and obstruct its passage. Once started, do not try to go back.
The casting off or dec of sts can only be done on the RB. By putting 2–3 Ns back down to A position on the MB while knitting it will leave a 'margin' without loops, which will be of help when it comes to seaming.

EASY STEPS TO PILE KNITTING
STEP 1: If pile knitting is something you have never heard of, or even if you just need a quick reminder, reading this part is a must before

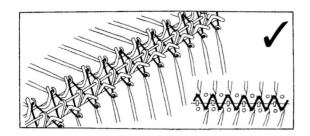 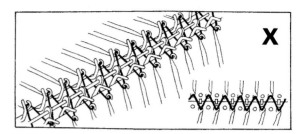

Fig 5.1 Correct and incorrect method of positioning teeth of casting-on comb against sinker pegs

embarking upon a full-sized garment. Wind together two strands of 'Bright' Acrylic (or any single strand of your choice) before beginning to knit.

Push the Ns you require to WP and set for FNR. Thread the yarn mast with double-stranded yarn in feeder A and single strand of industrial 2/30s in feeder B. Thread carr with double-stranded yarn and cast on, but there is a 'needle rule' that is extremely important, and for successful pile knitting, it must be obeyed: the casting-on comb needs to be placed with its 'teeth' in direct line with the sinker posts of the ribber bed in order to prevent the loose stitches from 'running away' later on (see Fig 5.1, above, for correct method). K a few rows, finishing with CAL.

STEP 2: Transfer the stitches from the MB Ns to the RB Ns, but leave the empty MB Ns in WP.

Fix the P-presser (see ribber manual) to the P-carriage. This should be with your ribber accessories. Place the P-carriage on the needle bed, just in front of the ribber carriage. Set the auxiliary-yarn feeder to P and, using the long yarn hook, thread the single-strand yarn through it, down the back of the feeder (see your ribber manual if unsure). This is made easier if the RB is lowered slightly at the left-hand side. Push it back into place before commencing! At this stage, lower the pile levers to widen the space between the beds (the ones with the blue spots on them). Set the stitch tension on the RB one whole number higher than the one on the MB.

STEP 3: Set R side lever back but leave L one forward. Set cam lever to slip. Move p-carr, steadily and without stopping, to the right. All the RB Ns will have moved to C position. K the row. Replace the p-carr on the ribber (rail) at L, and move it to the right (as before) K a row. Only the ribber will have knitted. CAL. Place the p-carr now on the rail of the MB (at R) and run it across the Ns to the left. Run it back to the right, and all the 'loops' from the MB Ns will have fallen off. Once again, place the p-carr on the ribber rail in front of the ribber (at L), run the p-carr across Ns (to the right), bringing them to C position. K the row, and repeat…

To re-cap…

Row 1, knits on the RB, but at the same time makes 'loops' on the MB.

Row 2, knits on the RB also, but locks the loops of the previous row. However, the loops on the MB must be dropped if we want to form the 'pile', so that is what happens when the p-carr is moved across the loops twice. The next row will reform the sts (loops) once again.

While it is recommended that the p-carr is used to bring the Ns to C position at the start of every row to ensure that the sts knit properly, I have found that it is rarely necessary to comply with this. By using the close-knit bar (see your instruction manual) throughout, and the correct thickness of yarns, I found no difficulty with the sts knitting off the Ns. It is, of course, necessary to use the p-carriage for the two movements on the MB, when the loops are removed. It is worth experimenting, trying both ways, because my way (if it works for you and your yarns) does save a great deal of time.

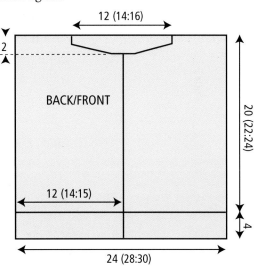

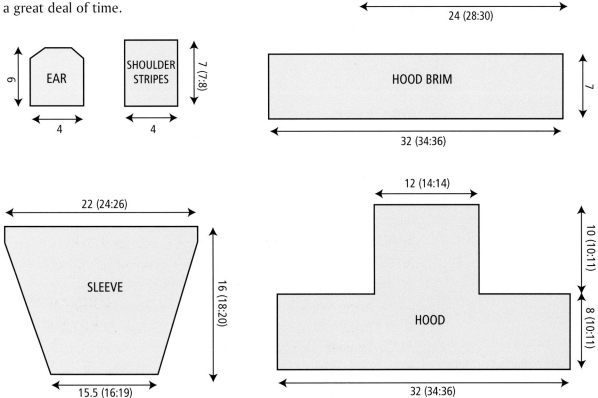

These instructions are written for standard gauge Silver Reed (Knitmaster) punchcard/electronic machines with pile knitting facility.

BACK
Use three ends MC for ribbed welts.

With RB in position set machine for 1 x 1 rib. Push 72[84:90] Ns on MB and corr Ns on RB to WP. Arrange Ns for 1 x 1 rib. Observing the casting-on comb rule (see patt notes) using three ends MC cast on and K2 tubular rows. T2/2, K12 rows. Using A, K2 rows. Using MC, K12 rows. Push empty Ns on both beds to WP.

RC000. Using MT for pile knitting, K3 rows. Transfer sts from MB to RB and start pile knitting sequence (see patt notes)*. K until RC shows 100[110:120]. Transfer sts to MB. Set MB carr for st st and K2 rows. WK.

RIGHT FRONT
Use three ends MC for ribbed welts.

With RB in position set machine for 1 x 1 rib. Push 36[42:46] Ns on MB and corr Ns on RB to WP. Work as given for back to *. K until RC shows 91[101:109]. CAL. (K1 extra row for L front).

Shape neck Working on RB Ns only and pushing empty MB Ns to NWP, cast off 13[14:14] sts at beg of next row, K1 row. Dec 1 st at neck edge on next 2 rows. 21[26:30] sts. K until RC shows 100[110:120].
Transfer sts to MB. Set MB carr for st st and K2 rows. WK.

LEFT FRONT
Work as given for R front, noting difference in rows to reverse the shaping.

SLEEVES
The sleeves are worked starting at the top edge and working down to the wrist, as it is easier to dec sts on pile knitting, than to inc them. It also makes the use of side weights unnecessary.

With RB in position set machine for FNR. Push 66[72:78] Ns on MB and corr Ns on RN to WP. Observing cast-on comb rule, using double-stranded MC, cast on and K2 tubular rows.

RC000. Using MT, K3 rows. CAL. Commence pile K sequence by

transferring sts from MB to RB. K until RC shows 10[12:12]. Dec on RB Ns only, pushing empty Ns to NWP and dec 1 st at each end of next and every foll 7[8:9] rows 9[8:9] times in all, K1 row. Dec 1 st at each end of next and every foll alt row 0[3:1] times in all. 46[48:56] sts. K until RC shows 80[90:100]. K2 rows Stockinet. Trans sts on both beds to adj Ns, setting machine for 1 x 1 rib. T2/T, and using three strands of yarn in main feeder, K12 rows. K2 rows with contrast yarn. K12 rows MC. Trans sts to MB. Cast off.

HOOD

With RB in position set machine for FNR. Push 90[96:102] Ns on MB and corr Ns on RB to WP. Using two strands MC, cast on and K4 tubular rows. RC000. Using T4/5 K32[40:44] rows. CAR. Cast off 28[28:30] sts at beg of next 2 rows. (Transfer them to MB first.) 34[40:42] sts. K40[40:44] rows. Transfer sts to MB and cast off.

Brim With RB in position set machine for FNR. Push 90[96:102] Ns on MB and corr Ns on RB to WP. Cast on observing cast on comb rule and K4 tubular rows. RC000 T3/4 K5 rows CAL. Transfer sts to RB and work pile knitting at MT for 40 rows. Transfer sts to MB and set carr for st st. K4 rows and cast off.

HELPFUL HINT

Use press studs if you wish to omit the button holes, and then sew on the buttons as trims.

'EARS'

Work two ears in MC and two ear linings in A. Use three strands MC and work on MB only. Push 17 Ns to WP and using MC cast on by hand ('e' wrap). T4, K10 rows. Dec 1 st at each end of next and foll alt row, K1 row. Dec 1 st at each end of next 2 rows. Cast off.

SHOULDER STRIPES

With RB in position set machine for 1 x 1 rib. Push 15 Ns on MB and corr Ns on RB to WP. Arrange Ns for 1 x 1 rib. Using MC cast on and K2 tubular rows.
RC000. T3/4, K4 rows. Using A, K4 rows. Cont in stripe patt as set and K until RC shows 24[28:32]. Transfer sts to MB and cast off.

FRONT BANDS

Buttonhole band With wrong side of coat facing, pick up R front edge and hang evenly on to Ns. Using three strands MC and T4, K6 rows. Work 5[6:6] evenly spaced buttonholes along the row. K5 rows. T9, K1 row. MT, K5 rows. Work another set of buttonholes to correspond with first set, K3 rows. Using A, K2 rows. Using MC, K2 rows and cast off loosely.

Button band Work as given for buttonhole band omitting buttonholes.

TO MAKE UP

If the cast-on comb was inserted correctly there should be no running loops. If there are, catch them with a darning needle and sew into place. Turn over the ribbed bands on coat hems, fronts, and sleeves, and sew down onto the pile knit side. Finish off the buttonholes. Sew side and sleeve seams, and join little striped shoulder pieces to back and front shoulder sections. Sew sleeves into armholes. Sew on buttons to correspond with buttonholes.

Hood Sew the ear sections together with the pink linings at the fronts. Baste them onto the hood, approx. 9cm apart, and 3cm back from the edge. Attach the pile knit brim to front of hood, turning under the rows of 'flat' plain knitting and enclosing the ears as you sew. Finally, sew the sides of the hood tog then attach it to neck edge of the coat, leaving the front bands free.

Girl's plated carry-cape

This carry-cape shows the stitch technique of 'plating' at its very best. Using a fine 3ply yarn in the main feeder and a single-ply silky yarn in the plating feeder meant that a higher tension than usual was required. On tension six (both beds) the resulting fabric was firm without being hard.

PATTERN INFORMATION

Sizes
One size to fit 0–5 months

Materials
1 cone acrylic 3ply in white (MC)
1 cone contrast yarn in 1ply
3m baby ribbon to match contrast
2.5mm crochet hook

Garment weight
Approx. 250g

Main tension
29 sts and 50 rows to 10cm, measured over tuck rib patt, (TD approx. 6/6 = MT). Tension must be matched exactly before starting garment.

Note
Knitted side is used as right side. Measurements are those of finished garment and should not be used to measure work on machine.

PATTERN NOTE
Program patt/punch card before starting to knit.
(Pattern is reproduced from card 3A in Silver (Knitmaster) basic pack.)
Arrange Ns for main patt as shown in Fig 5.2 (see page 104).

CROCHET EDGING
With right side of work facing, join in MC and work 1 row of dc all around. Join with sl st to first dc. Do not turn work.
Shells: *Miss 2 dc, 5 tr in next dc. Rep from * all the way around finishing by sl st into first st.

MACHINE KNITTED EDGING
Alternative machine knitted edging worked thus:
Arrange Ns as shown in Fig 5.3 (see page 104). Using two strands bright acrylic, cast on and K3 tubular rows. T4/5 K2 rows. Transfer sts as shown in Fig 5.4 (see page 104). Set carr for HP and push marked Ns to HP and K6 rows. Set carr so HP Ns will K and K2 rows. Rep this 8 row sequence throughout.

SPECIAL NOTE
Side weights need to be hung as the knitting progresses and moved up every 20–30 rows. With regards to the N positioning and the

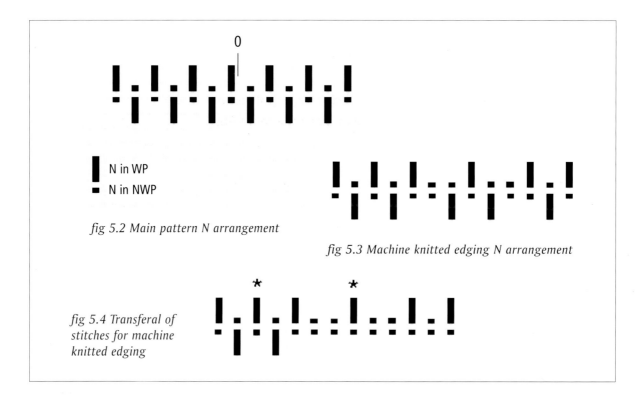

fig 5.2 Main pattern N arrangement

fig 5.3 Machine knitted edging N arrangement

fig 5.4 Transferal of
stitches for machine
knitted edging

pattern card – having arranged the Ns, lock the card on row 1, run
empty carr across (to select/memorize) and check that the Ns actually
'come out' as if they were going to pattern. If the Ns only come out
in a straight line, it means that the N setting is not correct and
therefore requires altering, or the punchcard has been inserted
upside down.

These instructions are written for standard gauge punchcard or
electronic machines with ribber.

BACK

With RB in WP set machine for FNR. Push 145
Ns on MB and corr Ns on RB to WP. Using MC
cast on and K2 tubular rows. Insert punchcard
and lock/program patt on first row. T4/5, K5
rows. CAL. Lower RB at L to ease threading
and place plating yarn in plating feeder. Close
ribber. Using MT, set carr to select/memorize
for patt and K1 row.
RC000. Set carr for tuck, release card and
work in tuck patt throughout. K until RC

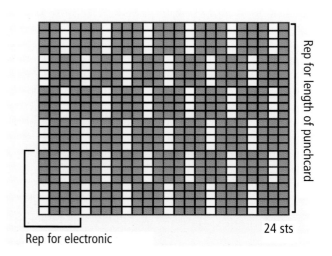

Rep for length of punchcard

24 sts

Rep for electronic

shows 240. Remove plating yarn and set carr for st st. T2/2. K4 rows. Transfer every third st to its adj N leaving empty Ns in WP. K6 rows and WK**.

Push 104 Ns on MB to WP. With wrong side facing pick up sts from below WY and hang on to Ns dec 41 sts evenly along the row. With RB in position set machine for 1 x 1 rib. Transfer alt sts to RB. Rep from * to *.

Push 70 Ns to WP. With wrong side facing pick up sts from below WY and hang on to Ns dec 34 sts evenly along the row. With RB in position set machine for 1 x 1 rib. Transfer alt sts to RB. Rep from * to * ending by transferring sts to MB and cast off (instead of WK).

FRONTS

Work two pieces alike

With RB in position set machine for FNR. Push 76 Ns on MB and corr Ns on RB to WP. Work as given for back to **.

Push 60 Ns on MB to WP. With wrong side facing pick up sts from below WY and hang on to Ns dec 16 sts evenly along the row. With RB in position set machine for 1 x 1 rib. Transfer alt sts to RB. Rep as for back from * to *.

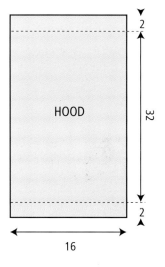

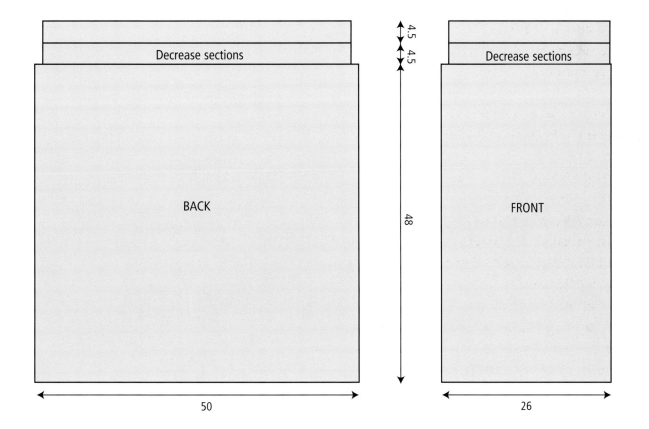

Push 50 Ns on MB to WP. With wrong side facing pick up sts from below WY and hang on to Ns dec 10 sts evenly along the row. With RB in position set machine for 1 x 1 rib. Transfer alt sts to RB. Rep as for back from * to * ending by transferring sts to MB and cast off (instead of WK).

HOOD

With RB in WP set machine for FNR. Push 46 Ns on MB and corr Ns on RB to WP. Using MC cast on and K2 tubular rows. T2/2, K4 rows. Transfer every third st to its adj N leaving empty Ns in WP. K5 rows. CAL. Lower RB at L to ease threading and place plating yarn in plating feeder. Close ribber. Insert punchcard and lock/program patt on first row. Using MT, set carr to select/memorize for patt and K1 row.

RC000. Using MT, release card and set carr for tuck and K160 rows. Remove plating yarn. T2/2 set carr for st st and K4 rows. Transfer every third st to its adj N leaving empty Ns in WP. K4 rows. Transfer sts to MB and cast off.

TO MAKE UP

If sewn up correctly, the garment is reversible. Sew both side and yoke seams. Run a coloured gathering thread around neck edge of cape, but leave loose. Sew back seam of hood. Baste the hood to neck edge, using the gathering thread to adjust the neck edge to fit. Sew hood to cape neck. Remove gathering thread and basting sts. Edge the cape if wished, using whichever method suits. Thread ribbons through yoke eyelets: on the centre ribbon, do not leave lengths to tie, but turn ends under and sew neatly in place. Leave ends for tying in neck and lower eyelets only.

For safety, put a couple of stitches in the ribbons at the front neck so they can not be pulled tight.

HELPFUL HINT

Plated fabric does not usually 'curl' at the edges. However, a crochet edging was added here to give a more 'finished' appearance. For those who find working with a crochet hook difficult, it can be given a machine knitted edge instead. Alternatively, gathered lace can be sewn around the edges.

'IMPOSSIBLE' YARNS

Any knitter could be forgiven for thinking that some yarns would not travel safely through a machine's system of hooked needles, sinker posts and cam brushes. But, in fact, you will find that many of these seemingly 'impossible' yarns machine knit extremely well.

If you have not yet discovered the range of viscose ribbon tapes and the ease with which they cope in our knitting machines, now is the time to try them. The ribbon, used so effectively on the waistcoat and beret (pages 109–118), knitted easily through the machine, albeit on a high tension. It is, however, advisable to choose the more expensive ribbon tapes, as thinner, cheaper tapes do not perform quite as well.

There is also a yarn that looks and feels like feathers. It knits beautifully at tension nine on stockinet, giving a wonderfully soft fabric. But for the hat featured on pages 119–120 I wanted a denser stitch, so I chose to alternate it with a thicker base yarn, which gave a lovely result. You do have to take extra care with this yarn, though, as the 'feathers' tend to catch on the needles. Fortunately, it is easy to unhook them.

Chenille is a popular yarn because it mostly behaves well on knitting machines, and its velvety texture makes it very pleasant to wear. If I were to criticize it at all, it would be because it does not respond to 'wear and tear' quite as well as some other yarns. It is, however, possible to overcome this problem by knitting chenille with another yarn as part of an all-over Fair Isle design. It then lasts a considerable time and launders well, too.

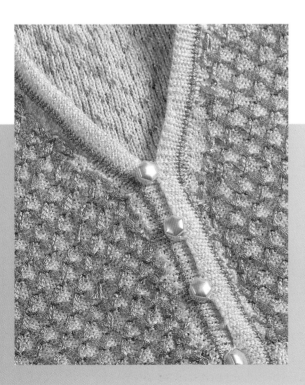 

Viscose-ribbon christening suit

This suit is knitted in the same beautiful yarn that was used for the christening gown on page 70. It is teamed with a waistcoat that is knitted using a viscose-ribbon tape to create a honeycomb effect, and a shiny yarn to form the background fabric.

PATTERN INFORMATION

Sizes
One size
To suit chest 46–51cm
Finished measurement waistcoat
60cm

Materials
1 cone Yeoman's Janeiro (knits as
3ply) in MC
Small amount of industrial bright
acrylic (single ply, knitted double
stranded) in contrast A
1 cone ribbon tape in contrast B
4 small cream buttons
Snap fasteners

Garment weight
For set approx. 275g

Main tension
32 sts and 52 rows to 10cm,
measured over st st, (TD approx.
3 = MT).
36 sts and 48 rows to 10cm
measured over 2 ends MC for
waistcoat and beret (TD approx.
4 = MT+1).
Tension must be matched exactly
before starting garment.

Note
Knitted side of st st and purl
side of ribbon is used as right
side. Measurements are those
of finished garment and should
not be used to measure work
on machine.

SPECIAL NOTE

This yarn needs the addition of weights at all stages of the knitting. Either use the knitting N method (see Glossary, page 140), or hang weights on WY only to prevent shredding of yarn. In the event of a dropped st, catch it at once or it will 'slip' away.

EASY STEPS TO KNITTING WITH RIBBON

STEP 1: Using WY, cast on 20–30 sts. K several rows, hang weights. MC and MT+1 for yarn, which is used double-stranded throughout. K4 rows. Stand the ribbon on the table behind your machine. With ribbon in feeder, and T9, K1 row, letting ribbon 'feed' through your fingers, not the yarn arm. CAL. Bring ribbon from feeder to stand on the floor at the side of your chair. Set cam box to move to the right without knitting. (Both side-levers forward and cam-lever set to 'slip', on Silver Reed/Knitmaster machines or part or empty for others). Re-thread with MC and MT.
RC000. Set cam lever to knit. Starting from the left, push the first and every fourth N to HP, but do not set the carr to HP. Taking the

HELPFUL HINT

Because of the smooth, silky texture of the viscose ribbon, there is a tendency for it to run too fast from the cone while it is being knit. To prevent this from occurring, cut the foot of a discarded nylon stocking, and place it over the cone. This will keep the ribbon moving freely but at a much slower rate.

ribbon and starting with the first N in HP, 'e' wrap the ribbon round every HP N to end.

STEP 2: K4 rows. Bring the third and every foll fourth N slightly forward, so that they stand out from the other Ns. Using your single-transfer tool, lift the ribbon loop that is directly beneath each N, and place it in the N 'hook', pulling each N (with its 'loop') fully out to HP. 'E' wrap these Ns with the ribbon, starting at whichever end the ribbon is laying. K4 rows, and rep the pick up and 'e' wrap sequence, as this forms the honeycomb pattern.

These instructions are written for standard gauge punchcard or electronic machines.

RIGHT BACK LEG AND BODY

Push 58 Ns to WP. Using WY cast on and K a few rows ending CAR (end CAL for L back leg). RC000. Using MC and MT, K12 rows. Inc 1 st at R on next and every foll 6 rows 6 times in all. 64 sts. K2 rows. Inc 1 st at R edge on next and every foll 3 rows 3 times, K1 row. Inc 1 st at R edge on next and every foll alt row 3 times. 70 sts. K until RC shows 78. Place a marker at R.

Shape crotch RC000. K2 rows. Dec 1 st at R on next row, K1 row. Dec 1 st at R on next and every foll alt row 4 times in all, K2 rows. Dec 1 st at R on next and every foll 3 rows 3 times in all. K3 rows Dec 1 st at R edge on next and every foll 5 rows 4 times in all. 58 sts. K until RC shows 120 and WK.

LEFT BACK LEG AND BODY

Work as given for R back leg and body noting difference in rows and reading R for L and vice versa to reverse shaping.

RIGHT FRONT LEG AND BODY

Push 52 Ns to WP. Using WY and A cast on and K a few rows ending CAR end CAL for L front leg and body). Hang weights. RC000. Using MC and MT, K13 rows. CAL. Inc 1 st at beg of next row, K1 row. Inc 1 st at L edge on next and every foll 5 rows, 9 times, K2 rows. Inc 1 st at L on next and every foll 3 rows, 6 times in all. 68 sts. K until RC shows RC 77. CAL. Mark L end st.

HELPFUL HINT

You may prefer to knit the suit with shorter legs. If so, simply knit less rows before reaching the crotch. But, you will need to cast on with far more stitches, and also knit a wider cuff to allow for the fact that a baby's leg is plumper at the calf than around the ankle.

Shape crotch RC000. K2 rows. Dec 1 st at beg of next row, K1 row. Dec 1 st at L edge on next and every foll 3 rows, 6 times in all. K2 rows. Dec 1 st at L edge on next and every foll 6 rows, 3 times in all. 58 sts. K until RC shows 120. WK.

LEFT FRONT LEG AND BODY

Work as given for R front leg and body reading R for L and vice versa to reverse shapings.

FRONT BODICE

Push 96 Ns to WP. Using WY cast on and K a few rows ending CAR. Place a marker thread in centre st.
RC000. Using MC and MT K32 rows. CAR.

Shape armholes RC000. Cast off 4 sts at beg of next 2 rows. 88 sts. Cast off 2 sts beg next 2 rows. 84 sts. Dec 1 st at both ends of next and every foll alt row 5 times in all. 74 sts. K until RC shows 26.

Shape neck Using a separate piece of MC cast off 14 sts at centre. Set carr for HP and push Ns at L to HP. Cont on rem 30 sts at R for

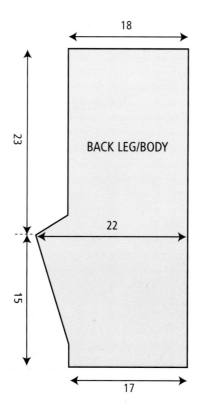

BACK LEG/BODY

18

23

15

22

17

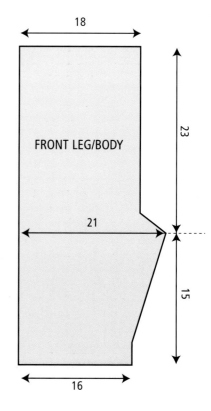

FRONT LEG/BODY

18

23

15

21

16

first side and K1 row. CAL. Dec 1st at neck edge on next 3 rows. Dec 1 st at neck edge on next and every foll alt row, 4 times in all. K1 row. Dec 1 st at neck edge on next and foll third row. 21 sts. K until RC shows 46 and WK. CAL. Reset RC at 26. Set carr so HP Ns will K and work L side to correspond with R.

LEFT BACK BODICE
Push 46 Ns to WP. Using WY cast on and K a few rows ending CAR (end CAL for R back bodice). RC000. Using MC and MT K32 rows. CAR.

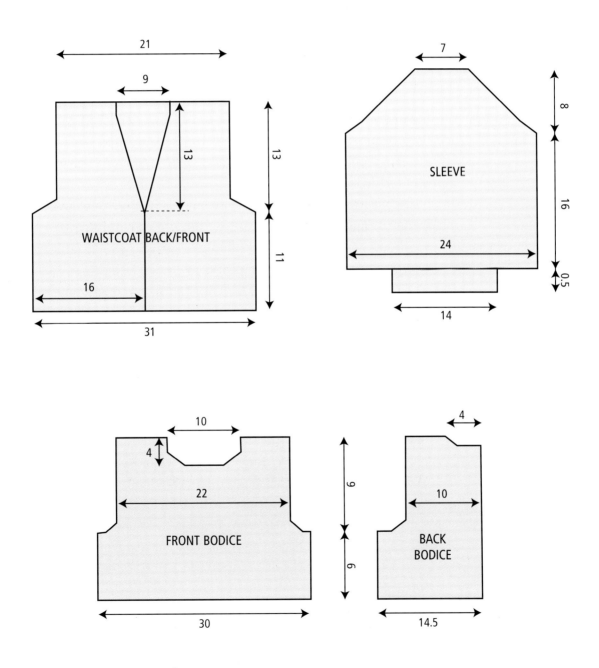

Shape armhole Cast off 4 sts at beg of next row, K1 row. Cast off 2 sts at beg of next row, K1 row. Dec 1 st at armhole edge on next and every foll alt row 5 times in all. 35 sts. K until RC shows 41. CAL.

Shape back neck Cast off 10 sts beg next row. Dec 1 st at neck edge on next row. 24 sts. Cast off 2 sts at beg of next row. Dec 1 st at neck edge on next row, K1 row. WK over rem 21 sts.

RIGHT BACK BODICE
Work as given for L back bodice reading R for L and vice versa to reverse shapings.

INTERIM MAKE UP
Push 21 Ns to WP. Join shoulder seams by rehanging sts below WY right sides together. Using MC and MK, K2 rows. T10+, K1 row and cast off.

SLEEVES
Push 76 Ns to WP. Using WY, cast on and K a few rows ending CAR. RC000. Using MC and MT K82 rows. CAR.

Shape cap Cast off 4 sts at beg of next 2 rows. 68 sts. Cast off 2 sts at beg of next 2 rows. 64 sts. Dec 1 st at both ends of next and every foll alt row, 16 times in all. 52 sts. Dec 1 st each end of every row, 5 times. 42 sts. Cast off 2 sts beg next 4 rows. K1 row. Cast off 3 sts at beg of next 4 rows. 34 sts. Cast off rem 22 sts.

JOINING BODICE TO LEG/BODY SECTIONS
With WY at top edges, and with right sides tog, sew front seam, matching markers at crotch. Push 96 Ns to WP. With wrong side facing pick up sts from below WY from bottom edge of front bodice. Matching centre body seam and centre marker on front bodice, rehang the MC sts onto bodice, spacing evenly along the row and gathering the excess sts. Using MT, K2 rows. T 10+ K1 row and cast off. Rep process for back bodice pieces and back leg/body pieces.

BACK FACINGS
Starting at neck edge, and with wrong side of work facing, pick up sts evenly down the back opening, as far as the stitching. Using

MC and MT, K7 rows. MT+5, K1 row. MT-1 K8 rows. T10+ K1 row and cast off. Rep for other side, then turn both facings under and sew down. Sew also, bodice sides and long, straight leg side seams, but leave inner leg seam open for now.

NECKBAND
Pick up sts around the neck opening, including the ones on back facings. Using MC and MT, K8 rows. MT-1, K4 rows. MT K8 rows. T10+ K1 row and cast off.
Turn hem to inside and sew down.

ANKLE CUFFS
Push 60 Ns to WP. Using WY, cast on and K a few rows. Using A and MT, K4 rows. MT+4, K1 row. MT K5 rows. Turn hem. Using MC, K1 row. Remove WY. With wrong side facing, add the MC bottom edge sts of the (now joined) back and front legs, gathering evenly across the row. MT, K7 rows. T10+ K1 row. Cast off loosely.
Rep process with other leg. Join inner leg, crotch and ankle cuff seams, neatening loose ends of yarn as you work.
Turn cuffs to inside and sew down.

SLEEVE CUFFS
Push 44 Ns to WP. Work as given for ankle cuffs ending by picking up bottom sleeve dec sts evenly along the row to fit.
When complete, neaten ends and sew cuffs and sleeve seams.
Set sleeves in armholes, easing the fit and gathering at shoulders.

NECK EDGING
Push 76 Ns to WP. Using WY cast on and K a few rows and hang weights. Using A and MT-1, K5 rows. MT+5, K1 row. MT K6 rows. Turn the hem. K2 rows. T10+ K1 row and cast off.
Sew this edging around the base of neckband. Sew snap fasteners to back facings.

WAISTCOAT BACK
Push 108 Ns to WP. *Using WY cast on and K a few rows and then hang weights. RC000. Using MC and MT (for double-stranded yarn) K4 rows. Working in honeycomb pattern with ribbon (see patt notes) K until RC shows 42.*

HELPFUL HINT
To prevent the weights from snagging the delicate main yarn, ensure that they are hung with their 'teeth' sunk into a wedge of waste yarn.

Shape armholes RC000. Cast off 4 sts at beg of next 2 rows. Cast off 3 sts at beg of next 2 rows. Cast off 2 sts at beg of next 2 rows. 90 sts. Dec 1 st at each end of next and every foll alt row 7 times in all. 76 sts. K until RC shows 58. Cast off.

LEFT FRONT
Push 54 Ns to WP. Using WY cast on and work as for back from *to*. K1 extra row for R front.

Shape armhole and V-neck RC000. Cast off 4 sts at beg of next row. Cast off 2 sts at beg of next row. Cast off 3 sts at beg of next row. Cast off 2 sts at beg of next 2 rows. Dec 1 st at each end of next and every foll alt row 8 times in all.
On front edge only: Dec 1 st every 4 rows, 3 times in all. K until RC shows 58. Cast off rem 22 sts.

RIGHT FRONT
Work as given for L front noting difference in rows to reverse the shaping.

BACK HEM
With wrong side facing pick up MC sts from bottom cast on edge and hang them evenly onto Ns. Using MC and MT-1, K6 rows. MT+5 K1 row. MT-1, K7 rows. Cast off.

FRONT HEMS
Work as given for back hem, picking up bottom front edge.

INTERIM MAKE UP
Join shoulder seams by picking up the R front shoulder 'loops' (made by the 22 cast-off sts) and with the wrong side of work facing you, and place on Ns. Now hang 22 loops from the R back, starting at the armhole edge, onto the same Ns. Using MC and MT, K2 rows. T10+ K1 row and cast off. Join L shoulder seam the same way. (This method is less bulky than a sewn seam.)

FRONT BANDS
With wrong side of work facing you, pick up the sts around one front edge, from shoulder to hem. Using MC and MT, K1 row. With

ribbon in feeder and loosely through fingers, T9, K1 row. MC and
MT-1, K5 rows. MT-2, K4 rows. MT-1, K5 rows. Cast off.

NECKBAND
Pick up the rem sts along back neck, (approx. 30), and knit as for
front bands.

ARMHOLE EDGES
Pick up sts around armholes and work as for front bands.

TO MAKE UP

Join side seams. Turn bands to
inside and sew down. Join
neckband to front bands. On
left front edge work four loop
buttonholes. Sew on buttons
to correspond.

BERET

Work four sections alike
Push 50 Ns to WP. Using WY
cast on and K a few rows
ending CAR. Hang weights.
RC000. Using MC (double) and
MT, K8 rows. Working Ff dec
throughout. Dec 1 st at both
ends of alt rows until RC shows
34. Dec 1 st each end of every
row until RC shows 42. Cast off
rem sts.
Working on one section at a
time, with wrong side facing

pick up MC sts from cast on edge. Using MC and MT, K4 rows. T10+
K1 row. MT K7 rows and WK.

With right side of work facing pick up MC sts from below WY, from
all four knitted sections and rehang them on Ns, but with each
section, put only 38 sts on out of the original 50, gathering the extra
12 sts per section, evenly across the Ns. Using MC and MT-1 K2
rows. T 9, thread ribbon into feeder and through fingers, K1 row.
Work one complete 'honeycomb' patt with the ribbon, finishing off
by knitting in the feeder, one final row of ribbon. MC and MT-1, K12
rows and cast off loosely.

TO MAKE UP

Neaten all loose ends. Sew the four sections together. Turn the
plain side of brim under and sew down. Lightly press (over a dry
cloth) the beret to shape, by laying it flat and pressing out the
natural flair of the circle, emphasizing the fold line made by the
high-tension row.

Feathered-yarn girl's hat and scarf

The combination of an unusual, feathery yarn, and a more solid, stabilizing 4ply yarn makes this matching hat and scarf modern in design, yet practical with regards to warmth and comfort. Knitted in simple stocking stitch, this set is ideal for knitters unaccustomed to experimenting with fancy yarns.

PATTERN INFORMATION

Sizes
The hat and scarf measurements are for one size only, but the hat can be made larger by the addition of more stitches and rows. Likewise, by using fewer rows and stitches, the hat can be made to a smaller size.

Materials
1 cone of Yeoman's Yarns 'Pellonia' in white (MC)
1 cone of any contrasting acrylic 4ply yarn (C)

Garment weight
Hat and scarf set approx. 150g

Main tension
26 sts and 42 rows to 10cm, measured over st st, (TD approx. 8 = MT).
Tension must be matched exactly before starting garment.

Note
Knitted side is used as right side. Measurements are those of finished garment and should not be used to measure work on machine.

SPECIAL NOTE

It is advisable to run your fingers behind the knitting and up against the needle bed every few rows to check there are no threads caught up on the gate pegs, although a firm tug will usually release them without damage to yarn or gate pegs. When the knitting is finished, check the brushes and wheels of the cam box assembly to ensure that stray threads of yarn have not become wound around them.

These instructions are written for all standard gauge machines with a ribber.

HAT

With RB in position set machine for 1 x 1 rib. Push 104 Ns on MB and corr Ns on RB to WP. Arrange Ns for 1 x 1 rib. Using C cast on and K3 tubular rows. T6/6, K6 rows. Transfer sts to MB. RC000. Using MT and C, K6 rows. Hang weights. *Thread fancy yarn in feeder (or run through fingers), K2 rows. Using C, K2 rows.* Rep these 4 rows, from *to* until RC shows 54. Cont in C only. K2 rows and WK. Push 84 Ns to WP and rehang the sts held on WY, dec 20 sts evenly across the row. On next row, work a row of eyelets by transferring every 4th st to its adj N, but leaving the empty Ns in WP. K8 rows and cast off.

PLAIT

Push 20 Ns to WP. Using C, cast on by hand ('e' wrap). Using MT K until work measures approx. 52cm long. Work a second strip using C, and a third strip using MC. Alternatively, the plait could be made using MC for all three strips.

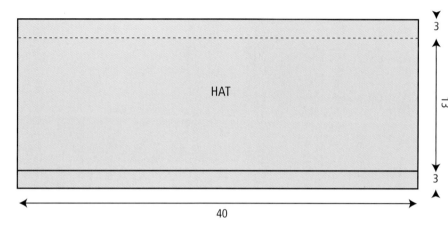

HAT

40

13

3

3

TO MAKE UP

Make a cord (either twisted or knitted) approx. 30cm long. Sew the back seam of hat. Thread the cord through the eyelets and pull tight before tying. Make two pom-poms using acrylic yarn, and attach to cord ends.

Lightly press plait strips (over a dry cloth). Fold each of the three strips in half lengthways, and sew seams. Securing the three ends together, plait the strips. Sew around the ribbed part of the hat, (loosely, so as not to restrict the stretch of brim) and join the open ends together.

SCARF

Push 80 Ns to WP. Using C, cast on by hand ('e' wrap). Using MT K6 rows. Begin the 4-row alt col sequence, as in the hat, for 24 rows. Cont in C only, until work measures approx. 70cm (or length preferred). Reconnect the fancy yarn and repeat the 4-row sequence again for 24 rows. Using C only, K6 rows and cast off.

TO MAKE UP

Fold scarf lengthways and sew seam. Press acrylic section only under a dry cloth and with a cool iron. Make fringe with acrylic yarn and attach to ends of scarf.

Chenille three-piece winter outfit

Chenille was the yarn chosen for this fashionably baggy, cosy three-piece outfit. Knitted alone, chenille can feel rather limp. But if you work chenille with a secondary yarn, such as acrylic, in a Fair Isle combination, you will see it at its best: both 'matt' and 'velvety' yarns are seen in contrast with one another and the Fair Isle patterning provides a warm and durable fabric.

PATTERN INFORMATION

Sizes
To suit chest 51[56:61]cm
Finished measurement 58[62:66]cm
Length 67[68:70]cm
Sleeve seam 22[25:27]cm
Figures in square brackets refer to larger sizes; where there is only one set of figures this applies to all sizes.

Materials
1 cone 4ply Chenille yarn in gold (MC)
1 cone 4ply acrylic yarn in cream (C)
Oddment of contrast 4ply yarn in blue (A)
Length of elastic for trouser waist

Garment weight
For outfit in size 41cm approx. 400g

Main tension
28 sts and 35 rows to 10cm, measured over Fair Isle patt, (TD approx. 7 = MT).
28 sts and 32 rows to 10cm measured over st st (TD approx. 7 = MT).
Tension must be matched exactly before starting garment.

Note
Knitted side is used as right side. Measurements are those of finished garment and should not be used to measure work on machine.

PATTERN NOTE
Program patt/punch card before starting to knit.
(Pattern is reproduced from card 265 in Silver (Knitmaster) pack 55.

PATTERN AND COLOUR SEQUENCE
Insert punchcard and lock/program patt on first row. Set carr to select/memorize for patt and K1 row. Release card and set carr for Fair Isle throughout. Using MC in feeder 1/a throughout change cols in feeder 2/b thus: *13 rows C, 1 row A, 13 rows C* Rep from * to * throughout. Note this stripe sequence can be omitted if desired and MC and C used together throughout.

SPECIAL NOTE
If a second contrast shade is desired (as in the pictured outfit), it is helpful if before the knitting process starts the patt card has been marked out. Mark rows 1, 14, 27, and 40 (Silver Reed machines).

HELPFUL HINT

If you find it difficult machine knitting the chenille, don't give up! Try waxing the yarn, either by fixing wax discs (available from knitting machine stockists) to your yarn arm, or by winding off balls of chenille and letting the yarn run lightly over a household candle. Any waxy residue left on the yarn will disappear during steaming.

These instructions are written for standard gauge punchcard or electronic machines.

SWEATER BACK

With RB in position set machine for 1 x 1 rib. Push 82[86:92] Ns on MB and corr Ns on RB to WP. Using MC cast on and K3 tubular rows. RC000. T3/3, K24 rows. Transfer sts to MB. RC000. Using MT K1 row. Start and work in Fair Isle patt and col sequence (see patt note) throughout. K until RC shows 106[108:116] and WK.

FRONT

Work as given for back until RC shows 88[90:94]. CAR.

Shape neck Note position in patt and col sequence. Using a separate piece of MC cast off 12[16:18] sts at centre. Using nylon cord K sts at L by hand taking Ns down to NWP. Cont over rem 35[35:37] sts at R for first side. K1 row. Dec 1 st at neck edge on next 6[6:7] rows, K1 row. Dec 1 st at neck edge on next and every foll alt rows 5 times in all. 24[24:25] sts. K until RC shows 106[108:116] and WK.

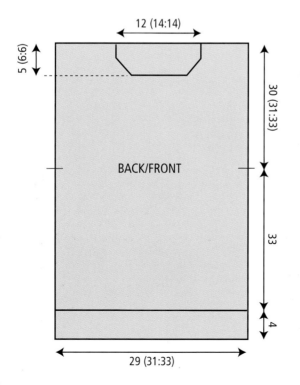

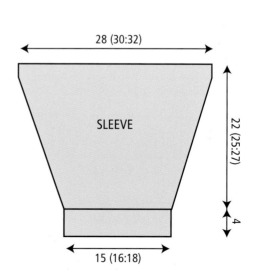

Return patt to noted row and lock. CAR. Unravel nylon cord over sts at L bringing Ns down to WP. Set carr to slip/part/empty and take to L. Reset RC at 88[90:94]. Release card and set carr for Fair Isle. Keeping col sequence correct from noted position complete to correspond with first side, reversing shapings.

SLEEVES

With RB in position set machine for 1 x 1 rib. Push 42[44:50] Ns on MB and corr Ns on RB to WP. Using MC cast on and K3 tubular rows. RC000. T3/3, K24 rows. Transfer sts to MB. RC000. Using MT K1 row. Start and work in Fair Isle patt and col sequence (see patt note) throughout. K until RC shows 4. Inc 1 st at each end of next and every foll 4 rows 18[20:20] times in all. 78[88:90] sts. K until RC shows 78[88:94]. Mark centre st and cast off.

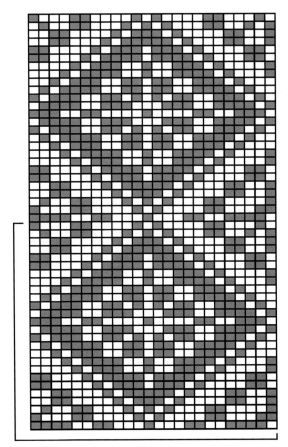

Repeat for electronics

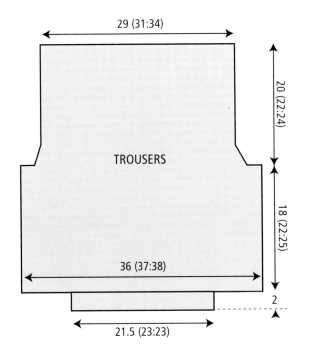

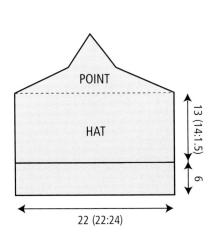

HELPFUL HINT

The hat's 'point' can be omitted if preferred. Work a cast-off edge where you would start decreasing for the start of the point. A pom-pom can also be made instead of the bears head.

NECKBAND

Push 24[24:25] Ns to WP. With right side facing, pick up sts from below WY from R front shoulder and hang on Ns. With wrong side of back facing pick up the same number of sts for the R back shoulder, unravelling them from WY. When both sets of sts are on the Ns, using MC and MT K2 rows, joining the right shoulder seam. T10+ K1 row and cast off.

With wrong side of work facing pick up sts (starting at the back) from around the neck and hang evenly on to Ns. Count the sts used from back for R shoulder, and mark the same number of sts in readiness for the L shoulder. (The rem sts are for the back neck). Pick up sts from side, then centre then side front and hang evenly alongside back sts. Using MC and MT, K2 rows. Push RB to WP and transfer sts for 1 x 1 rib. Weight evenly. T3/3. K6 rows. T5/5 K8 rows. T3/3 K6 rows. WK.

TO MAKE UP

Join L shoulder in the same way as for R. Fold neckband in half and sew loosely on the inside. Sew sleeve seams, set sleeves into place, lining marker threads to shoulder seams. Join side seams.

HAT

With RB in position set machine for 1 x 1 rib. Push 62[62:68] Ns on MB and corr Ns on RB to WP. Arrange Ns for 1 x 1 rib. Using MC, cast on and K3 tubular rows. T3/3 K26 rows. Transfer sts to MB. RC000. Using MT, K1 row. Start and work patt (see patt note) and K until RC shows 46[50:52].

Shape for 'point' Dec 1 st at each end of next 14[12:12] rows. K1 row. Dec 1 st at each end of next and every foll alt row until 3 sts rem. Cast off.

'BEAR' POM-POM (OPTIONAL)

Push 10 Ns to WP. Using WY cast on and K a few rows. Using MC, K4 rows. Inc 1 st at each end of next 3 rows, K6 rows. Dec 1 st at each end of next 3 rows. K4 rows and WK.

EARS

Work two alike.

Push 10 Ns to WP. Using MC, cast on by hand ('e' wrap) and K3 rows. Dec 1 st at each end of next 3 rows. Cast off rem 4 sts.

TO MAKE UP

Fold the head section in half. Make a small 'tuck' in the centre of both ears, and sew them to the inside of the head. Sew front and back of head tog, leaving the WY still in place. Fill the head with stuffing. Embroider eyes/nose/mouth. Remove WY and run a strong thread through open sts, drawing them tight. Fasten off thread. Attach pom-pom to 'point' of hat.

TROUSER LEG

Work two alike.
Push 100[104:106] Ns to WP. Using WY cast on and K a few rows.
RC000. Using MC and MT, K58[70:80] rows.

Shape crotch RC000. Cast off 4 sts at beg of next 2 rows. Dec 1 st at beg of next 6 rows. 86[90:92] sts. K until RC shows 64[70:76]. Using MT-1, K5 rows. MT+3, K1 row. MT-1, K5 rows and cast off.

CUFF

With RB in position set machine for 1 x 1 rib. Push 60[64:64] Ns on MB and corr Ns on RB to WP. Arrange Ns for 1 x 1 rib. Using MC cast on and K3 tubular rows. T3/3 K26 rows. Transfer sts to MB. Using MT, K2 rows. With wrong side of leg facing, pick up sts from below WY and hang on to Ns dec 40[40:42] sts evenly along the row. T10+ K1 row and cast off.

TO MAKE UP

Place two halves tog, matching at the crotch. Sew front and back seams. Sew from ankle at one side across the crotch to ankle at the other. Turn cuffs to inside and slip st into place. Turn top over at the high tension 'fold' and slip st this down, leaving opening for elastic. Thread elastic into casing and fasten off securely.

KNIT A NURSERY

In this final chapter, the pièce de résistance of all babies' requirements – the nursery – is considered. Planning a nursery can be thoroughly enjoyable but it can be made all the more gratifying by utilizing your knitting skills to contribute to the finished room.

Many of the techniques discussed in earlier chapters are brought into focus again here, providing further opportunities for them to be practised. For the quilt and bumper set on pages 136–139 I took inspiration from the first chapter on Decorative Trimmings and added lace and ribbons. Lovers of the plain and simple, can, of course, make them without these extra trimmings. Handtooling, explored in the second chapter, has been used to pick up the stitches and rows in the pin-tucking on the nursing-chair cushion seen on pages 133–135, while another version of slip stitch, explored in chapter four, is also featured on this item. Finally, chenille, dicussed in the chapter on 'Impossible Yarns', was ideal for knitting the bears in the cot mobile (see pages 129–132).

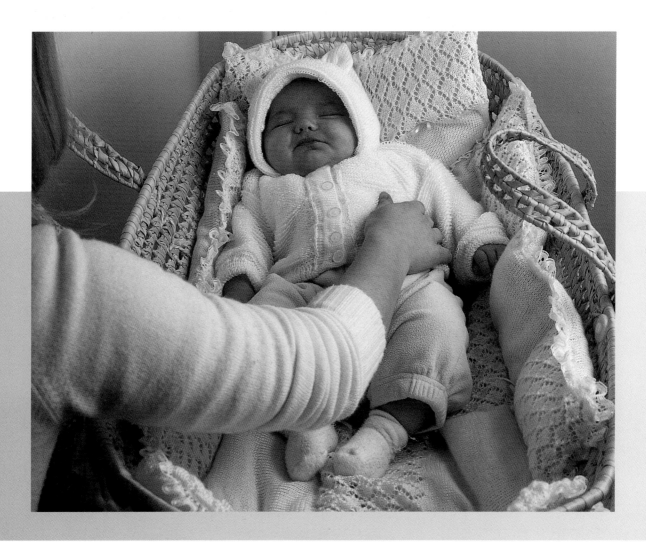

Teddy and balloons cot mobile

This fun mobile makes a perfect addition to any nursery and is not too difficult to make. It can be easily hung from the ceiling with ribbon looped over a hook.

PATTERN INFORMATION

Materials

2 white plastic coat hangers with hooks on the underside (wire ones can be used, but will need covering with tape or ribbon)
Length of wide white satin ribbon
2m narrow white ribbon
Oddments of white and coloured yarn

4 small, durable cardboard boxes or baskets
Strong glue
4 knitted teddy bears
Bag of stuffing (one that is considered safe for stuffing soft toys)

METHOD

Cut the hook arrangement from one of the hangers. Push this hanger through the hanger with the hook remaining (see Fig 7.1, below), glue the two together in appropriate places, and bind where the two crossbars meet in the centre with ribbon or tape for added strength. Make two large satin bows from the wide ribbon and tie where they look most effective.

BALLOONS

Each balloon is made up of four sections: two white, (MC) two coloured. (C) K4 balloons.
Push 6 Ns to WP and work a closed edge cast on with MC.
RC000. T6 K6 rows. Inc 1 st at each end of every 3 rows, until RC shows 34. K12 rows. Dec 1 st at both ends of every foll alt row until RC shows 58. Dec 1 st at each end of next 4 rows. K until RC shows 64. Run rem sts onto a darning N and gather up tight.
All of the sections are made in the same way. K8 white, and eight coloured sections.

Fig 7.1 To make frame of mobile cut off hook from one hanger and push through base of second hanger

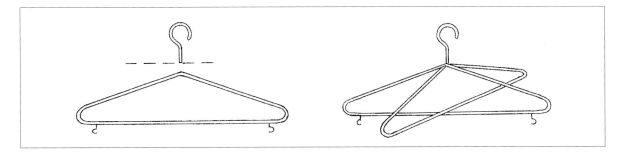

TO MAKE UP

Sew together two white and two coloured sections for each balloon. Fill with stuffing and gather top opening, enclosing a ribbon loop, made from the narrow white ribbon. Sew four ribbons to inside of each balloon, before pushing them through to the outside, where they are fastened to the boxes. The balloons are hung from the hooks on the hangers, with the bears sitting in the boxes (or baskets). It is possible to obtain musical boxes that can be added to cot mobiles, but these are entirely optional.

Baskets (or boxes) Small baskets can be purchased from craft shops or florists. We chose small, strong boxes. Four holes need to be punched in the sides to accommodate the ends of the ribbons.

TEDDY BEARS
Materials
Oddments of gold chenille yarn
Safety stuffing for filling the bears
Black wool or embroidery silk for eyes and noses
Lace trimming if bears are to be 'dressed'

BODY

(Legs body and head are made in one piece. The back and front of a bear is identical.)
Push 12 Ns to WP. Using MC cast on with a closed edge. T7 K20 rows for first leg section. WK. Rep from*to*. Return sts on WY to Ns, making 24 sts in all. RC000. K24 rows. Cast off 3 sts at beg of next two rows 18 sts. K2 rows. Inc 1 st at both ends of next 2 rows. K12 rows. Cast off 1 st each end of next 6 rows. Cast off 10 rem sts.

ARMS

Work four alike per bear.
Push 10 Ns to WP. Using MC cast on with a closed edge. T7 K14 rows. Dec 1 st at each end of next 3 rows. Cast off rem 4 sts.

EARS

Push 10 Ns to WP. Using MC cast on with a closed edge. T7 K2 rows. Dec 1 st at each end of next 3 rows. Cast off rem 4 sts.

TO MAKE UP

Sew two arm sections for bear's L side and two arm sections for bear's R side, leaving open at widest part for stuffing. Sew front and back body/head/leg, sections, leaving an opening either side for attaching ready-stuffed arms. Stuff the head section and embroider eyes and nose/mouth (see Fig 7.2). Sew in one arm. Use the other opening to complete stuffing the bear. Attach the other arm into opening. Tie strong yarn around the bear's neck, and pull to shape bear's head.

When finished, the bears can be 'dressed' according to your own imagination and skill, if desired.

Fig 7.2 embroidery for nose and mouth

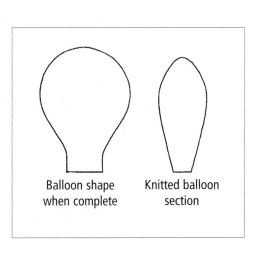

Balloon shape when complete   Knitted balloon section

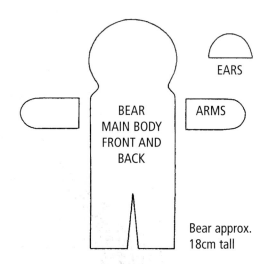

EARS

BEAR MAIN BODY FRONT AND BACK

ARMS

Bear approx. 18cm tall

Nursing-chair cushion

This soft, comfortable cushion will look attractive in the nursery and certainly be useful. It has pretty, coloured stripes at the sides and a teddy bear pattern in the centre. The lace adds a delicate touch.

PATTERN INFORMATION

Size
Approx. 46 x 36cm

Materials
Oddments of yarn, including white (MC), Mint (A), Rose (B), Gold (C) and Blue (D)
1 cushion pad, approx. 46 x 36cm in size

Main tension
Owing to the complexity and mixture of stitch patterns on the side panels, it was not possible to give an accurate stitch tension for them, but the stitch tension for the back cover, which is worked in st st, is 28 sts and 40 rows to 10cm (TD approx. 5).
MT for Fair Isle panel: 32 sts and 37 rows to 10cm (TD approx. 6).

PATTERN NOTE

Punch card/program patts on page 8 and 134 before starting to knit.
Note: You can use card 3 from basic pack, locked on first row as patt on page 8.

FRONT COVER

The front cover consists of two identical panels, K sideways, and one centre panel, K lengthways.

SIDE PIECES

Work two pieces alike.
Push 104 Ns to WP. Using MC cast on with a closed edge. T5, K6 rows. Using B, K4 rows. C K8 rows. B K4 rows. Using the single transfer tool, pick up every fifth st from the last row K in B, and place it on every fifth N. K2 rows. Insert punchcard/program patt A for 'ripple stitch' patt. Card stays locked throughout. K2 rows st st.* Set carr to knit slip/part/empty. MC K8 rows. A, K2 rows st st*. Rep from *to*, 2 more times. MC, K4 rows. B, K4 rows. MC K4 rows. C K4 rows. MC K4 rows. A K4 rows. T10+ K1 row and cast off.

CENTRAL PANEL

Push 74 Ns to WP. Using MC cast on with a closed edge.
RC000. Using MT, K11 rows. Insert card B/program patt B on first row. Set carr to select/memorize for patt and K1 row. *Release card and

HELPFUL HINT

If desired, turn the card over before knitting the second set of bears so that they face in the opposite direction.

set carr for Fair Isle. Using MC in feeder 1/a throughout change yarns in feeder 2/b thus: 4A, 6D, 3MC, 38 chenille. RC shows 63. Reset and lock the patt card on first row*. K7 rows MC. Rep from * to * one more time. MC K until RC shows 126 and cast off.

BACK COVER
This part of the cushion cover is knit sideways,
Push 108 Ns to WP and using MC, cast on with a closed edge.
RC000. MT K184 rows.

TO MAKE UP
Pin out the back and centre panels and steam lightly. When dry, sew lace edging along the last row of A. Sew front panel to both side panels, sewing in edges of loose yarn. Join front and back covers. Fit over cushion pad and sew opening. If the cushion pad purchased is too big for the knitted cover, cut pad to size, then over sew the cut ends. The pad and cover can be laundered together. If an edging is desired for the cushion, it can be crocheted, as illustrated with the carry-cape (see page 103) or machine knitted and sewn on.

Lace-trimmed cot quilt and bumper set

This quilted and lace-trimmed set will provide comfort for your baby while also looking pretty.

PATTERN INFORMATION

Size
To fit a standard swinging crib or small cot

Materials
2 cones of 2/30s Bright acrylic (white)
2m of non-iron, silky lining, in contrasting or matching shade
2m narrow ribbon to match
2m white narrow ribbon for ties
1m Terylene wadding

Notes
• The use of tension swatches is considered unnecessary for this design, as there does not appear to be any set measurements for these items, only perhaps small, medium and large. By following the instructions, any quilt and bumper set should turn out at what is considered a small size, ideal for most swinging cribs or small cots. Their sizes are not unduly affected by a few centimetres either way.
• On Silver Reed (Knitmaster) machines: To eliminate unnecessary changing of the two carriages, (lace and main carr) the main carriage is used only for the purpose of working a closed-edge

cast-on, then the lace carr knits both the lace panels and the stockinet ones.
Brother/Toyota machines: Substitute an appropriate alternative lace pattern.
• Yarn is used doubled throughout.
• The use of a fabric lining (coloured or otherwise) makes for a smoother fitting of the knitted outer covers. It also lessens the possibility of the wadding fibres showing through the fine yarn. Lining the set is optional, but I think that it gives an interesting touch of colour and added lustre which compliments the choice of yarn used.
• The quilting technique here is different from the one described in the pattern for the bodywarmer on pages 60–63. Not only does this give knitters a chance to see that quilting can be worked in this alternative way, it allows for a larger quilting area than the 24-stitch one, previously used.
• Patt card L–1 from Silver Reed's (Knitmaster's) basic pack is used (see page 72), but knitters can use any lace pattern of their choice.

QUILT
Easy Steps

STEP 1: Lock patt card on row 1. The quilt is worked in three 'strips'. Strips one and three are worked the same, both beginning and ending with a lace pattern panel.
Push 64 Ns to WP. Using WY, cast on and K a few rows ending CAR.
Push Ns to HP and using MC, starting from the L side, work an 'e'

wrap cast on (over the WY, which is pulled out later.)
Hang weights. K2 rows. Change to lace carr.

RC000. Using MT for lace (2). K2 rows. Release patt card and set carr
to knit lace patt.

K to RC 62. Lock patt card. Change tension to 3, and carr to K st st.

RC000. K64 rows. Cont in this manner until you have a strip of
knitting that starts with a lace panel, then a st st panel, another lace
panel, another st st panel, finishing with a lace panel.

STEP 2: Work strip two, starting with the same number of sts as strip
one. Cast on in the same manner, including the 'e' wrap, but this
time, start with a st st panel, then a lace panel, ending with a st st
panel. When finished, work another strip the same as the first one
(for strip three). Remove WY from cast-on edges, and sew panels tog
with strip two in the centre.

STEP 3: Pin out joined piece and steam lightly. When dry, take
measurements of width and length of piece. Mark out these
measurements on the wadding, then cut out. Lay the lining fabric
double and mark out the measurements here also, but leave a
margin or seam allowance round the edges of approx. 1cm. Cut out.

STEP 4: Stitch (hand or machine) the lining back and front tog,
leaving the bottom edge open. Insert the wadding. Sew the bottom
edges tog. K the back of the quilt.

Using MC cast on 160 sts (WY and 'e' wrap method), with main carr.
Change to lace carr.

RC000. T3 K240 rows, finishing with several rows of WY. Only cast

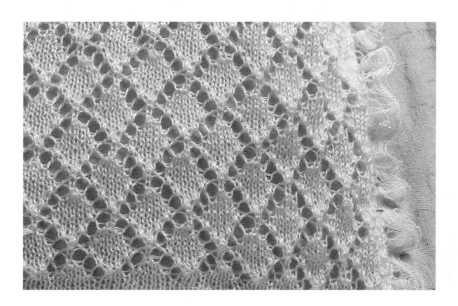

off properly when certain that the knitted back is exactly the same length as the knitted front. This can be done quickly and efficiently with fine knitting Ns or the piece put back onto the machine and the required number of rows knitted. If the piece turns out to be too long for the front, pull the necessary rows back then cast off the preferred way.

STEP 5: Pin out the back piece and steam lightly. Sew gathered lace around the inside edge of the front quilt cover. Sew back of cover to front, 'sandwiching' the lace in between, but leaving an opening along the bottom edge. Place the wadding (lined or otherwise) inside, and close the opening with small stitches. Sew with little running sts along the panel seams, passing the N through all the layers, catching them all together. Now rep the process along the rows where the lace panels meet the st st ones (see Fig 7.3). Finally, make small bows and sew them securely to each of the panel joins.

Dotted lines indicate where small stitches should be sewn

Fig 7.3

BUMPER SET

The set comprises one top bumper and two (identical) side bumpers.

TOP BUMPER

Front cover Push 160 Ns to WP. Using WY cast on and K a few rows ending CAR. Using MC, work an 'e' wrap cast on. T3, K2 rows. Insert punchcard/program patt on first row. Using lace carr and MT, K2 rows. Release card and set for lace knitting.
RC000* K52 rows. Set carr for st st T3 and K150 rows. Cast off.

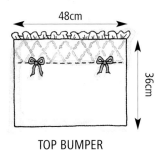

TOP BUMPER

Back cover Work as front cover to *. K186 rows and cast off. Alternatively WK as for back of quilt and check the 'fit' compared to the front cover.

TO MAKE UP

Work as for quilt. Pin out, steam and take measurements, transferring the measurements onto wadding and lining before cutting out. Make up in the same manner as for quilt, sewing bows to front as pictured and ribbons to side for tying.

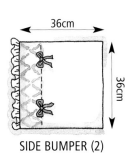

SIDE BUMPER (2)

SIDE BUMPERS

Push 130 Ns to WP. Work as given for top bumper.

GLOSSARY

Blocking-out Garment pieces pinned to size on a pressing pad, usually prior to steaming.

Casting-off loosely Machine-knitted cast-offs can sometimes pull tight, without the knitter being aware of it. Where it is desirable to have a really loose cast-off edge, the addition of a claw weight on the sts being cast off drags them slightly, elongating the chain of the stitch, and gives a cast-off as loose as you want.

'E' wrap This is where a needle is pushed into holding position and the yarn is wound (by hand) around the needle, anti-clockwise.

'Ease' of garments Occasionally, part of a garment, e.g. a sleeve cap, needs to have 'ease' so that it can be either gathered into place, or eased to fit neatly into its round armhole. Also, garments are designed and knitted with 'ease' in them. This is an allowance of width, as garments are rarely comfortable if they fit skin-tight. Garments that are meant to be worn over other garments more 'ease' than others to allow for the extra layer(s)underneath.

Fabric The name sometimes given to a piece of knitting.

Hand knitting During the course of machine knitting, we often need to 'hand knit' a stitch or stitches. Push out the needle(s) so that the stitch it is holding slips back over the latch. Put the stitch (or yarn) that we need to hand knit into the hook of the needle and pull it through, letting the original stitch move back into place and, in doing so, knit the stitch.

Knitting needle method This refers to a way of weighting your knitting, and is excellent where the fabric of the knitting or yarn (or both) is fine, and the claw weights seem rough. Weave one or two fine knitting needles in and out of the fabric from end to end, then hang the weights evenly along the needles, not on your fabric.

Latch off This is most commonly used when we want to cast off a stitch or stitches. Usually, the last row of knitting will have been done at a very high tension, leaving a row of loose stitches. With the latch tool, the first stitch is picked up into the latch, allowed to slide back over the latch while we pick up a second stitch. This stitch is then pulled through the stitch at the back of the latch, making a chain effect.

Marking stitches This is done when we want to instantly recognize a stitch, or a place in the knitting, for whatever purpose. It is often used for matching up when seaming, much as the way dressmakers use 'tailors' tacks'. A short length (or loop) of contrast yarn is passed into the stitch with the help of the latch tool, then drawn back on itself without affecting the actual stitch.

Measurements These are given on the pattern and should not (except in certain circumstances) be used to measure anything on the machine, as you will not be able to get a true reading.

Steaming Most yarns benefit from being steamed after leaving the machine. Pieces of knitting are pinned out to size, and a damp cloth laid over them. Sometimes this is sufficient to 'set' the fabric, but, occasionally, a hot iron passed over the damp cloth to release some steam is even more beneficial to the fabric's finish. For any yarn you are unsure of, read the spinners directions.

Short Row This means that only part of the row is knitted, and is used for shaping or as an alternative method for casting off. Certain needles are put to 'hold' (as in toes on bootees or socks), while the rest of the row is knitted.

WK This abbreviation refers to the part of knitting where the stitches need to be knitted with waste yarn before being released from the machine.

FURTHER READING

Allen, John, The Machine Knitting Book, Dorling Kindersley, 1985

Allen, John, John Allen's Treasury of Machine Knitting Stitches, David & Charles, 1989

The Complete Harmony Guide to Machine Knitting Stitches and Designs, Lyric, 1992

Devaney, Barbara (Ed.), The Harmony Guide to Machine Knitting Stitches, Lyric, 1988

Guagliumi, Susan, Hand Manipulated Stitches for Machine Knitters, Taunton Press, 1990

Kinder, Kathleen, The Machine Knitters Book of the Ribber, K. Kinder, 1984

Musk, Denise, The Technique of Slipstitch, Batsford, 1989

Ratcliffe, Hazel, The Pan Book of Machine Knitting, Pan, 1986

Sharp, Sheila, Textured Patterns for Machine Knitting, Batsford, 1986

ABOUT THE AUTHOR

Christine Eames lives in north-east England with her husband Clive. She began machine knitting over 40 years ago, enjoying to design and make garments for her children. She went on to become an in-store demonstrator, tutor, knitwear designer, and eventually ran her own business selling knitting machines and knitted garments. Her love of knitting is as great today as it was when she first embarked on her career, and she continues to design and knit for her 30 grandchildren.

INDEX

GMC Publications

BOOKS

Woodcarving

Beginning Woodcarving	*GMC Publications*
Carving Architectural Detail in Wood: The Classical Tradition	*Frederick Wilbur*
Carving Birds & Beasts	*GMC Publications*
Carving the Human Figure: Studies in Wood and Stone	*Dick Onians*
Carving Nature: Wildlife Studies in Wood	*Frank Fox-Wilson*
Carving on Turning	*Chris Pye*
Celtic Carved Lovespoons: 30 Patterns	*Sharon Littley & Clive Griffin*
Decorative Woodcarving (New Edition)	*Jeremy Williams*
Elements of Woodcarving	*Chris Pye*
Essential Woodcarving Techniques	*Dick Onians*
Figure Carving in Wood: Human and Animal Forms	*Sara Wilkinson*
Lettercarving in Wood: A Practical Course	*Chris Pye*
Relief Carving in Wood: A Practical Introduction	*Chris Pye*
Woodcarving for Beginners	*GMC Publications*
Woodcarving Made Easy	*Cynthia Rogers*
Woodcarving Tools, Materials & Equipment (New Edition in 2 vols.)	*Chris Pye*

Woodturning

Bowl Turning Techniques Masterclass	*Tony Boase*
Chris Child's Projects for Woodturners	*Chris Child*
Contemporary Turned Wood: New Perspectives in a Rich Tradition	*Ray Leier, Jan Peters & Kevin Wallace*
Decorating Turned Wood: The Maker's Eye	*Liz & Michael O'Donnell*
Green Woodwork	*Mike Abbott*
Intermediate Woodturning Projects	*GMC Publications*
Keith Rowley's Woodturning Projects	*Keith Rowley*
Making Screw Threads in Wood	*Fred Holder*
Segmented Turning: A Complete Guide	*Ron Hampton*
Turned Boxes: 50 Designs	*Chris Stott*
Turning Green Wood	*Michael O'Donnell*

Turning Pens and Pencils	*Kip Christensen & Rex Burningham*
Woodturning: Forms and Materials	*John Hunnex*
Woodturning: A Foundation Course (New Edition)	*Keith Rowley*
Woodturning: A Fresh Approach	*Robert Chapman*
Woodturning: An Individual Approach	*Dave Regester*
Woodturning: A Source Book of Shapes	*John Hunnex*
Woodturning Masterclass	*Tony Boase*
Woodturning Techniques	*GMC Publications*

Woodworking

Beginning Picture Marquetry	*Lawrence Threadgold*
Celtic Carved Lovespoons: 30 Patterns	*Sharon Littley & Clive Griffin*
Celtic Woodcraft	*Glenda Bennett*
Complete Woodfinishing (Revised Edition)	*Ian Hosker*
David Charlesworth's Furniture-Making Techniques	*David Charlesworth*
David Charlesworth's Furniture-Making Techniques – Volume 2	*David Charlesworth*
Furniture-Making Projects for the Wood Craftsman	*GMC Publications*
Furniture-Making Techniques for the Wood Craftsman	*GMC Publications*
Furniture Projects with the Router	*Kevin Ley*
Furniture Restoration (Practical Crafts)	*Kevin Jan Bonner*
Furniture Restoration: A Professional at Work	*John Lloyd*
Furniture Restoration and Repair for Beginners	*Kevin Jan Bonner*
Furniture Restoration Workshop	*Kevin Jan Bonner*
Green Woodwork	*Mike Abbott*
Intarsia: 30 Patterns for the Scrollsaw	*John Everett*
Kevin Ley's Furniture Projects	*Kevin Ley*
Making Chairs and Tables – Volume 2	*GMC Publications*
Making Classic English Furniture	*Paul Richardson*
Making Heirloom Boxes	*Peter Lloyd*
Making Screw Threads in Wood	*Fred Holder*
Making Woodwork Aids and Devices	*Robert Wearing*

Gardening

How to Attract Butterflies to your Garden
John & Maureen Tampion

Marginal Plants *Bernard Sleeman*

Orchids are Easy: A Beginner's Guide to their Care
and Cultivation *Tom Gilland*

Plant Alert: A Garden Guide for Parents *Catherine Collins*

Planting Plans for Your Garden *Jenny Shukman*

Sink and Container Gardening Using Dwarf Hardy Plants
Chris & Valerie Wheeler

The Successful Conservatory and Growing Exotic Plants
Joan Phelan

Success with Cuttings *Chris & Valerie Wheeler*

Success with Seeds *Chris & Valerie Wheeler*

Tropical Garden Style with Hardy Plants *Alan Hemsley*

Water Garden Projects: From Groundwork to Planting
Roger Sweetinburgh

Photography

Close-Up on Insects *Robert Thompson*

Digital Enhancement for Landscape Photographers
Arjan Hoogendam & Herb Parkin

Double Vision *Chris Weston & Nigel Hicks*

An Essential Guide to Bird Photography *Steve Young*

Field Guide to Bird Photography *Steve Young*

Field Guide to Landscape Photography *Peter Watson*

How to Photograph Pets *Nick Ridley*

In my Mind's Eye: Seeing in Black and White
Charlie Waite

Life in the Wild: A Photographer's Year *Andy Rouse*

Light in the Landscape: A Photographer's Year
Peter Watson

Outdoor Photography Portfolio *GMC Publications*

Photographers on Location with Charlie Waite
Charlie Waite

Photographing Fungi in the Field *George McCarthy*

Photography for the Naturalist *Mark Lucock*

Photojournalism: An Essential Guide *David Herrod*

Professional Landscape and Environmental Photography:
From 35mm to Large Format *Mark Lucock*

Rangefinder *Roger Hicks & Frances Schultz*

Underwater Photography *Paul Kay*

Viewpoints from Outdoor Photography *GMC Publications*

Where and How to Photograph Wildlife *Peter Evans*

Wildlife Photography Workshops *Steve & Ann Toon*

Art Techniques

Oil Paintings from your Garden: A Guide for Beginners
Rachel Shirley

Videos

Drop-in and Pinstuffed Seats *David James*

Stuffover Upholstery *David James*

Elliptical Turning *David Springett*

Woodturning Wizardry *David Springett*

Turning Between Centres: The Basics *Dennis White*

Turning Bowls *Dennis White*

Boxes, Goblets and Screw Threads *Dennis White*

Novelties and Projects *Dennis White*

Classic Profiles *Dennis White*

Twists and Advanced Turning *Dennis White*

Sharpening the Professional Way *Jim Kingshott*

Sharpening Turning & Carving Tools *Jim Kingshott*

Bowl Turning *John Jordan*

Hollow Turning *John Jordan*

Woodturning: A Foundation Course *Keith Rowley*

Carving a Figure: The Female Form *Ray Gonzalez*

The Router: A Beginner's Guide *Alan Goodsell*

The Scroll Saw: A Beginner's Guide *John Burke*

Magazines

WOODTURNING • WOODCARVING
FURNITURE & CABINETMAKING • THE ROUTER
NEW WOODWORKING • THE DOLLS' HOUSE MAGAZINE
OUTDOOR PHOTOGRAPHY • BLACK & WHITE PHOTOGRAPHY
TRAVEL PHOTOGRAPHY • MACHINE KNITTING NEWS
GUILD OF MASTER CRAFTSMEN NEWS

The above represents a full list of all titles currently
published or scheduled to be published. All are available
direct from the Publishers or through bookshops,
newsagents and specialist retailers. To place an order, or
to obtain a complete catalogue, contact:

**GMC Publications,
Castle Place, 166 High Street, Lewes,
East Sussex BN7 1XU United Kingdom
Tel: 01273 488005 Fax: 01273 402866
E-mail: pubs@thegmcgroup.com**
Orders by credit card are accepted